SMP 16–19

Methods

Foundations of pure mathematics,
statistics and probability

CAMBRIDGE
UNIVERSITY PRESS

Much of this book is based on earlier SMP books to which the following people contributed.
Simon Baxter
Chris Belsom
Robert Black
David Cundy
Stan Dolan
Doug French
Jackie Gallard
Howard Gilbert
Andy Hall
Barrie Hunt
Michael Leach
Sarah Lightfoot
Chris Little
Timothy Lewis
Lorna Lyons
Fiona McGill
Richard Peacock
Paul Roder
Mary Rouncefield
Jeff Searle
David Tall
Brian Wardle
Thelma Wilson
Phil Wood

PUBLISHED BY THE PRESS SYNDICATE OF THE UNIVERSITY OF CAMBRIDGE
The Pitt Building, Trumpington Street, Cambridge, United Kingdom

CAMBRIDGE UNIVERSITY PRESS
The Edinburgh Building, Cambridge, CB2 2RU, UK
40 West 20th Street, New York, NY 10011–4211, USA
477 Williamstown Road, Port Melbourne, VIC 3207, Australia
Ruiz de Alarcón 13, 28014 Madrid, Spain
Dock House, The Waterfront, Cape Town 8001, South Africa

http://www.cambridge.org

First published 2000
Reprinted 2001 (twice)

Printed in the United Kingdom at the University Press, Cambridge

Typeface Minion and Officina   *System* QuarkXpress®

A catalogue record for this book is available from the British Library

ISBN 0 521 78796 3 paperback

Cover photograph: Images Colour Library
Cover design: Angela Ashton

Contents

Using this book

Each section within a chapter consists of work developing new ideas followed by an exercise for practice in using those ideas.

Within the development sections, some questions are labelled with a **D**, for example **2D**, and are enclosed in a box. These involve issues that are worth exploring through discussion – either teacher-led discussion in the whole class or discussion by students in small groups, who may then feed back their conclusions to the whole class.

Questions labelled **E** are more demanding.

At the end of some chapters there is support material. This is referred to at the point in the chapter where some students may need it to consolidate a basic idea or technique before moving further with the main flow of the work.

Important note

In this book much use is made of a graphical calculator – mostly as a graph plotter – as an exploratory tool to help in understanding new ideas. However you will only be allowed to use an ordinary scientific calculator for the Methods part of the examination*. So after working through the development section for a new topic using your graphical calculator, you should switch to an ordinary scientific calculator for the subsequent exercise(s) and any past examination papers you may try.

The way the statistical functions work varies from calculator to calculator. So it is particularly important to practise statistical work on the ordinary scientific calculator that you plan to use for the exam.

*For AQA's 2001/2002 AS/A level examination: you should check the position for subsequent years.

---

1 Linear and other graphs

A Introduction (answers p. 166)

Drawing and sketching graphs is an important and useful skill in mathematics, often helping to illustrate an idea, or as an aid to solving a problem.

Solving the following problem is greatly simplified by drawing appropriate graphs.

1   A market trader finds that she can sell 60 transistor radios each week if she reduces her profit margin to zero, but sales drop when she increases her price. In fact, at £6.00 profit per radio she sells none at all. What profit margin should she choose to achieve the greatest possible total profit?

To help decide what profit margin to choose, the trader models her sales figures with the straight-line graph shown.

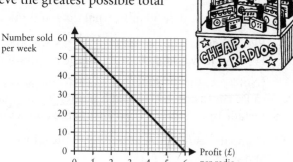

(a) Use the graph to copy and complete this table.

Profit (£) per radio	0	1	2	3	4	5	6
Number of radios sold	60						0
Total profit (£) from sales						50	

(b) Draw a graph from the table, plotting total profit against profit per radio. (The solution to the trader's problem should now be quite easy to see.)

(c) What profit per radio should she choose?

2D   Suppose the profit is £x per radio.

(a) Find the number of radios that the trader sells per week in terms of x.

(b) What is her total profit from sales in terms of x?

(c) What are the equations of the straight-line graph shown above and the graph that you have drawn?

In the following work you should use a graph plotting calculator (or computer package) to explore properties of the graphs of a variety of functions. Many of the functions will be new to you but you will soon become more familiar with them.

3   Use a graph plotter to draw each of the following basic functions and their graphs. Sketch them and note any features which you think are interesting. Look out for and note any features such as reflection or rotational symmetry.

(a) $y = x$ (b) $y = x^2$ (c) $y = x^3$ (d) $y = x^4$

(e) $y = \sqrt{x}$ (f) $y = \sqrt[3]{x}$ (g) $y = \dfrac{1}{x}$ (h) $y = \dfrac{1}{x^2}$

(i) $y = \sin x$ (j) $y = \cos x$ (k) $y = \tan x$ (l) $y = \log x$

(m) $y = 3^x$ (n) $y = (\tfrac{1}{2})^x$ (o) $y = |x|$ (p) $y = \text{int}(x)$

Judging from their graphs, what do you think $|x|$ and $\text{int}(x)$ mean?

4   Plot the graphs of $y = -x$, $y = -x^2$, $y = -x^3$ and $y = -x^4$.
How are they related to some of the graphs of question 3?

(Note: $-x^2$ means square first, then change sign. Sometimes this can cause confusion with a graph plotter, and it may be necessary to include brackets, $-(x^2)$, to ensure the correct meaning.)

5   Compare and comment on the graphs of $y = x^2$ and $y = \sqrt{x}$, and $y = x^3$ and $y = \sqrt[3]{x}$.

Linear graphs

When a function has a straight-line graph, it is said to be **linear**.

Examples of straight-line graphs may be found in a wide range of subjects.

(a) The distance-against-time graph of a body moving with constant speed is a straight line.

(b) Economists often assume that the demand for a commodity decreases linearly with price (as with the transistor radios on p. 1).

(c) The amount by which a metal rod expands when it is heated is proportional to its temperature and so the graph of length against temperature is linear.

Linear graphs are simple to deal with. Sometimes you can approximate more complex graphs by linear graphs, as in the example which follows.

6 A long-distance walker aims to cover the 800 miles from John O'Groats to Land's End at the rate of 30 miles per day.

The graphs below illustrate his progress after t days.

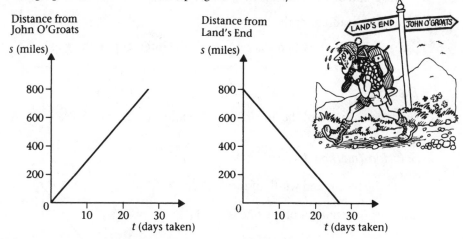

(a) What distance has the walker covered after one day and how far is he from Land's End?

(b) How far has he walked after two days and how far is he from Land's End?

(c) How far has he walked after t days and how far is he from Land's End?

(d) What are the equations of the two graphs of distance against time?

7D What assumptions have been made to obtain straight-line graphs? Do you think these assumptions are reasonable?

The graphs have the following features.

- They are both straight-line or **linear** graphs. For this reason, $30t$ and $800 - 30t$ are called **linear functions** of t.

- The graph of $s = 30t$ passes through the origin and has a **gradient** of 30.

- The graph of $s = 800 - 30t$ crosses the s-axis at 800. The number 800 is called the **intercept** on the s-axis. This function is decreasing, the graph having a **negative gradient** of -30.

An introduction to straight-line graphs is provided in the support material S1.1 on p. 8.

y is a **linear function** of x if it can be expressed in the form $mx + c$.

The graph of y against x is then a straight line.

m is the **gradient** of the line.

c is the value of y when x is zero and is the **intercept** on the y-axis.

Example 1

Find the equation of the line joining the points $(1, 2)$ and $(3, 8)$.

Solution (method 1)

From the height and width of the smaller triangle, the gradient of the line is $\dfrac{6}{2} = 3$.

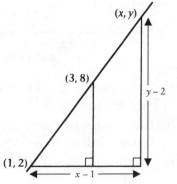

For any point (x, y) on the line, the gradient is also $\dfrac{y - 2}{x - 1}$.

(You can see this from the larger triangle.)

So $y - 2 = 3(x - 1)$

$\implies \quad y = 3x - 1 \qquad$ ($\implies$ means 'implies')

A straight line of slope m passing through the point (x_1, y_1) has equation $\dfrac{y - y_1}{x - x_1} = m \quad$ or $\quad y - y_1 = m(x - x_1)$.

Solution (method 2)

The gradient is $\dfrac{6}{2} = 3$.

So in the form $\quad y = mx + c$
the equation is $\quad y = 3x + c$.

The line goes through $(1, 2)$ so we substitute these values:

$$2 = 3 + c$$
$$\implies c = -1$$

The line has the equation $y = 3x - 1$.

Exercise A (answers p. 167)

1 Draw these straight lines.

(a) $y = 2x + 4$ (b) $s = -2t + 7$ (c) $2y = 4x - 3$

(d) $x = -y + 4$ (e) $y = 5$ (f) $x = 3$

2 Write down the equation for each of the following straight lines.

(a)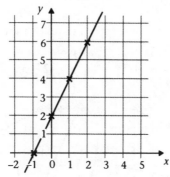

(b)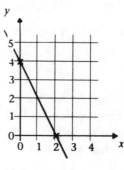

(c)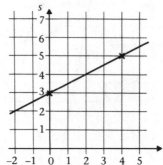

(d)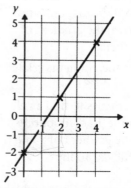

3 Find the equations of the straight lines passing through these points.

(a) $(0, 3)$ and $(2, 7)$ (b) $(1, 4)$ and $(2, 6)$

(c) $(5, 4)$ and $(10, 19)$ (d) $(1, -5)$ and $(-4, 0)$

(e) $(1, 2)$ and $(-2, 1)$ (f) $(-3, -2)$ and $(-1, 2)$

4 Find the equation of each of these straight lines.

(a) Gradient $= 4$, passing through $(3, -2)$

(b) Gradient $= 0.25$, passing through $(-1, 6)$

(c) Gradient $= -4$, passing through $(-2, -5)$

5 State whether each of these equations gives a straight-line graph.

(a) $y = x^2 - 2$ (b) $2y + x = 4$ (c) $x^2 + y^2 = 9$

(d) $3x + 4y - 2 = 0$ (e) $xy = 5$ (f) $x - 5y + 6 = 0$

(g) $x = 5 - 2y$ (h) $x - y = 2x - y + 6$ (i) $y - 3 = 4(x + 1)$

(j) $\dfrac{x}{2} + \dfrac{y}{3} = 1$ (k) $\sqrt{y} = \sqrt{x} + 1$ (l) $-2x + 3y + 8 = 0$

B Perpendicular and parallel lines (answers p. 167)

1 Superimpose these lines on a graph plotter.

$$y = 0.7x + 1 \qquad y = 0.7x - 2 \qquad y = 0.7x + 8$$

What do you find?

2 Plot another set of graphs of the form $y = mx + c$, where m is the same for all of them and c varies. What happens?

3 Use what you have found to sort these into three sets of parallel lines.

$$y = 3x - 4 \qquad y = -\tfrac{1}{2}x + 2 \qquad y = 3x + \tfrac{1}{2} \qquad y = -3x + 4$$
$$y = 7 - \tfrac{1}{2}x \qquad y = 7 - 3x \qquad y = -\tfrac{1}{2} + 3x \qquad y = -2 - 3x$$

4 Some of these lines are at right angles (perpendicular) to one another. Which is perpendicular to which?

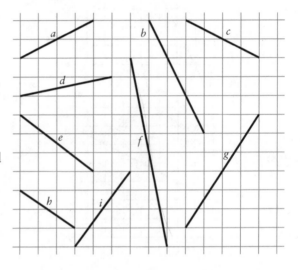

5 Select a pair of perpendicular lines from the diagram and write down the gradient of each of them.

How are the gradients related to one another?

Try other pairs to find a rule relating the gradient of one line to the gradient of a line perpendicular to it.

6 Use your rule to decide which of these straight lines are perpendicular to one another.

$$y = 2x + 4 \qquad y = 2 - 5x \qquad y = -\tfrac{1}{2}x - 3$$
$$y = \tfrac{1}{5}x - 2 \qquad y = 3 - 2x \qquad y = \tfrac{1}{2}x + 5$$

Lines that are **parallel** have the **same gradient**.

If two lines with gradients m_1 and m_2 are **perpendicular**,

$$m_2 = \frac{-1}{m_1} \quad \text{or} \quad m_1 m_2 = -1.$$

You saw in question 5 of Exercise A that a straight line could be written in various forms including $ax + by + c = 0$. You can rearrange such equations into the familiar form $y = mx + c$ by making y the subject of the formula.

7 For each of these equations,
  (i) rearrange it into the form $y = mx + c$
  (ii) give the gradient
  (iii) give the intercept on the y-axis.
  (a) $3x + y + 7 = 0$ (b) $x + 2y - 8 = 0$
  (c) $4x + 5y + 1 = 0$ (d) $3x - 2y - 6 = 0$
  (e) $-7x + 2y + 3 = 0$ (f) $-4x - 6y + 9 = 0$

8 Generalising from your answers to question 7, what is the gradient of a straight line in the form $ax + by + c = 0$?

Mid-points

If a straight line is drawn between $(1, 2)$ and $(5, 8)$ it is easy to see from the diagram that their **mid-point** (the point halfway between them) is $(3, 5)$.

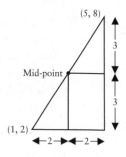

9 Give the mid-point of each of these pairs of points. Draw a sketch if you need to.
  (a) $(4, 4)$ and $(6, 10)$ (b) $(3, 1)$ and $(7, 8)$
  (c) $(2, 5)$ and $(9, 1)$ (d) $(4, -2)$ and $(8, 4)$
  (e) $(-1, 3)$ and $(3, -1)$ (f) $(-4, 5)$ and $(-1, -2)$

> The **mid-point** of (x_1, y_1) and (x_2, y_2) is $\left(\dfrac{x_1 + x_2}{2}, \dfrac{y_1 + y_2}{2}\right)$.

Exercise B (answers p. 168)

1 Which of these lines are parallel to the line $y = 4x - 2$?
  $y = 2 - 4x$ $y = 4x + 8$ $4x + y + 6 = 0$ $-8x + 2y - 7 = 0$

2 Which of these lines are parallel to the line $2x + 3y - 4 = 0$?
  $3x - 2y + 1 = 0$ $y = \frac{2}{3}x + 6$ $4x + 6y + 3 = 0$ $y = -\frac{2}{3}x$

3 Which of these lines are **perpendicular** to the line $y = 3x + 1$?
  $y = \frac{1}{3}x - 1$ $6x - 2y + 3 = 0$ $y = -\frac{1}{3}x + 2$ $x + 3y = 1$

4 Which of these lines are perpendicular to the line $5x - 3y + 2 = 0$?

  $y = \frac{3}{5}x + 4$ $3x - 5y - 10 = 0$ $y = 6 - \frac{3}{5}x$ $-3x - 5y + 1 = 0$

5 Give the equations of straight lines fitting these conditions.
   (a) Parallel to $y = 4x + 1$ and passing through $(2, 5)$
   (b) Parallel to $2x + 3y + 4 = 0$ and passing through $(3, 2)$
   (c) Perpendicular to $y = 7x - 2$ and passing through $(0, 0)$
   (d) Perpendicular to $x + 9y - 4 = 0$ and passing through $(6, 7)$

6 A quadrilateral is drawn with its vertices at the points shown.

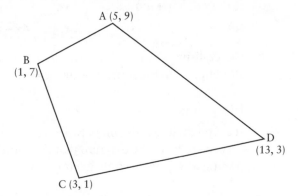

   (a) Give the mid-points of the four sides.
   (b) A new quadrilateral is formed by joining the four mid-points. Work out the gradient of each side of this new quadrilateral.
   (c) What do your answers to (b) tell you about this new quadrilateral?

7 A line is drawn from $(1, 2)$ to $(6, 4)$.
   Find the equation of a line that goes through its mid-point and is perpendicular to it.

After working through this chapter you should

1 be able to find the gradient and the equation of a line joining two points

2 be familiar with linear functions and the equations of straight lines

3 be able to identify parallel and perpendicular straight-line graphs from their equations.

S1.1 The equation of a straight line (see p. 3, answers p. 168)

1 (a) Use a graph plotter to sketch the graph of $y = 2x + c$ where $c = -2, -1, 0, 1, 2$.
   (b) Describe the effect of varying c.

2 (a) Use a graph plotter to sketch the graph of $y = mx + 3$ where $m = -2, -1, 0, 1, 2$.
   (b) Describe the effect of varying m.

A gradient of 1 in 5, i.e. a rise of 1 unit for every 5 horizontal units travelled, is described mathematically as a gradient of $\frac{1}{5}$ or 0.2 .

> The gradient of a line measures how steeply it rises. Gradient is measured as
>
> $$\frac{\text{vertical } \mathbf{increase}}{\text{horizontal } \mathbf{increase}}$$
>
> Notice that if y decreases, then the 'vertical increase' will be negative.

Example

Find the gradient of the line AB.

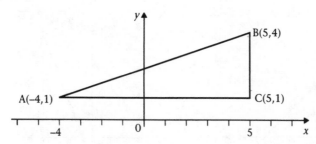

Solution

The gradient is $\dfrac{BC}{AC} = \dfrac{3}{9} = \dfrac{1}{3}$.

3 Plot the points A (1, 2) and B (3, 10) and calculate the gradient of the line AB.

4 Find the gradient of the line AB for these points.

   (a) A (−1, 2), B (2, 11)   (b) A (3, 1), B (−1, 9)   (c) A (4, 1), B (1, 1)

5 (a) Find the gradient of the line.

   (b) Where does the line cross the y-axis?

   (c) The equation of the line is $y = 2x + 1$. Show that the points (0, 1) and (2, 5) satisfy this equation.

   (d) How is the equation $y = 2x + 1$ related to your answers to (a) and (b)?

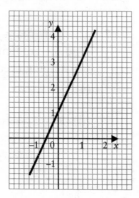

6 (a) Find the gradient of the line.

    (b) Where does the line cross the *y*-axis?

    (c) The equation of the line is $y = -3x - 1$. Choose two points on the line, and show that their coordinates satisfy this equation.

    (d) How is the equation $y = -3x - 1$ related to your answers to (a) and (b)?

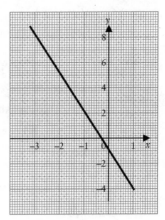

7 Find the equations of the lines.

(a)

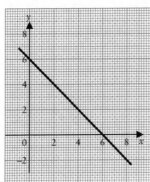

(b)

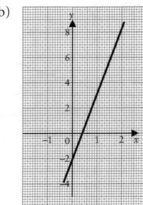

Any equation in the form $y = mx + c$ represents a straight line.

Its gradient is *m* and its intercept on the *y*-axis is *c*.

---

8 There are many alternative ways of writing equations of straight lines. Find the gradients and *y*-intercepts of the following straight lines by rearranging them into the form $y = mx + c$.

    (a) $y = 9 - 4x$

    (b) $2y = 6x + 3$

    (c) $2y - 4x = 5$

    (d) $3x + 5y + 10 = 0$

    (e) $y - 3 = 5(x - 2)$

    (f) $\dfrac{x}{4} + \dfrac{y}{5} = 1$

2 Quadratic graphs and equations

A Quadratic functions (answers p. 169)

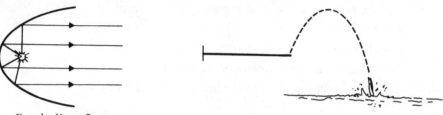

Parabolic reflector   Parabolic path of body under gravity

You can see the curve known as a **parabola** in various everyday situations and it arises in mathematics most simply as the graph $y = x^2$.

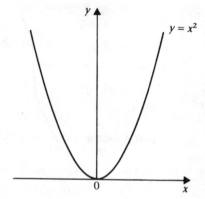

The graph of $y = x^2$ has line symmetry in the y-axis, and a **vertex** at the origin. In this case the vertex is the minimum point. For inverted parabolas it would be the maximum point.

In this section we will concentrate on **functions** of the form
$$y = ax^2 + bx + c \qquad \text{(where } a \neq 0\text{)}$$
A function of this form is called a **quadratic function**.

1D | Use a graph plotter to see whether the graph of $ax^2 + bx + c$ is always a parabola, whatever the values of a, b and c ($a \neq 0$). Note, for example, the effect of making a negative.

We will now look at some other ways of writing a quadratic function.

2 Plot the graph of $y = x^2$ and superimpose the graph of $y = x^2 + 3$.

3 Superimpose various graphs of the form $y = x^2 + q$, for both positive and negative values of q. Write down your conclusions.

4 Plot the graph of $y = x^2$ and superimpose the graph of $y = (x + 4)^2$. Describe carefully the relationship between the graphs.

5 Superimpose various graphs of the form $y = (x + p)^2$ for both positive and negative values of p.

Describe carefully how they are related to $y = x^2$.

6 Plot the graph of $y = x^2$ and superimpose the graph of $y = (x + 5)^2 + 2$.

(a) How are the two curves related?

(b) What are the coordinates of the vertex of $y = (x + 5)^2 + 2$?

(c) What is the equation of the line of symmetry of $y = (x + 5)^2 + 2$?

7 Repeat question 6 comparing $y = x^2$ with other graphs of the form $y = (x + p)^2 + q$.

(a) What is the effect of the value p?

(b) What is the effect of the value q?

(c) What are the coordinates of the vertex of the parabola $y = (x + p)^2 + q$?

(d) What is the equation of its line of symmetry?

The graph of $y = (x + p)^2 + q$ is a **translation** of the graph of $y = x^2$.

Using **vector notation**, this translation can be described as $\begin{bmatrix} -p \\ q \end{bmatrix}$

i.e. the curve is moved by $-p$ units in the x direction and by q units in the y direction.

This is an important result which will be used later.

Example 1

Sketch the graph of $y = (x + 3)^2 - 7$.

Solution

The graph of $y = (x + 3)^2 - 7$ is obtained by translating the graph

of $y = x^2$ through $\begin{bmatrix} -3 \\ -7 \end{bmatrix}$.

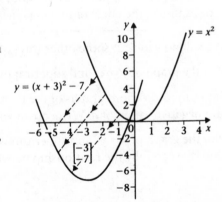

As the vertex of $y = x^2$ is at $(0, 0)$, you can see that the vertex of $y = (x + 3)^2 - 7$ is at $(-3, -7)$.

8 Suggest *possible* equations for the following curves. The curve $y = x^2$ is shown dotted in each case and the coordinates of the vertex are given. Use a graph plotter to check your equations.

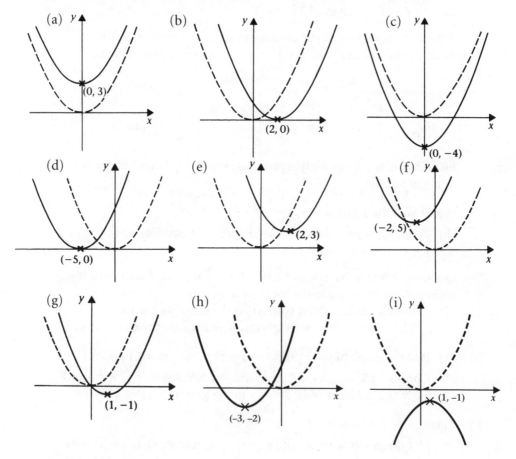

Completing the square

Before going further you may find it helpful to revise how to multiply brackets.

Example 2

Multiply out: $(x + 5)(x - 3)$.

Solution

$$(x + 5)(x - 3) = x(x - 3) + 5(x - 3)$$
$$= x^2 - 3x + 5x - 15$$
$$= x^2 + 2x - 15$$

With practice you should be able to write down the answer straight away.

$(\overbrace{x+5})(x-3)$ gives x^2

$(\overbrace{x+5})(x-3)$ gives $2x$ } which combine to give $x^2 + 2x - 15$.

$(\overbrace{x+5})(x-3)$ gives -15

A table is a good way of showing the process of multiplying two brackets and is useful when you have to reverse the process later.

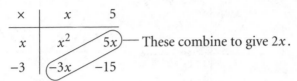

These combine to give $2x$.

Further practice in multiplying brackets is provided in the support material S2.1 on p. 30.

9 (a) Sketch the graph of $y = (x+5)^2 + 3$.

(b) By multiplying out the bracket, express the equation in the form $y = x^2 + bx + c$.

Question 9 shows that it is not difficult to convert an equation in the form $y = (x+p)^2 + q$ into the form $y = x^2 + bx + c$.
The following work is about converting the other way, from $y = x^2 + bx + c$ to $y = (x+p)^2 + q$ (**completed square form**).

10 (a) Plot the graph of $y = x^2$ and superimpose the graph of $y = x^2 + 2x$.

(b) Consider the vertices to decide what translation maps $y = x^2$ onto $y = x^2 + 2x$. Hence write $x^2 + 2x$ in the form $(x+p)^2 + q$.

11 Taking values of b as (a) 10   (b) −6   (c) 7

(i) plot the graph of $y = x^2$ and superimpose the graph of $y = x^2 + bx$

(ii) write down the translation which maps $y = x^2$ onto $y = x^2 + bx$, and hence write $x^2 + bx$ in the form $(x+p)^2 + q$.

12 (a) On the basis of your work in question 11 write $x^2 + 4x$ in the form $(x+p)^2 + q$.

(b) Hence write $x^2 + 4x + 9$ in the form $(x+p)^2 + q$.

(c) Check your answer to part (b) by plotting the graph of $x^2 + 4x + 9$ and a graph of the expression you have written.

To convert any quadratic to completed square form without depending on experiments with a graphic calculator you can use algebra. The method depends on the idea of a quadratic that is a **perfect square**.

13 (a) Expand these perfect squares.

   (i) $(x+5)^2$ (ii) $(x-3)^2$

   (b) Express these perfect squares in the form $(x+p)^2$.

   (i) x^2+4x+4 (ii) $x^2+12x+36$ (iii) $x^2-10x+25$

14 (a) Express x^2+6x+9 in the form $(x+p)^2$.

   (b) Hence express x^2+6x in the form $(x+p)^2+q$.

   (c) Hence express x^2+6x+5 in the form $(x+p)^2+q$.

   (d) Sketch the graph of $y=x^2+6x+5$.

15 (a) Express x^2+12x in the form $(x+p)^2+q$.

   (b) Hence write $x^2+12x+20$ in completed square form.

16 (a) Express x^2-14x in the form $(x+p)^2+q$.

   (b) Hence write $x^2-14x+80$ in completed square form.

> The method developed in questions 14, 15 and 16 is called
> **completing the square**. It can be used for any quadratic. The
> process is summarised in the following example.

Example 3

Express x^2-8x+3 in the form $(x+p)^2+q$.

Solution

$$x^2-8x=(x-4)^2-16$$

Find the square which fits the first two terms.

$$\Rightarrow x^2-8x+3=(x-4)^2-16+3$$

Adjust your answer to take into account the constant term.

$$\Rightarrow x^2-8x+3=(x-4)^2-13$$

With practice you may be able to obtain this line immediately.

17 Write these in the form $(x+p)^2+q$.

   (a) $x^2+14x+2$ (b) x^2-3x+1 (c) x^2+8x-3

18 (a) Express x^2-2x+1 in completed square form.

   (b) Explain why x^2-2x+1 can never be negative.

19E (a) Express $x^2 + bx + c$ in completed square form.

(b) Write down the coordinates of the vertex of the graph of
$y = x^2 + bx + c$.

(c) What is the relationship that must be satisfied by b and c if the
expression $x^2 + bx + c$ is always positive?

In order to complete the square for $x^2 + bx + c$,

(a) write $x^2 + bx$ in the form $(x + p)^2 + q$
where $p = \frac{1}{2}b$ and $q = -p^2$

(b) adjust the constant term by adding on c.

Exercise A (answers p. 170)

1 Write each of these equations in the form $y = x^2 + bx + c$.

(a) $y = (x + 3)^2 + 7$ (b) $y = (x - 1)^2 + 4$

(c) $y = (x - 6)^2 - 8$ (d) $y = (x + 4)^2 - 1$

2 For each of the following equations,

(i)   complete the square

(ii) check your answer by multiplying out

(iii) without using a graph plotter, sketch the corresponding graph.

(a) $y = x^2 + 8x + 5$ (b) $y = x^2 - 4x - 3$

(c) $y = x^2 - 5x + 6$ (d) $y = x^2 - 7x - 3$

3 (i) Write down a possible completed square form for the quadratic
functions whose graphs are shown below.

(ii) Hence write down the equations of the quadratic functions in the
form $y = x^2 + bx + c$.

(a)

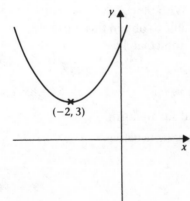

$(-2, 3)$

(b)

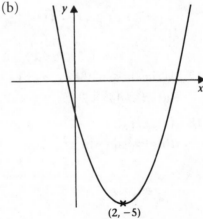

$(2, -5)$

4 Write in completed square form and hence sketch (*without* the aid of a graph plotter) the graphs of these expressions.

(a) $x^2 + 4x - 2$ (b) $x^2 - 5x + 3$ (c) $x^2 + 12x - 5$

5E The graph of $y = d(x + e)^2 + f$ has its vertex at $(6, 3)$ and also passes through the point $(4, 11)$. Find the values of d, e and f.

B Zeros of quadratics (answers p. 171)

The axis of symmetry and the vertex are important features of a parabolic graph, but they are by no means the only ones. Also useful are the points at which the graph crosses the axes, if it does! The graphs of all quadratic functions of x must cross the y-axis, but some graphs, such as those below, do not cross the x-axis.

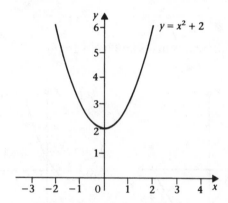

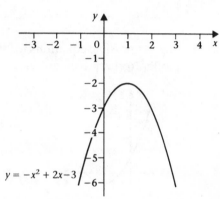

For the graph of any function, the point of intersection with the y-axis is easily found by putting $x = 0$ in the function. The values of x at the points of intersection with the x-axis are called the **roots** of the equation $y = 0$, and are also known as the **zeros** of the function because they make the function equal to zero. The zeros of $x^2 - x - 6$ are -2 and 3.

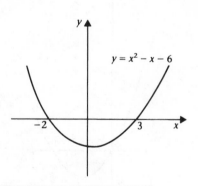

1D (a) If the product of two numbers ab equals 0, what can you say about either a or b?

(b) State all solutions of these equations.

(i) $x + 2 = 0$ (ii) $x - 1 = 0$ (iii) $(x - 1)(x + 2) = 0$

2 (a) Plot the graph of $y = (x+1)(x+5)$. What is the significance of the numbers 1 and 5 with respect to the graph?

   (b) Investigate the graph of $y = (x+\alpha)(x+\beta)$ for various values of α and β, including positive and negative values, zero and the case where $\alpha = \beta$. What is the significance of α and β for the graph?

3 What is the relationship between the graphs of

$$y = (x+\alpha)(x+\beta) \qquad \text{and} \qquad y = -(x+\alpha)(x+\beta)\,?$$

> The quadratic expressions above are in **factorised form**.
> Factorised form gives important information about the graph of
> the function and, as you will see later in this section, provides one
> way of solving equations.

4 Suggest possible equations for the following curves and use a graph plotter to check your answers.

(a)

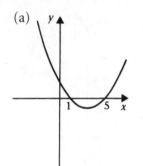

(b)

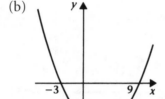

(c)

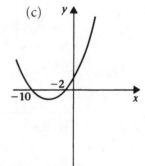

(d)

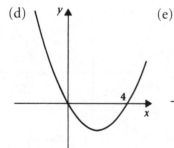

(e)

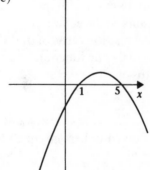

(f)

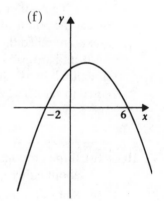

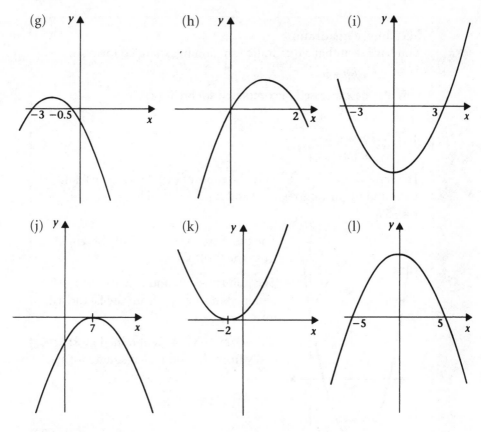

(g) with x-intercepts at -3 and -0.5

(h) with x-intercept at 2

(i) with x-intercepts at -3 and 3

(j) with x-intercept at 7

(k) with x-intercept at -2

(l) with x-intercepts at -5 and 5

5 Without the aid of a graph plotter, make sketches of the graphs of these functions.

(a) $y = (x+2)(x-1)$ (b) $y = (x-2)^2$ (c) $y = -(x+1)^2$

Sketching a quadratic

You have seen that a quadratic function in expanded form such as

$$x^2 + 6x + 5$$

may also be expressed in completed square form

$$(x+3)^2 - 4$$

or in factorised form

$$(x+1)(x+5)$$

The zeros of $(x+1)(x+5)$ are the roots of $(x+1)(x+5) = 0$ and are found by putting $x+1 = 0$ and $x+5 = 0$ to give $x = -1$ and $x = -5$.

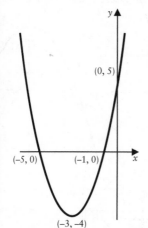

The point $(0, 5)$ is most easily obtained from the form $y = x^2 + 6x + 5$.

The points $(-1, 0)$ and $(-5, 0)$ are obtained most easily from the factorised form $y = (x+1)(x+5)$.

The vertex $(-3, -4)$ is obtained most easily from the completed square form $y = (x+3)^2 - 4$.

Factorising quadratics

If you have a quadratic function in the form $ax^2 + bx + c$, converting it to factorised form will tell you where it crosses the x-axis.

We will begin with the simple case where $a = 1$ using a table of the kind shown on p. 14.

Example 4

Factorise the quadratic $x^2 - 9x + 18$.

Solution

It is straightforward to fill in the table this far.

×	x
x	x^2
	18

You now have to put positive and negative values here that have 18 as their product.

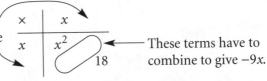

These terms have to combine to give $-9x$.

With a little experimenting values that work can be found.

×	x	-3
x	x^2	$-3x$
-6	$-6x$	18

Here is another way of illustrating the relationships.

$$+18 = (-3) \times (-6)$$
$$x^2 - 9x + 18 = (x-3)(x-6)$$
$$-9 = (-3) + (-6)$$

With practice, you should be able to factorise simple quadratics in a single step.

6   Factorise the following.

(a) $x^2 + 7x + 12$ (b) $x^2 - 2x - 3$ (c) $x^2 - 7x + 10$

(d) $x^2 - 4$ (e) $x^2 - 7x$ (f) $x^2 - 6x + 9$

(g) $x^2 + 3x + 2$ (h) $x^2 + 4x + 4$ (i) $x^2 - 49$

Further practice with basic factorisation is provided in the support material S2.2 on p. 31.

Some quadratics cannot be factorised using the approach above (even though they cross the x-axis).

From your work on graph plotting you know that some quadratic functions do not have zeroes (do not have to cut the x-axis). They cannot be factorised either.

7   Use a graph plotter to plot the graphs of these functions.

(a) $y = x^2 + 3x + 2$ (b) $y = x^2 + x - 1$ (c) $y = x^2 - x + 1$

In each case determine whether

(i)   the quadratic function has any zeros

(ii)   the quadratic expression can be factorised with factors of the form $(ax + b)$ where a and b are whole numbers (and, if so, factorise it).

The following example shows how to solve a quadratic equation in the form $ax^2 + bx + c = 0$ if the quadratic function can be factorised.

Example 5

Solve the equation $x^2 + x - 12 = 0$.

Solution

$$x^2 + x - 12 = 0$$
$$\Rightarrow (x+4)(x-3) = 0$$
$$\Rightarrow \quad \text{either } x+4 = 0 \quad \text{or} \quad x-3 = 0$$
$$\Rightarrow \qquad\qquad x = -4 \text{ or } 3$$

8 Solve the following equations by factorisation.

(a) $x^2 + 5x + 6 = 0$ (b) $x^2 + 6x + 5 = 0$ (c) $x^2 - 8x + 15 = 0$

(d) $x^2 - 8x + 12 = 0$ (e) $x^2 - 9 = 0$ (f) $25 - x^2 = 0$

(g) $x^2 + 3x - 18 = 0$ (h) $x^2 - 3x - 10 = 0$ (i) $x^2 - 4x = 0$

(j) $x^2 - 6x + 9 = 0$

The solutions to some equations seem obvious though care needs to be taken not to miss solutions: for example, $x^2 = 9$ clearly has $x = 3$ as a solution, but it also has the solution $x = -3$.

Other equations may need some rearrangement before solving.

Example 6

Solve the equation $x = \dfrac{16}{x}$.

Solution

$$x = \frac{16}{x}$$
$$\Rightarrow x^2 = 16 \text{ (multiplying both sides by } x)$$
$$\Rightarrow x = \pm 4$$

9 Rearrange these into the form $x^2 + bx + c = 0$ and solve them.

(a) $x^2 = 15 - 2x$ (b) $x = 12 - x^2$ (c) $90 = x^2 + x$

(d) $x^2 = 49$ (e) $9 = x^2$ (f) $x = \dfrac{9}{x}$

(g) $x^2 + 2x = 35$ (h) $x^2 = 5x$ (i) $x - \dfrac{1}{x} = 0$

Harder factorisation

You will usually need to experiment more when the value of a in a quadratic of the form $ax^2 + bx + c$ is not 1.

Example 7

Factorise the function $4x^2 + 4x - 3$.

Solution

The first step is not so obvious as when you just had x^2 because there are two possible ways of getting $4x^2$.

$\times$	$2x$
$2x$	$4x^2$
	-3

$\times$	$4x$
x	$4x^2$
	-3

Only the left-hand table leads to values that work.

$\times$	$2x$	3
$2x$	$4x^2$	$6x$
-1	$-2x$	-3

10 Factorise these.

(a) $2x^2 + 7x + 3$ (b) $4x^2 - 27x - 7$ (c) $2x^2 + 5x + 3$

(d) $2x^2 + 5x - 3$ (e) $3x^2 - x$ (f) $2x^2 - 7x - 4$

(g) $6x^2 - 7x + 2$ (h) $9x^2 + 13x + 4$ (i) $4x^2 + 4x - 15$

(j) $6x^2 + 71x - 12$ (k) $9x^2 - 6x - 8$

Exercise B (answers p. 173)

1 Find the possible values of x for each of these.

(a) $(x + 1)(x + 3) = 0$ (b) $(x - 1)(x + 9) = 0$

(c) $(x - 1)(2x + 3) = 0$ (d) $(4x - 1)(x + 2) = 0$

(e) $(5x - 2)(x + 4) = 0$ (f) $x(2x - 7) = 0$

(g) $(3x - 4)(1 - 2x) = 0$ (h) $(4x + 5)(2x + 3) = 0$

2 Solve these equations by factorisation.

(a) $x^2 + 2x - 24 = 0$ (b) $x^2 - 6x - 16 = 0$

(c) $3x^2 - 14x + 8 = 0$ (d) $3x^2 + 2x - 1 = 0$

(e) $2x^2 + 5x + 2 = 0$ (f) $2x^2 + 7x + 5 = 0$

3 Rearrange these equations and solve them by factorisation.

(a) $2x^2 = 5x + 3$ (b) $2x^2 = 2 - 3x$

(c) $3x^2 + 3 = 10x$ (d) $5x^2 = 14x + 3$

(e) $x(5x - 4) = 2 - x$ (f) $2x(5x - 3) = 5x + 6$

4 Sketch a graph for each of these functions, marking the exact values of the coordinates of the points where the curve crosses the x-axis.

(a) $y = (2x - 1)(3x + 7)$ (b) $y = 3x(5x - 1)$

5 Simplify $(x - 1)(x - 5) + (x - 1)(x + 2)$.
Hence solve the equation $(x - 1)(x - 5) + (x - 1)(x + 2) = 0$.

6 Find the two times when a projectile is at a height of 140 m, if the height h metres, after time t seconds, is given by the expression $h = 40t - 5t^2 + 80$.

C Solving quadratic equations by completing the square
(answers p. 173)

The path round the square lawn is 1 metre wide. If the area of the path is equal to the area of the lawn, the dimensions of the lawn may be found as follows.

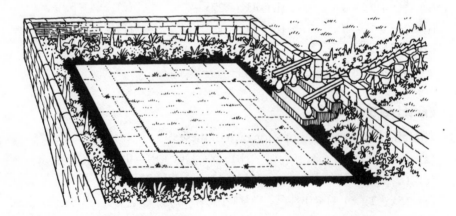

Let x be the length of a side of the lawn.

Area of lawn $= x^2$

Area of path $= 4(x + 1)$

So $x^2 = 4x + 4$

$x^2 - 4x - 4 = 0$

This equation does not factorise to give integer roots!

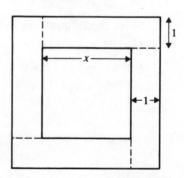

1D Instead, rewrite the equation with its left-hand side in completed square form.

Now see if you can solve the equation.

Do you get two roots? Does this give you the dimensions of the lawn?

Using the completed square form gives an alternative approach to solving a quadratic equation.

Example 8

Solve the equation $x^2 + 4x + 1 = 0$ using the method of completing the square.

Solution

$$x^2 + 4x + 1 = 0$$
$$\Rightarrow \quad (x+2)^2 - 4 + 1 = 0$$
$$\Rightarrow \quad (x+2)^2 = 3$$
$$\Rightarrow \quad x + 2 = \pm\sqrt{3}$$
$$\Rightarrow \quad x = \sqrt{3} - 2 \text{ or } -\sqrt{3} - 2$$

$\sqrt{3} - 2$ and $-\sqrt{3} - 2$ are the exact solutions to the equation.

-0.27 and -3.73 are approximate solutions to two decimal places.

A calculator value for $\sqrt{3}$ cannot be exact because $\sqrt{3}$ cannot be expressed as a fraction. It is called an irrational number.

2 Solve the following equations by the method of completing the square.

  (a) $x^2 + 6x + 4 = 0$ (b) $x^2 - 3x - 2 = 0$ (c) $x^2 + 5x + 3 = 0$

Give your answers (i) as exact solutions and (ii) to 2 d.p.

You can also use completing the square to solve equations where the coefficient of x is not 1.

Example 9

Solve $2x^2 + 5x - 1 = 0$ by completing the square.

Solution

$$2x^2 + 5x - 1 = 0$$
$$\Rightarrow \quad x^2 + \tfrac{5}{2}x - \tfrac{1}{2} = 0 \qquad \text{(dividing both sides by 2)}$$
$$\Rightarrow \quad (x + \tfrac{5}{4})^2 - \tfrac{25}{16} - \tfrac{1}{2} = 0$$
$$\Rightarrow \quad x + \tfrac{5}{4} = \pm\sqrt{\tfrac{33}{16}}$$
$$\Rightarrow \quad x = -\tfrac{5}{4} \pm \sqrt{\tfrac{33}{16}}$$

3 Solve the following equations by the method of completing the square.

(a) $2x^2 + 6x + 3 = 0$ (b) $3x^2 - 3x - 2 = 0$ (c) $4x^2 + 6x + 1 = 0$

Give your answers (i) as exact solutions and (ii) to 2 d.p.

Completing the square can be used to establish a general formula for solving quadratic equations.

$$ax^2 + bx + c = 0$$

$$x^2 + \frac{b}{a}x + \frac{c}{a} = 0 \qquad (1)$$

$$\left(x + \frac{b}{2a}\right)^2 - \frac{b^2}{4a^2} + \frac{c}{a} = 0 \qquad (2)$$

$$\left(x + \frac{b}{2a}\right)^2 = \frac{b^2}{4a^2} - \frac{c}{a} \qquad (3)$$

$$\left(x + \frac{b}{2a}\right)^2 = \frac{b^2 - 4ac}{4a^2} \qquad (4)$$

$$x + \frac{b}{2a} = \pm \sqrt{\frac{b^2 - 4ac}{4a^2}} \qquad (5)$$

$$x = \frac{-b}{2a} \pm \frac{\sqrt{b^2 - 4ac}}{\sqrt{4a^2}} \qquad (6)$$

$$x = \frac{-b \pm \sqrt{b^2 - 4ac}}{2a}$$

4D

(a) What has happened in line 1?

(b) Where has the $\dfrac{b^2}{4a^2}$ come from in line 2?

(c) Why has the c in line 3 become $4ac$ in line 4?

(d) Why has the $\pm$ appeared in line 5?

(e) The change to the square root between lines 5 and 6 is like

saying $\sqrt{\dfrac{9}{16}} = \dfrac{\sqrt{9}}{\sqrt{16}}$. Could you convince someone that

$\sqrt{\dfrac{9}{16}} = \dfrac{\sqrt{9}}{\sqrt{16}}$?

The formula for solving the general quadratic equation
$ax^2 + bx + c = 0$, $a \neq 0$, is

$$x = \frac{-b \pm \sqrt{b^2 - 4ac}}{2a}.$$

Example 10

Solve the equation $5x^2 - 3x - 4 = 0$, giving the solutions correct to 2 decimal places.

Solution

Using $x = \dfrac{-b \pm \sqrt{b^2 - 4ac}}{2a}$, where $a = 5$, $b = -3$, $c = -4$,

$$x = \frac{3 \pm \sqrt{9 - 4 \times 5 \times (-4)}}{2 \times 5}$$

$$\Rightarrow x = \frac{3 \pm \sqrt{89}}{10}$$

$$\Rightarrow x = 1.24 \text{ or } x = -0.64 \text{ (to 2 decimal places)}$$

Note that the solution may be given in one of two forms:

$\dfrac{3 \pm \sqrt{89}}{10}$ are the **exact** solutions;

1.24 or −0.64 are the **approximate** solutions, written to 2 decimal places.

5 Use the formula to solve these.

(a) $2x^2 + 7x + 4 = 0$ (b) $3x^2 - 9x + 4 = 0$ (c) $x^2 + 3x - 5 = 0$

Give your answers (i) as exact solutions (ii) to 2 d.p.

6 Plot each of these quadratic functions on your graph plotter.

(a) $y = 3x^2 - 2x + 1$ (b) $y = 2x^2 + 6x - 1$ (c) $y = 5x^2 + 10x + 5$

(d) $y = -x^2 + 5x + 4$ (e) $y = x^2 + 4x + 4$ (f) $y = x^2 + 3x + 4$

Given that they are in the form $y = ax^2 + bx + c$, calculate the value of $b^2 - 4ac$ for each of them.

Does this show a relationship between the value $b^2 - 4ac$ and the number of roots of the equation $ax^2 + bx + c = 0$?

> The expression $b^2 - 4ac$ is called the **discriminant** of the quadratic equation $ax^2 + bx + c = 0$.
>
> The value of the discriminant tells you this:
>
> $b^2 - 4ac > 0$, there are two solutions (roots) to the equation (the graph of $y = ax^2 + bx + c$ crosses the x-axis twice).
>
> $b^2 - 4ac = 0$, there is only one solution (the graph of $y = ax^2 + bx + c$ just touches the x-axis).
>
> $b^2 - 4ac < 0$, there are no real solutions to the equation* (the graph of $y = ax^2 + bx + c$ does not cross the x-axis).
>
> *In advanced work mathematicians talk about 'imaginary' roots of such equations, but for our purposes there are no solutions.

Exercise C (answers p. 174)

1   Use the method of completing the square to solve these equations, giving your answers (i) as exact solutions and (ii) to 2 d.p.

   (a) $x^2 + 4x - 7 = 0$ (b) $x^2 - 8x + 5 = 0$

   (c) $x^2 + 6x + 7 = 0$ (d) $x^2 - 3x - 3 = 0$

2   Use the quadratic equation formula to solve the following, giving your answers (i) in exact form, and (ii) to 2 decimal places.

   (a) $x^2 + 5x + 3 = 0$ (b) $3x^2 + 6x + 2 = 0$

   (c) $3x^2 + 4x - 1 = 0$ (d) $5x^2 - 8x - 1 = 0$

   (e) $-2x^2 + 7x + 1 = 0$ (f) $3x^2 - 7x - 2 = 0$

3   By considering the discriminant, state whether each of these equations has two solutions, one solution or no real solutions.

   (a) $3x^2 + 7x + 2 = 0$ (b) $x^2 - 4x + 5 = 0$

   (c) $x^2 - 10x + 5 = 0$ (d) $5x^2 + 11x + 6 = 0$

4   Rearrange the following equations and then solve them, giving your answers to 2 decimal places.

   (a) $x^2 + 2x = 4$ (b) $5x^2 = 3x + 4$

   (c) $8 = 7x - x^2$ (d) $6x^2 + 10x - 4 = x^2 + 7x - 3$

5   Solve the following equations where possible, giving your answers to 2 decimal places. Use factors, where possible, otherwise use either the formula or completing the square.

   (a) $8x - x^2 = 0$ (b) $x^2 + 2x = 5x + 4$ (c) $x^2 + x - 1 = 0$

   (d) $x^2 = 25$ (e) $x^2 + x + 1 = 0$ (f) $25 = 10x - x^2$

6

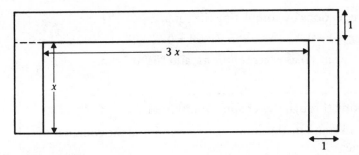

A rectangular lawn which is three times as wide as it is long has a 1 metre path round three sides only, as shown above. The area of the path is equal to the area of the lawn.

(a) If the dimensions of the lawn are x metres $\times 3x$ metres as shown, explain why
$$3x^2 = 5x + 2.$$

(b) Hence find the dimensions of the lawn.

7 Two numbers differ by 1 and have a product of 10. Let n be the smaller number.

(a) Explain why
$$n^2 + n - 10 = 0.$$

(b) Hence find the two numbers exactly.

8 (a) Use the formula to solve, where possible, the equation $y = 0$ for each of these functions.

(i) $y = x^2 - 2x + 4$ (ii) $y = x^2 - 4x + 4$ (iii) $y = x^2 - 6x + 4$

(b) The graph of each of the functions is given below. Use the information about the roots that you found in part (a) to match each function to its graph.

A   B   C

(c) Describe how the value of $b^2 - 4ac$ (the **discriminant** of the quadratic equation) relates to the number of roots.

9   Solve these equations by completing the square.

(a) $3x^2 + 2x - 4 = 0$ (b) $2x^2 - 7x + 4 = 0$ (c) $4x^2 + 2x - 1 = 0$

Give your answers (i) as exact solutions, and (ii) to 2 d.p.

After working through this chapter you should

1   be able to translate the graph of $y = x^2$ and find the equation of its image

2   know how to complete the square to find the position of the vertex and the equation of the line of symmetry for the graph of a quadratic function

3   be able to find, when possible, the zeros of a quadratic function from the factorised form

4   be able to rewrite a quadratic in a different form using this scheme

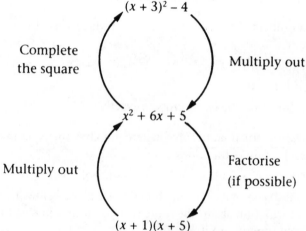

5   be able to solve a quadratic equation by completing the square

6   be able to solve a quadratic equation using the formula

7   be able to say how many roots (solutions) a quadratic equation has by calculating the discriminant.

S2.1 Multiplying brackets (see p. 14, answers p. 175)

You have met expressions like $3(x + 2)$ before.

$3(x + 2)$ means '3 lots of $(x + 2)$' or '3 lots of x' plus '3 lots of 2'.

i.e. $3(x + 2) = 3x + 6$.

1   Multiply out these expressions.

(a) $5(x + 3)$ (b) $2(x - 4)$ (c) $8(2x + 5)$

(d) $-2(x + 6)$ (e) $-4(x - 7)$ (f) $6(x - 2y)$

Complicated expressions can sometimes be simplified by first multiplying out any brackets, for example

$$6x(x-1) - 2(2x-3) = 6x^2 - 6x - 4x + 6$$
$$= 6x^2 - 10x + 6$$

2 Multiply out and gather together like terms for these expressions.

(a) $3 + 2(x+3)$ (b) $3(x-4) - x$ (c) $a + 5(8-a)$

(d) $t - 4(1-t)$ (e) $p - 1 + 2(3p-8)$ (f) $5 - 6(5x-9)$

(g) $y - 9(y-2)$ (h) $4x - x(2-x)$ (i) $2 - 3x(1+2x)$

You have seen how to multiply out expressions of the form $2x(x+1)$. You can now consider expressions like $(x+2)(x+4)$.

$(x+2)(x+4)$ means 'x lots of $(x+4)$' *plus* '2 lots of $(x+4)$'.

So: $(x+2)(x+4)$ becomes $x(x+4) + 2(x+4)$, which you can then multiply out.

3 Multiply out these expressions.

(a) $(x+2)(x+4)$ (b) $(x-3)(x+1)$

(c) $(x+4)(x-1)$ (d) $(x-5)(x-2)$

(e) $(x+5)(x-7)$ (f) $(x+8)(x+2)$

(g) $(x-2)(x-9)$ (h) $(x-4)(x+7)$

Expressions of the form $(x+2)^2$ are called **perfect squares**. $(x+2)^2$ means $(x+2)(x+2)$ and can be multiplied out in the standard way.

4 (a) Multiply out these expressions.

(i) $(x+3)^2$ (ii) $(x+7)^2$ (iii) $(x-9)^2$ (iv) $(x-6)^2$

(b) If $(x+p)^2 = x^2 + bx + c$, express

(i) b in terms of p (ii) c in terms of p

S2.2 **Further factorisation** (see p. 21, answers p. 175)

1 (a) Write these in the form $x^2 + bx + c$.

(i) $(x+2)(x+3)$ (ii) $(x-2)(x-3)$

(iii) $(x+4)(x+5)$ (iv) $(x-4)(x-5)$

(b) How is the constant term c related to the numbers in the brackets?

(c) How is b related to the numbers in the brackets?

When you multiply the brackets $(x+4)(x+7)$, you find

the coefficient of x (the number of xs) by *adding* 4 to 7,

and the constant term by *multiplying* 4 by 7.

$$(x+4)(x+7) = x^2 + (4+7)x + 4 \times 7$$
$$= x^2 + 11x + 28$$

When you factorise $x^2 + 11x + 28$ you have to do the opposite and find two numbers

(a) whose product is +28 and (b) whose sum is +11 .

Since 28 has a limited set of factors, i.e. $(\pm 28, \pm 1)$, $(\pm 14, \pm 2)$, $(\pm 7, \pm 4)$, it is not hard to see that the numbers must be 7 and 4 .

2 Factorise these expressions.

(a) $x^2 + 9x + 14$ (b) $x^2 + 13x + 40$ (c) $x^2 - 9x + 14$

(d) $x^2 + 12x + 36$ (e) $x^2 - 7x - 8$ (f) $x^2 + 3x - 28$

(g) $x^2 - 8x + 12$ (h) $x^2 - 5x - 36$ (i) $x^2 - 2x - 48$

(j) $x^2 + 2x - 24$

You should be familiar with the following important special cases.

- If the constant term is missing, x will be a factor, for example
  $x^2 + 6x = x(x + 6)$.

- If the expression has the form $x^2 - a^2$, then it factorises into
  $(x - a)(x + a)$, for example
  $x^2 - 16 = x^2 - 4^2 = (x - 4)(x + 4)$.

- Expressions of the form $x^2 + a^2$ will not factorise.

3 Factorise these expressions where possible.

(a) $x^2 + 2x$ (b) $x^2 - 9$ (c) $x^2 - 8x$

(d) $x^2 + 25$ (e) $x^2 + 25x$ (f) $x^2 - 25$

(g) $x^2 + 1$ (h) $x^2 - 1$ (i) $x^2 - x$

3 Simultaneous equations and inequalities

A Simultaneous linear equations
(answers p. 175)

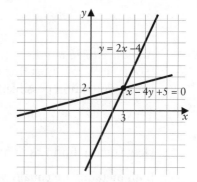

The graphs of two equations are shown here.

The one point that fits both equations is $(3, 2)$.
This means that $x = 3$ and $y = 2$ are the solution of the pair of simultaneous equations $y = 2x - 4$ and $x - 4y + 5 = 0$.

A pair of simultaneous equations can be solved either by plotting the graphs, or by algebra as in the following example.

Example 1

Solve the simultaneous equations $y = -\frac{1}{2}x + 4$
$$2x - y - 1 = 0.$$

Solution (method 1)

Label the two equations.

$$y = -\tfrac{1}{2}x + 4 \qquad\qquad (1)$$
$$2x - y - 1 = 0 \qquad\qquad (2)$$

Rearrange equation 2 to make y the subject (it doesn't have to be y: choose the variable that gives you a *simple* equation).

$$y = 2x - 1$$

Substitute this expression for y into equation 1.

$$2x - 1 = -\tfrac{1}{2}x + 4$$

Solve this to find the value of x.

$$\Rightarrow \tfrac{5}{2}x = 5$$
$$\Rightarrow x = 2$$

Substitute $x = 2$ into rearranged equation 2, say, to find the value of y.

$$y = (2 \times 2) - 1 = 3$$

Check by substituting solutions for x and y into equation 1.

Left-hand side = 3; right-hand side = $-(\tfrac{1}{2} \times 2) + 4 = 3$, so both sides agree.

Solution (method 2)

Rearrange so that one x term is under the other, and similarly with the y terms and the constant terms.

$$\tfrac{1}{2}x + y = 4 \qquad (1)$$
$$2x - y = 1 \qquad (2)$$

Add the two equations together to 'eliminate' the y term.
(Sometimes you must first multiply both sides by some number to make elimination possible.)

$$\tfrac{5}{2}x \quad = 5$$
$$\Rightarrow \qquad x = 2$$

Now you can find y as in method 1.

Both methods are equally valid, but method 1 is more easily adapted to the more advanced simultaneous equations that you will meet in Section B of this chapter. So if you are familiar with method 2 but not method 1 you should do Exercise A using method 1 to gain confidence with it.

Exercise A (answers p. 175)

In this exercise, solve the simultaneous equations using algebra.
Always check using substitution.
Check by superimposing straight line graphs on your graph plotter if you wish.

1 Solve the pair of simultaneous equations represented by the straight line graphs on p. 33.

2 Solve the following pairs of simultaneous equations.

(a) $3x - 7y = 1$ and $y = 2x - 8$

(b) $5 - 3y = x$ and $3x + 4y = 0$

(c) $3x - 2y + 12 = 0$ and $y = 6x + 3$

3 Find the point of intersection of each of these pairs of lines.

(a) $y = 5x - 4$ and $7x - 2y - 2 = 0$

(b) $x + 6y - 1 = 0$ and $3x - 8y - 16 = 0$

(c) $3x + 2y - 11 = 0$ and $7x - 4y - 4 = 0$

4 These three straight lines make a triangle.

$5x + 3y - 47 = 0$, $y = 3x - 3$ and $x - 5y + 13 = 0$

Find the coordinates of the vertices of the triangle.

5 These three straight lines all go through one point.

$y = 2x - 7$, $3x + 2y - 21 = 0$ and $x - 4y + c = 0$

Find the value of c.

6 Solve the following pairs of simultaneous equations.

(a) $2(x-3) = y - 1$ and $x + 4y = 7$

(b) $x = 2y + 1$ and $2(7 - x) = 3(y - 3)$

(c) $2(x + 1) = 3(y + 2)$ and $-2(x + 1) = y + 2$

7 A market stall sells some articles at £1 each and others at £2 each.

(a) One day their takings totalled £160.
Write an equation for this beginning $x + 2y =$ ...
Explain carefully what the variables x and y stand for.

(b) 117 items were sold altogether.
Write a linear equation for this using your variables x and y.

(c) Solve the pair of simultaneous equations to get information about the stall's sales.

8 A father is 25 years older than his son.
7 years ago the father was 6 times as old as his son.
What are their ages now?

9 For each of these pairs of simultaneous equations,

(i) what happens when you try to solve the pair?

(ii) by showing the pair as superimposed straight lines on your graph plotter, explain why there is a difficulty.

(a) $2x + 3y - 12 = 0$ and $6x + 9y - 36 = 0$

(b) $x + 5y - 8 = 0$ and $2x + 10y + 3 = 0$

B Simultaneous equations, only one linear (answers p. 176)

A linear graph may intersect a curved graph (such as a quadratic graph).

1 Superimpose graphs of $y = 2x - 5$ and $y = x^2 - 6x + 10$ on a graph plotter. Give the coordinates of the points of intersection.

The points of intersection can also be found by algebra, treating the equations of the two lines as a pair of simultaneous equations.
The following example uses the graphs you have just plotted.

Example 2

Solve the simultaneous equations $y = 2x - 5$ (1)

$$y = x^2 - 6x + 10.$$ (2)

Solution

Substitute equation 1's expression for y into equation 2.

$$2x - 5 = x^2 - 6x + 10$$

Rearrange this into familiar quadratic form.

$$x^2 - 8x + 15 = 0$$
$$\Rightarrow \quad (x-3)(x-5) = 0$$
$$\Rightarrow \qquad\qquad x = 3 \text{ or } 5$$

Substitute into equation 1.

When $x = 3$, $y = 1$; when $x = 5$, $y = 5$.

Example 3

Solve the simultaneous equations $x + 2y - 8 = 0$ (1)

$$y = x^2 + x - 3.$$ (2)

Solution

Rearrange equation 1 to make y the subject

$$y = -\tfrac{1}{2}x + 4$$

Substitute this expression for y into equation 2.

$$-\tfrac{1}{2}x + 4 = x^2 + x - 3$$

Rearrange this into familiar quadratic form.

$$x^2 + \tfrac{3}{2}x - 7 = 0$$

Multiply through by 2 to deal with the fraction.

$$\Rightarrow \qquad\qquad 2x^2 + 3x - 14 = 0$$
$$\Rightarrow \qquad\qquad (x-2)(2x+7) = 0$$
$$\Rightarrow \qquad\qquad\qquad x = 2 \text{ or } -3\tfrac{1}{2}$$

Substitute into the rearranged equation 1.

When $x = 2$, $y = 3$; when $x = -3\tfrac{1}{2}$, $y = 5\tfrac{3}{4}$.

2D   Why is equation 1 rearranged as $y = -\tfrac{1}{2}x + 4$ rather than $x = 8 - 2y$?

Example 4

Solve the pair of simultaneous equations $x^2 + y^2 = 4$ (1)

$x + y = 1$.   (2)

Solution

$$y = 1 - x \qquad \text{(from equation 2)}$$

$$x^2 + (1 - x)^2 = 4 \qquad \text{(substitute for } y \text{ in equation 1)}$$

$$\Rightarrow \quad 2x^2 - 2x - 3 = 0 \qquad \text{(expand and simplify)}$$

$$\Rightarrow \qquad x = \frac{2 \pm \sqrt{4 - 4 \times 2 \times (-3)}}{4} = \frac{1 \pm \sqrt{7}}{2}$$

When $x = \dfrac{1 + \sqrt{7}}{2}$, $y = 1 - x = \dfrac{1 - \sqrt{7}}{2}$

When $x = \dfrac{1 - \sqrt{7}}{2}$, $y = \dfrac{1 + \sqrt{7}}{2}$

Exercise B (answers p. 176)

1 Solve each of these pairs of simultaneous equations.

   (a) $y = 3x + 2$ and $y = x^2 + 2x + 2$

   (b) $y = 4x - 3$ and $y = 2x^2 - x - 6$

   (c) $y = \frac{1}{2}x + 3$ and $y = x^2 - x + 2$

2 Solve each of these pairs of simultaneous equations.

   (a) $y = x^2 + 3x - 28$ and $x + y - 4 = 0$

   (b) $x + 3y - 7 = 0$ and $y = x^2 - 2x + 3$

3 Sketch the curves $y = (x - 3)^2 + 2$ and $y = 11$ and find the coordinates of the points where they meet.

4 Find the coordinates of the points of intersection of these pairs of graphs.

   (a) $y = 5x^2$ and $y = 3x + 4$ (b) $y = x - x^2$ and $y = 8 - 6x$

   (c) $xy = 4$ and $y - 2x = 1$

5 Solve this pair of simultaneous equations.

$$2x + y = 5$$

$$x(3x + 4y) = 0$$

6 The straight line $x + y = 2$ intersects the circle $x^2 + y^2 = 9$.

   (a) Show that the x-coordinates of the points of intersection satisfy the equation $2x^2 - 4x - 5 = 0$.

   (b) Hence find the coordinates of the points of intersection, giving your answers to 2 d.p.

C Inequalities (answers p. 176)

Some problems lead to an inequality rather than an equation.

> **1D**   Eve employs a part-time gardener. She pays him a 'retainer' of £11.00 per week plus £8.00 for every hour she asks him to work. A National Insurance contribution has to be paid if the total weekly payment is greater than £73.00. For what amounts of hours worked do National Insurance payments have to be paid?

This question is easy enough to answer using common sense, but it can also be used to illustrate an algebraic approach.

The weekly pay can be written as $8t + 11$, where t is the time worked in hours.

So National Insurance will have to be paid when

$$8t + 11 > 73.$$

This can be solved like an equation.

$$8t > 62 \qquad \text{(subtracting 11 from both sides)}$$
$$t > 7.75 \qquad \text{(dividing both sides by 8)}$$

So National Insurance will have to be paid if the gardener works more than $7\frac{3}{4}$ hours.

$t > 7.75$ is called the **solution set** of the inequality $8t + 11 > 73$. It describes the set of values of t that make $8t + 11 > 73$ true.

$8t + 11 > 73$ is an example of a **linear inequality** (the functions $y = 8t + 11$ and $y = 73$ are straight lines). The following example also deals with a linear inequality.

Example 5

Find the solution set for the inequality $t + 2 > 6t + 7$.

Solution

$$t + 2 > 6t + 7$$
$$\Rightarrow \qquad -5t > 5 \qquad \text{(gathering together like terms)}$$
$$\Rightarrow \qquad t < -1 \qquad \text{(dividing both sides by a negative value –}$$
$$\text{note the change in the inequality sign)}$$

> When manipulating inequalities algebraically, normal algebraic rules are obeyed, except that when both sides are multiplied or divided by a negative number the inequality sign is reversed.

Further practice with linear inequalities is provided in the support material S3.1 (p. 41).

A graphical approach is helpful in solving **quadratic inequalities**.

The graph of $y = (x + 1)(x - 2)$
is shown by this curve.

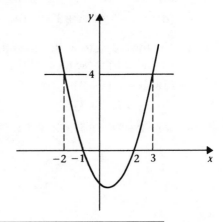

2D Find the solution set for the following inequalities.
(a) $(x + 1)(x - 2) > 0$
(b) $(x + 1)(x - 2) > 4$

When you solve a quadratic inequality you are seeking the set of values for which it is true. It is usually simplest to solve the corresponding *equation* and refer to a sketch graph to find the ranges of values which satisfy the inequality.

Example 6

Find the solution set for these inequalities.
(a) $x^2 > 6 - x$ (b) $x^2 < 6 - x$

Solution

Solving $x^2 = 6 - x$,

$$x^2 + x - 6 = 0$$
$$(x + 3)(x - 2) = 0$$
$$x = -3 \text{ or } x = 2$$

From the graph you can see that

(a) $x^2 > 6 - x$ when *either* $x < -3$ *or* $x > 2$.

(b) $x^2 < 6 - x$ when *both* $x > -3$ *and* $x < 2$. This solution set is usually written as $-3 < x < 2$. You can think of this as meaning 'x lies between -3 and 2'.

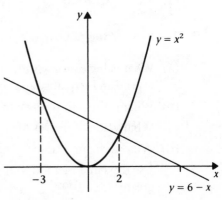

Exercise C (answers p. 176)

1   Solve these using an algebraic method.

   (a) $5x < -10$ (b) $1 - 2x < 3x + 6$ (c) $2(x - 3) < 8$

   (d) $3(x + 5) < 2x + 3$ (e) $-3x < 6$

2   Use the graph to write down the
   solutions of these inequalities

   (a) $(x - 1)(x + 3) < 0$

   (b) $(x - 1)(x + 3) > 5$

   (c) $(x - 1)(x + 3) < 2x + 1$

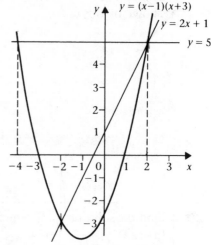

3   Use sketch graphs or an algebraic method to solve these inequalities.

   (a) $(x + 5)(x - 2) > 0$ (b) $(x + 4)(x + 6) < 0$

   (c) $(x - 1)(x - 7) > 0$ (d) $(x - 2)(3 - x) < 0$

4   Find the range of possible values for x if $(2 - x)^2 > 0$.

5   Find the solution set for each of these inequalities.

   (a) $x(x + 1) < 20$ (b) $2x^2 - 3 > 5x$

6   Solve these inequalities.

   (a) $x^2 < 3x$ (b) $3x^2 + 2x < 2x^2 + 3x$

   (c) $x(x - 3) < 10$ (d) $x^2 + x > 1$

7   Find the range of values of x for which $(x - 3)(2x + 5) < 0$.

8   Find the solution set for these inequalities.

   (a) $-x^2 - 2x + 8 < 0$ (b) $x(3x - 1) > 2$

9   The value of the nth triangle number is given by $\dfrac{n(n + 1)}{2}$.

   (a) What value of n gives the first triangle number greater than 50?
      (Write an inequality and solve it.)

   (b) What is the first triangle number greater than 50?

   (c) What value of n gives the first triangle number greater than 100?

   (d) What is the first triangle number greater than 100?

   (e) Use the same method to find the value of the first triangle number
      greater than 1000.

After working through this chapter you should

1   understand how a pair of simultaneous equations may be
    represented as graphs

2   be able to solve a pair of simultaneous equations algebraically when
    at least one of them is linear

3   be able to find the solution set for a linear inequality (solve the
    inequality) by
    ● testing with values
    ● drawing graphs
    ● using algebra

4   be able to find the solution set for a quadratic inequality.

S3.1 Linear inequalities (see p. 39, answers p. 177)

There are three approaches to finding the solution set for an inequality:

● Testing with values
● Drawing graphs
● Using algebra.

Results from the three methods should be consistent with one another.

1   Find the solution set for the inequality $t + 3 > 5$ using the following
    methods.

    (a) Try different whole number values of t to see which make the
         inequality true.

    (b) Superimpose the graphs of $y = t + 3$ and $y = 5$. For what values of t
         is the graph of $y = t + 3$ *above* (greater than) the graph of $y = 5$?

    (c) 'Solve' $t + 3 > 5$ as though it was an equation, 'doing the same thing
         to both sides'.

2   The diagram shows the graphs of $y = 2p + 1$ and
    $y = p + 6$ superimposed.

    (a) Use it to give the solution set for
         $2p + 1 > p + 6$ (the range of values of p that
         make $2p + 1 > p + 6$ true).

    (b) Use it to give the solution set for
         $2p + 1 < p + 6$.

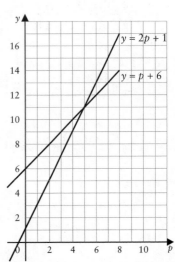

3 Use all three of the methods in question 1 to find the solution set for each of these inequalities. Note whether the results from all three methods are consistent.

(a) $x - 4 > -3$ (b) $4x > 12$ (c) $3x + 2 < 10$

(d) $8x + 4 > 3x - 9$ (e) $5(x - 3) < 3x + 2$ (f) $-4x > 8$

Your algebraic solution of question 3(f) may have started like this.

$$-4x > 8$$

$$-x > 2 \qquad \text{(dividing both sides by 4)}$$

If you then divided or multiplied both sides by -1 for the next step you would get the result $x > -2$, which disagrees with the results from drawing a graph and testing values. The correct solution is $x < -2$. This illustrates the following fact.

> When manipulating inequalities algebraically, normal algebraic rules are obeyed except that when both sides are multiplied or divided by a negative number the inequality sign is reversed.

4 Complete the following algebraic solution.

$$2x - 5 > 5x + 1$$

$$-3x > 6 \text{ (subtracting } 5x \text{ from both sides and adding 5 to both sides)}$$

...   .

Check your solution by testing with values of x or by sketching superimposed graphs of $y = 2x - 5$ and $y = 5x + 1$.

5 Use an algebraic method to find the solution set for each of these.

(a) $5x + 1 < 2x + 7$ (b) $2x - 1 > 5 - x$

(c) $1 - 2x < x - 7$ (d) $3 > 1 + 2x$

(e) $1 - \frac{1}{3}x < 4$ (f) $3 - 2x > 2 - 3x$

(g) $3(x + 2) < 11(x - 2)$ (h) $2(5 - x) > 3(x - 10)$

4 Polynomials

A Factorising (answers p. 177)

For this chapter you will need to be confident in expanding expressions such as $(x-1)(x+3)(x-4)$. Further practice in expanding brackets is provided in the support material S4.1 on p. 48.

Polynomial functions of x are formed by adding together powers of x.

Examples are
$$3x+1$$
$$x^2 + 5x - 2$$
$$x^3 + 3x^2 - 6x - 8$$
$$5x^4 - 3x^3 + 2x^2 + 7x - 5$$

Note that the powers of x must be non-negative whole numbers.

You have already met examples like the first two. They are linear and quadratic functions. The third example, $x^3 + 3x^2 - 6x - 8$, is called a cubic function.

The highest power present is the **degree** of the polynomial. So a cubic polynomial is a polynomial of degree 3.

Let us use $P(x)$ to denote the polynomial $x^3 + 3x^2 - 6x - 8$.

1 By expanding the brackets, show that

$(x+1)(x-2)(x+4) = P(x)$

Each of these brackets is a **factor** of $P(x)$.

2D

(a) What are the zeros of $(x+1)(x-2)(x+4)$? (In other words, what values of x make $(x+1)(x-2)(x+4)$ equal to zero?)

(b) Substitute each of your answers to (a) into $x^3 + 3x^2 - 6x - 8$. Are the results what you expected?

(c) What is the relationship between the zeros of $P(x)$ and the factors of $P(x)$?

By looking for the zeros of a polynomial you discover whether it has a simple factor.

3 Now consider the polynomial $P(x) = x^3 - 13x - 12$.

(a) Calculate these values.

  (i) $P(1)$ (the value of $P(x)$ when $x = 1$)   (ii) $P(2)$ (iii) $P(3)$
  (iv) $P(4)$ (v) $P(-1)$ (vi) $P(-2)$ (vii) $P(-3)$ (viii) $P(-4)$

(b) Write down three factors of $P(x)$.

(c) Confirm your answers to (b) by multiplying the three factors together.

4 The cubic polynomial $P(x)$ is $x^3 - x^2 - 10x - 8$.

  (a) To check whether $x + 2$ is a factor of $P(x)$, for which value of a should you choose to calculate $P(a)$?

  (b) Is $x + 2$ a factor of $P(x)$?

5 (a) If $P(x) = (x - 2)(x^2 - x - 2)$, explain why $P(2) = 0$.

  (b) More generally, if $P(x) = (x - a)Q(x)$, where $Q(x)$ is a polynomial, explain why $P(a) = 0$.

In question 5(b) you proved this fact:

> If $x - a$ is a factor of $P(x)$, then $P(a) = 0$.

This is the converse, and more useful, result:

> If $P(a) = 0$, then $x - a$ is a factor of $P(x)$.
>
> This is known as the **factor theorem**.
>
> $P(x)$ can then be written as $(x - a)Q(x)$, where $Q(x)$ is a 'simpler' polynomial.

6 Use the factor theorem to factorise $x^3 - 3x^2 - x + 3$.

Often it is quite easy to spot one factor, but finding all three can be much harder.
Questions 7–11 show how you can find the remaining factors without relying too much on inspiration!

7 Expand these polynomials.

  (a) $(x - 3)(x^2 + 5x + 6)$ (b) $(x + 4)(x^2 + x - 2)$

8 If $x^3 - 19x + 30 = (x + 5)(x^2 - 5x + a)$, find a.

9 (a) Expand the polynomial $P(x)$ if
$$P(x) = (x + 1)(x^2 - bx + 2).$$

  (b) What is the value of b if
$$P(x) = x^3 - 2x^2 - x + 2?$$

10 For each polynomial use the method of question 9 to find b and hence factorise the polynomial completely.

  (a) $x^3 + x^2 - 5x + 3 = (x - 1)(x^2 + bx - 3)$

  (b) $x^3 - 9x^2 + 6x + 56 = (x - 7)(x^2 + bx - 8)$

11 If $(x+2)$ is a factor of $P(x) = x^3 - x^2 - 10x - 8$, then

$x^3 - x^2 - 10x - 8 = (x+2)(ax^2 + bx + c)$.

(a) (i) What is the value of a?

    (ii) What is the value of c?

(b) Find b.

(c) Hence write $P(x)$ as the product of three factors.

12 Use the factor theorem to find one factor, and then find the remaining factors of each of the following polynomials.

(a) $x^3 + 9x^2 + 2x - 48$ (b) $x^3 + 4x^2 - x - 4$

(c) $x^3 - 4x^2 + x + 6$ (d) $x^3 - 3x^2 - 6x + 8$

(e) $x^3 + 10x^2 + 29x + 20$ (f) $x^3 + x^2 - 9x - 9$

(g) $x^3 + 5x^2 - 2x - 24$

Example 1

Consider the function $f(x) = x^3 - 3x^2 - 10x + 24$.

(a) Find the factors of $f(x)$.

(b) Find the roots of the equation $f(x) = 0$.

Solution

(a) The possible factors of 24 are $\pm 1, \pm 2, \pm 3, \pm 4, \pm 6, \pm 8, \pm 12$ and ± 24.

By trial,

$f(2) = 8 - 12 - 20 + 24 = 0$,

so

$x - 2$ is a factor.

Therefore, you can write $x^3 - 3x^2 - 10x + 24$ as $(x-2)(x^2 + ax - 12)$.

Comparing the coefficients of x^2 gives

$\qquad -3 = -2 + a$

$\qquad \Rightarrow a = -1$

and so

$\qquad f(x) = (x-2)(x^2 - x - 12)$

$\qquad\qquad = (x-2)(x+3)(x-4)$

(b) $f(x) = 0$

$\qquad \Rightarrow (x-2)(x+3)(x-4) = 0$

$\qquad \Rightarrow x = -3, 2, 4$

When you have found one linear factor, there is an alternative approach to finding the remaining factor or factors. This is to use the approach of algebraic division.

The process is usually set out in the style of numerical long division.

$$
\begin{array}{r}
x^2 - x - 12 \\
x-2\overline{)x^3 - 3x^2 - 10x + 24} \\
\underline{x^3 - 2x^2} \\
-x^2 - 10x \\
\underline{-x^2 + 2x} \\
-12x + 24 \\
\underline{-12x + 24} \\
0
\end{array}
$$

Exercise A (answers p. 178)

1 $P(x) = x^3 - 2x^2 - 11x + 12$.

   (a) Show that $x + 3$ is a factor of $P(x)$.

   (b) Find $Q(x)$, if $P(x) = (x + 3)Q(x)$.

2 $P(x) = x^3 - 5x^2 + 2x + 8$.

   (a) Use the factor theorem to find one factor of $P(x)$.

   (b) Factorise $P(x)$ completely.

   (c) Write down the solutions of $P(x) = 0$.

3 Solve the equation $x^3 + 5x^2 + 3x - 9 = 0$.

4 Solve the equation $x^3 + 4x^2 + 2x - 4 = 0$ by finding one simple factor and then solving a quadratic equation.

5 What happens if you try to factorise these polynomials completely?

   (a) $x^3 - 8$

   (b) $x^3 - 3x^2 + x - 3$

   (c) $x^4 - 16$

6 The function $f(x) = x^3 - 7x^2 + ax + 40$ has $(x + 2)$ as a factor. Find the value of a and completely factorise $f(x)$.

B Sketching polynomials (answers p. 179)

Factorising a polynomial helps in sketching the graph of the polynomial.

Example 2

Sketch the graph of the function $f(x) = x^3 - 3x^2 - 10x + 24$.

Solution

In Example 1 (page 45) the factors of f(x) have been found and the roots of the equation f(x) = 0 shown to be −3, 2 and 4.

So the graph of $x^3 - 3x^2 - 10x + 24$ goes through $(-3, 0)$, $(2, 0)$ and $(4, 0)$.

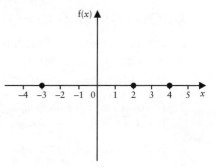

Before sketching the graph it is a good idea to find the value of f(x) for some other values of x.

In this case,

f(−4) = −48

f(0) = 24

f(3) = −6

f(5) = 24

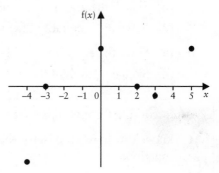

So the sketch looks something like this.

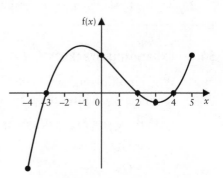

With practice it is possible to sketch a polynomial graph from the zeros, without finding so many additional points. The easiest point to find is by letting $x = 0$.

Exercise B (answers p. 179)

When you sketch a graph in this exercise, make sure you show clearly the values where it cuts each of the axes.

1 If $P(x) = (x+5)(x-2)(x+1)$, sketch the graph of $P(x)$.

2 (a) Find the zeros of the function $f(x) = x^3 - 4x^2 - 3x + 18$ and hence factorise the function.

    (b) Sketch the graph of the function.

3 By means of a sketch graph, determine the ranges of values of x for which $x(2x-5)(x-3) < 0$.

4 Sketch the graph of the function $-x^3 + 2x^2 + 5x - 6$.

5 (a) Find all the zeros of, and hence factorise, the function

        $P(x) = x^4 - x^3 - 7x^2 + x + 6$.

    (b) Sketch the graph of the function.

    (c) Solve the inequality $P(x) > 0$.

6 (a) Solve the equation $x^3 - 2x + 4 = 0$.

    (b) Sketch a graph of the function to explain the solution.

After working through this chapter you should

1 know how to use the factor theorem to help factorise polynomial functions

2 be able to sketch and use graphs of polynomial functions.

S4.1 Expanding brackets (see p. 43, answers p. 179)

When multiplying out more than two brackets, a well-organised and careful approach is important if mistakes are to be avoided.

With three sets of brackets this approach can be used.

$(x-1)(x+3)(x-4)$

$\qquad = (x-1)(x^2 - x - 12)$ Expand brackets in pairs only.

$\qquad = x(x^2 - x - 12) - (x^2 - x - 12)$ This may be omitted, but errors with signs are common and this is when they usually occur.

$\qquad = x^3 - x^2 - 12x - x^2 + x + 12$

$\qquad = x^3 - 2x^2 - 11x + 12$ Gather together like terms.

1   Expand these polynomials.

    (a) $(x+1)(x+2)(x-4)$ (b) $(x-2)(x-3)(x-4)$

    (c) $(x-1)(x+1)(x+5)$ (d) $(x-1)^2(x+3)$

With more than three sets of brackets, pairs of brackets may be expanded in any order. With practice, a good choice of brackets may speed up the process.

$$(x+1)(x-2)(x-3)(x+2)$$
$$= (x+1)(x^2-4)(x-3)$$
$$= (x+1)(x^3-3x^2-4x+12)$$
$$= x^4-3x^3-4x^2+12x+x^3-3x^2-4x+12$$
$$= x^4-2x^3-7x^2+8x+12$$

2   Expand these polynomials.

    (a) $(x+1)(x-1)(x+2)(x-2)$ (b) $(x+2)^2(x-2)^2$

    (c) $(x-1)(x+3)^3$ (d) $(x+1)(x-2)(x+3)(x-4)$

5 Powers and surds

A Rules of indices (answers p. 180)

Indices (the plural of 'index') are the values printed in small raised type like the 4 in 2^4.

Since $2^4 = 16$ we talk about 16 being a **power** of 2, in this case the fourth power of 2. Similarly x^2, x^3, x^4 and so on are all powers of x.

1 Work these out on your calculator.

(a) (i) 2^6 (ii) $2^2 \times 2^4$ (iii) $2^3 \times 2^3$

(b) (i) 4^7 (ii) $4^3 \times 4^4$ (iii) $4^5 \times 4^2$ (iv) $4^2 \times 4^2 \times 4^3$

2 Use your answers to question 1 to describe a quick way of working out c if you are told that $3^3 \times 3^5 = 3^c$.

3D How can you use what you have discovered to work out d if you are told that $6^7 \div 6^3 = 6^d$?

Check with your calculator to see if the method works.

4 (a) $a^4 \times a^4 \times a^4$ can be written as $(a^4)^3$. Explain why $(a^4)^3 = a^{12}$.

(b) Write these expressions as simply as possible.

(i) $(a^4)^2$ (ii) $(b^4)^4$ (iii) $(x^3)^5$ (iv) $(a^5)^6$

The methods you have discovered are called the **rules of indices**.

The rules can be written like this.

- $x^a \times x^b = x^{a+b}$
- $x^a \div x^b = x^{a-b}$
- $(x^a)^b = x^{ab}$

Using the second rule we get $x^3 \div x^5 = x^{-2}$.

But we know that $x^3 \div x^5 = \dfrac{x^3}{x^5} = \dfrac{x \times x \times x}{x \times x \times x \times x \times x} = \dfrac{1}{x^2}$.

So x^{-2} means $\dfrac{1}{x^2}$.

In general, $x^{-a} = \dfrac{1}{x^a}$.

5D   (a) Express 2^{-4} and 2^{-3} as fractions.

(b) Multiply the two fractions in part (a).

(c) Use the rule $x^a \times x^b = x^{a+b}$ to simplify $2^{-4} \times 2^{-3}$.

(d) Does your answer to part (c) agree with your answer to part (b)?

Again using the second rule we get $x^5 \div x^5 = x^0$.

But we know that $x^5 \div x^5 = 1$.

So in general $x^0 = 1$ (but not when $x = 0$).

Exercise A (answers p. 180)

1   Express the following as single powers of 2.

(a) $2^2 \times 2^3$ (b) 2×2^9 (c) $2^{12} \div 2^7$ (d) $(2^5)^3$

2   Write these down, as single powers of p.

(a) $p^3 \times p^5$ (b) $(p^6)^2$ (c) $p^2 \times p^3 \times p^5$

(d) $p^7 \div p^4$ (e) $p^4 \times p^2 \div p^3$ (f) $(p^2 \times p^4 \div p^3) \times p^2$

3   Evaluate these expressions.

(a) 6^1 (b) 3^{-2} (c) 10^{-3} (d) $3^{-2} \times 3^5$ (e) $5^2 \div 5^{-1}$

4   Simplify these expressions.

(a) $y^3 \times y^{-5}$ (b) $c^3 \div c^{-2}$ (c) $x^{-5} \times x^5$ (d) $(x^{-2})^{-3}$

5   Decide which of the following are equal.

$(\frac{1}{2})^3$ $\dfrac{1}{2^3}$ 8 2^{-3} $\frac{1}{8}$ 3^{-2}

6   Work out the value of each of the following without using a calculator.

(a) 4^{-2} (b) 3^{-3} (c) $(\frac{1}{2})^2$ (d) $(\frac{1}{2})^{-2}$

(e) $(\frac{1}{2})^0$ (f) $(-2)^4$ (g) $(-2)^{-4}$ (h) $(-2)^0$

Now check your answers with a calculator.

B Fractional indices and surds (answers p. 180)

1D | (a) If $2^{\frac{1}{2}}$ is to obey the rules in Section A, what must $(2^{\frac{1}{2}})^2$ equal?

(b) What does this suggest that $2^{\frac{1}{2}}$ should be used to mean?

(c) Using the same approach, what should these mean?

(i) $2^{\frac{1}{3}}$ (ii) $3^{\frac{1}{2}}$ (iii) $3^{\frac{1}{3}}$ (iv) $4^{\frac{1}{2}}$ (v) $2^{\frac{1}{n}}$ (vi) $a^{\frac{1}{n}}$

Experiment to see whether your calculator treats fractional indices the way your answers to parts (b) and (c) suggest.

2 Find (a) $9^{\frac{1}{2}}$ (b) $8^{\frac{1}{3}}$ (c) $256^{\frac{1}{4}}$ (d) $81^{0.5}$

3 Evaluate these, checking your answers using the x^y or $x^{\frac{1}{y}}$ key on your calculator.

(a) $4^{\frac{1}{2}}$ (b) $25^{-\frac{1}{2}}$ (c) $1\,000\,000^{\frac{1}{3}}$ (d) $0.01^{\frac{1}{2}}$ (e) $0.0016^{\frac{1}{4}}$

> In general, then, $x^{\frac{1}{a}} = {}^{a}\sqrt{x}$.

4 Evaluate these.

(a) (i) $(\sqrt{4})^3$ (ii) $\sqrt{4^3}$

(b) (i) $({}^{3}\sqrt{27})^2$ (ii) ${}^{3}\sqrt{27^2}$

(c) (i) $({}^{4}\sqrt{625})^3$ (ii) ${}^{4}\sqrt{625^3}$

5 Evaluate these.

(a) (i) $(49^{\frac{1}{2}})^3$ (ii) $(49^3)^{\frac{1}{2}}$

(b) (i) $(8^{\frac{1}{3}})^4$ (ii) $(8^4)^{\frac{1}{3}}$

(c) (i) $(81^{\frac{1}{4}})^3$ (ii) $(81^3)^{\frac{1}{4}}$

Using the rule $(x^a)^b = x^{ab}$, the expressions $(49^{\frac{1}{2}})^3$ and $(49^3)^{\frac{1}{2}}$ can both be written in the form $49^{\frac{3}{2}}$.

6 Use the power buttons on your calculator to check that $49^{\frac{3}{2}}$ gives the same result as your answers to question 5(a).

7 Write the expressions in questions 5(b) and (c) in the form $x^{\frac{a}{b}}$.

> In general, $x^{\frac{a}{b}} = ({}^{b}\sqrt{x})^a$ or ${}^{b}\sqrt{(x^a)}$

Example 1

Evaluate $8^{-\frac{2}{3}}$.

Solution

$$8^{-\frac{2}{3}} = \frac{1}{8^{\frac{2}{3}}}$$

$$= \frac{1}{(8^{\frac{1}{3}})^2}$$

$$= \frac{1}{(\sqrt[3]{8})^2} = \frac{1}{2^2} = \frac{1}{4}$$

8 Evaluate these.

  (a) $8^{\frac{1}{3}}$ (b) $16^{-\frac{1}{4}}$ (c) $27^{\frac{2}{3}}$ (d) 3^{-2}

  (e) $16^{\frac{3}{4}}$ (f) $1000^{-\frac{1}{3}}$ (g) 25^0 (h) $100^{\frac{3}{2}}$

  (i) $(\frac{1}{4})^{-2}$ (j) $1^{\frac{3}{5}}$ (k) $(\frac{1}{2})^{-3}$ (l) 0.1^{-4}

  (m) $81^{\frac{3}{4}}$ (n) $125^{-\frac{2}{3}}$ (o) $1\,000\,000^{\frac{1}{3}}$ (p) $0.01^{-\frac{3}{2}}$ (q) $25^{-\frac{3}{2}}$

9 The diagram shows a spiral of right-angled triangles.
Find the lengths of the hypotenuses labelled u_1, u_2 and u_3.

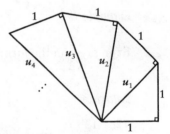

It is best in this example to work in *exact* form, giving the lengths as $\sqrt{2}$, $\sqrt{3}$ and $\sqrt{4}$. This suggests that the next might be $\sqrt{5}$, which it is, and that the nth length u_n will be $\sqrt{n+1}$.

This pattern would never be apparent if you worked in approximate form, where the first few lengths would be

1.414, 1.732, 2, 2.236, 2.449, ...

Numerical expressions which contain one or more irrational roots of numbers, such as $3 + \sqrt{5}$, are known as **surds**. Familiarity with the methods of working with surds often means that patterns can be easily spotted, and that numbers containing irrational parts can be written and dealt with in *exact form*.

10 Evaluate these, leaving your answers in exact form.

  (a) $(3 + \sqrt{5})^2$ (b) $(2 - \sqrt{13})^2$ (c) $(3 - 2\sqrt{5})^2$

11 Evaluate these.

(a) (i) $\sqrt{4 \times 9}$ (ii) $\sqrt{4} \times \sqrt{9}$

(b) (i) $\sqrt{\dfrac{4}{9}}$ (ii) $\dfrac{\sqrt{4}}{\sqrt{9}}$

From examples like those in question 11 you can see these facts.

$$\sqrt{a \times b} = \sqrt{a} \times \sqrt{b}$$

and

$$\sqrt{\dfrac{a}{b}} = \dfrac{\sqrt{a}}{\sqrt{b}}$$

You can use these facts to simplify surds.

Example 2

Express $\sqrt{18}$ as the simplest possible surd.

Solution

$$\sqrt{18} = \sqrt{(9 \times 2)} = \sqrt{9} \times \sqrt{2} = 3\sqrt{2}$$

Example 3

Express $\dfrac{12}{\sqrt{3}}$ in the form $a\sqrt{b}$, where a and b are integers.

Solution

$$\dfrac{12}{\sqrt{3}} = \dfrac{12\sqrt{3}}{(\sqrt{3})^2} \quad \text{(multiplying top and bottom by } \sqrt{3}\text{)}$$

$$= \dfrac{12\sqrt{3}}{3} = 4\sqrt{3}$$

Example 4

Expand and simplify $(8 + 2\sqrt{3})(8 - 2\sqrt{3})$.

Solution

$$(8 + 2\sqrt{3})(8 - 2\sqrt{3}) = 64 + 16\sqrt{3} - 16\sqrt{3} - (2\sqrt{3})^2$$

$$= 64 - 4(\sqrt{3})^2$$

$$= 64 - 12$$

$$= 52$$

Notice that in example 4 we were expanding brackets of the form $(a+b)(a-b)$, giving $a^2 - b^2$, which had no surds in it.

This technique can be used to remove surds from the denominator of a fraction. This process is called rationalising the denominator.

Example 5

By rationalising the denominator, simplify $\dfrac{3 - \sqrt{5}}{1 + \sqrt{5}}$.

Solution

$$\frac{3 - \sqrt{5}}{1 + \sqrt{5}} = \frac{(3 - \sqrt{5})(1 - \sqrt{5})}{(1 + \sqrt{5})(1 - \sqrt{5})} \quad \text{(multiplying top and bottom by } (1 - \sqrt{5}))$$

$$= \frac{3 - \sqrt{5} - 3\sqrt{5} + 5}{1 + \sqrt{5} - \sqrt{5} - 5} \quad \text{(expanding brackets)}$$

$$= \frac{8 - 4\sqrt{5}}{-4} = -2 + \sqrt{5}$$

Exercise B (answers p. 180)

1 Evaluate these.

    (a) $27^{\frac{1}{3}}$ (b) $4^{\frac{5}{2}}$ (c) $27^{-\frac{1}{3}}$ (d) $\left(\dfrac{9}{49}\right)^{\frac{1}{2}}$

    (e) $125^{-\frac{1}{3}}$ (f) $144^{\frac{3}{2}}$ (g) $\left(\dfrac{1}{4}\right)^{\frac{3}{2}}$ (h) $\left(\dfrac{1}{9}\right)^{-\frac{3}{2}}$

    (i) $\left(\dfrac{81}{4}\right)^{-\frac{3}{2}}$ (j) $\left(\dfrac{8}{27}\right)^{\frac{2}{3}}$

2 Write these surds using fractional indices.

    (a) $\sqrt{7}$ (b) $\sqrt[3]{10}$ (c) $(\sqrt{5})^3$ (d) $\sqrt[3]{7^2}$

    (e) $\dfrac{1}{\sqrt[4]{10}}$ (f) $\dfrac{1}{(\sqrt{3})^5}$ (g) $\dfrac{1}{\sqrt{7^3}}$ (h) $\dfrac{1}{\sqrt[3]{3^2}}$

3 Evaluate these.

    (a) $(0.49)^{\frac{1}{2}}$ (b) $(0.64)^{-\frac{1}{2}}$ (c) $(0.25)^{\frac{3}{2}}$ (d) $(0.01)^{-\frac{3}{2}}$

4 Express each of the following in terms of the simplest possible surds.

    (a) $\sqrt{8}$ (b) $\sqrt{60}$ (c) $\sqrt{32}$ (d) $\dfrac{\sqrt{512}}{\sqrt{64}}$

5 Solve these, leaving your solutions in simplified surd form.

    (a) $x^2 + 5x + 1 = 0$ (b) $x^2 - 3x - 9 = 0$ (c) $3x^2 + 7x - 3 = 0$

6 A circle has an area of 50 cm^2. Show that the radius is $5\sqrt{\dfrac{2}{\pi}}$ cm and the circumference is $10\sqrt{2\pi}$ cm.

7 Solve the following equations, giving each solution in the form $a \pm \sqrt{b}$ where a and b are integers.

    (a) $x^2 - 6x + 6 = 0$ (b) $x^2 + 8x + 3 = 0$ (c) $x^2 + 4x - 2 = 0$

8 Simplify these.

    (a) $\sqrt{3}\,(\sqrt{27} - 1)$ (b) $(\sqrt{3} - \sqrt{2})^2$ (c) $(\sqrt{3} - 1)(\sqrt{3} + 2)$

9 Solve the following equations, giving each solution in the form $a \pm b\sqrt{c}$ where a, b and c are integers and $b \neq 1$.

    (a) $x^2 - 8x - 2 = 0$ (b) $x^2 + 8x + 4 = 0$ (c) $x^2 - 14x - 5 = 0$

10 Rationalise the denominators of the following.

    (a) $\dfrac{1}{1 + \sqrt{3}}$ (b) $\dfrac{1 + \sqrt{2}}{1 - \sqrt{3}}$ (c) $\dfrac{\sqrt{2} + \sqrt{3}}{\sqrt{5}}$ (d) $\dfrac{\sqrt{5} + 4}{\sqrt{2} + 1}$ (e) $\dfrac{2}{\sqrt{2} + \sqrt{5}}$

11 Express $\dfrac{(2 - \sqrt{2})^2}{2 + \sqrt{2}}$ in the form $a + b\sqrt{2}$ where a and b are integers.

After working through this chapter you should

1 Understand the meaning of expressions involving integer and fractional indices (both positive and negative), in particular that

$$x^{-a} = \frac{1}{x^a}$$

$$x^0 = 1$$

$$x^{\frac{1}{a}} = \sqrt[a]{x}$$

$$x^{\frac{a}{b}} = \left(\sqrt[b]{x}\right)^a \quad \text{or} \quad \left(\sqrt[b]{x^a}\right)$$

2 be able to use the use the following rules in manipulating expressions with integer and fractional indices

$$x^a \times x^b = x^{a+b}$$

$$x^a \div x^b = x^{a-b}$$

$$\left(x^a\right)^b = x^{ab}$$

3 know that an expression is exact if it is left in surd form

4 be able to manipulate surds using the following

$$\sqrt{a \times b} = \sqrt{a} \times \sqrt{b}$$

$$\sqrt{\frac{a}{b}} = \frac{\sqrt{a}}{\sqrt{b}}$$

5 be able to rationalise the denominator of an expression (be able to rewrite it so that the denominator is not in surd form).

6 Rates of change

A Linear functions (answers p. 181)

Everything changes! Indeed, the rate at which things change may well be of very great significance – the rate at which populations grow, the rate at which a radioactive material decays or the temperature of an object falls are but a few examples where the study of **rates of change** is important.

The area of mathematics developed to deal with problems involving rates of change is known as the **calculus**. It is extremely important in mathematics and in many related disciplines and forms a considerable part of any study of mathematics at this and higher levels.

Rates of change do not always involve time; for example, a **conversion rate** (like currency exchange rates) enables us to convert from one unit to another.

In this section we consider only rates of change for linear functions; later we extend these ideas to more general functions.

This is a **temperature conversion graph** relating F (temperature in °F) to C (temperature in °C).

The graph cuts the F axis at $F = 32$.

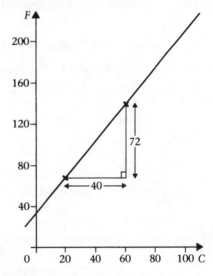

1D   (a) If the temperature changes by 10 degrees Celsius, what is the change in degrees Fahrenheit? Repeat for temperature changes of 20 and 50 degrees Celsius.

(b) Find the gradient of the line, and explain its significance.

(c) Find an equation expressing F in terms of C and explain the numbers which occur in your equation.

For linear functions, a 'rate of change' is the gradient of a straight-line graph.

The gradient of any linear graph of y against x can be found by choosing any two points on the line and calculating

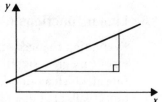

$$\frac{\text{the difference in } y\text{-coordinates}}{\text{the difference in } x\text{-coordinates}}$$

The symbol $\dfrac{dy}{dx}$ is used to represent the gradient of such a straight line. The gradient of the graph of Fahrenheit against Celsius would be written as $\dfrac{dF}{dC}$.

2 What is the value of $\dfrac{dF}{dC}$?

3D A particle moves according to the formula

$$s = 4t + 5,$$

where s is its distance from a fixed point and t is the time elapsed.

(a) Sketch a graph of the motion, with t on the horizontal axis and s on the vertical axis.

(b) Find $\dfrac{ds}{dt}$.

$\dfrac{ds}{dt}$ tells you 'how the distance changes as time passes' or, more formally,

$\dfrac{ds}{dt}$ is the rate of change of s with respect to t.

4 For the line with equation $y = 3x + 2$, copy and complete these statements.

(a) gradient of line =   (b) $\dfrac{dy}{dx} =$

5 Look at the graph of $y = 6 - 3x$.

(a) What are the 'difference in y-coordinates' and the 'difference in x-coordinates' from A to B?

(b) Find $\dfrac{dy}{dx}$.

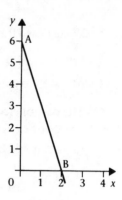

6D

(a) What can be deduced about the equation of a line which has gradient given by $\dfrac{dy}{dx} = 3$?

(b) Using $y = mx + c$, obtain the equation of the line with $\dfrac{dy}{dx} = 3$ passing through $(2, 5)$.

(c) What can be said about the gradient, $\dfrac{dy}{dx}$, of lines with equations such as $y = 4$ or $x = 6$?

Question 6D illustrates this fact: if all you know is the rate of change of a linear function and one point on its graph, then you can derive the expression for the function.

Exercise A (answers p. 182)

1 Write down the gradient, $\dfrac{dy}{dx}$, for each of the lines with these equations.

(a) $y = 5 - 7x$ (b) $y = 4 + x$

(c) $y = -2x$ (d) $y = \frac{1}{2}x - 1$

2 The graph of $2y + x = 4$ is as shown.

(a) What are the 'difference in y-coordinates' and the 'difference in x-coordinates' from A to B?

(b) Find $\dfrac{dy}{dx}$.

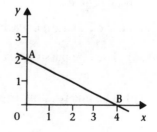

3 Write down the gradient, $\dfrac{dy}{dx}$, for each of the lines with these equations.

(a) $2y = x + 4$ (b) $y + x = 7$

(c) $x - y = 6$ (d) $2y + x = 4$

4 The cost of electricity consists of a standing charge of 702p and a charge of 2.87p for each unit of electricity used.

(a) Write the total cost, C pence, in terms of the number of units, n.

(b) Find $\dfrac{dC}{dn}$ and explain what it means.

5 Copy and complete these.

(a) $s = 3 - 8t \Rightarrow \dfrac{ds}{dt} =$

(b) $y = 4t + 2 \Rightarrow$

(c) $z = 2 - y \Rightarrow$

(d) $y = 5(2x + 1) \Rightarrow y = 10x + 5$

$\Rightarrow \dfrac{dy}{dx} =$

(e) $y = 4(3 - 5x) \Rightarrow$

6 The circumference, C, of a circle of radius r is given by the formula $C = 2\pi r$.

(a) Find $\dfrac{dC}{dr}$. Explain what this rate of change represents.

(b) A wire is placed taut around the Earth's equator. Approximately how much extra wire would be needed to enable the wire to be pulled 2 metres away from the surface at all points?

(c) Answer part (b) for a similar wire pulled taut around the Moon.

7 A linear graph has $\dfrac{dy}{dx} = 5$ and passes through the point $(-1, 2)$.

Find its equation.

8 Find the equation of each of the following lines.

(a) The line passing through $(3, 2)$ with $\dfrac{dy}{dx} = -2$

(b) The line passing through $(4, 3)$ with $\dfrac{ds}{dt} = \frac{1}{2}$

(c) The line passing through $(-6, -1)$ with $\dfrac{dp}{dx} = \frac{2}{3}$

9 A line passes through the points $(1, 5)$ and $(4, 11)$. Find $\dfrac{dy}{dx}$ and the equation of the line.

10 (a) A plumber charges £5 for a call-out plus £7 per hour for labour.

      (i) Write the charge £C as a formula in terms of t, the number of hours taken to do the job.

      (ii) What is the value of $\dfrac{dC}{dt}$?

   (b) Another plumber charges £6 per hour for labour, and for a job lasting 3 hours the bill is £26.

      (i) Write down the value of $\dfrac{dC}{dt}$.

      (ii) Hence obtain the charge £C as a formula in terms of t, the number of hours taken to do the job.

11 The marks obtained in a test ranged from 25 to 50. They have to be rescaled to range from 0 to 100. Copy and complete this table.

Test mark, T	25	26		50
Rescaled mark, R	0		. 96	100

(a) Find $\dfrac{dR}{dT}$.

(b) Hence express R in terms of T.

B Gradients of curves (answers p. 182)

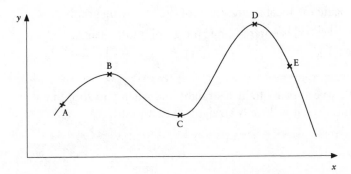

In Section A you found a single result for the gradient of any particular straight line graph. If you imagine moving from left to right along the curve sketched above, then the steepness of the curve constantly changes. Because of this we talk about the **gradient at a point** on the curve. If you zoomed in closely to the points marked you would see the following.

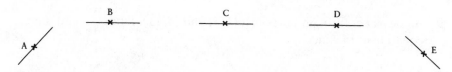

The gradient at A is positive, at B, C and D it appears to be zero, and at E it is negative. In every case the curve is **locally straight**.

In each of the following questions you need to use a graph plotter to zoom in on a chosen part of a graph.

1   Input the graph of $y = x^3 - 7x^2 + 8x + 7$ for $0 \leqslant x \leqslant 5$.

Zoom in to the point with $x = 2$ and redraw.

Repeat, increasing the magnification. What do you notice?

Zoom in at $x = 4$. Note your observation.

When you zoom in at some point on a sufficiently smooth curve, the curve starts to look more and more like a straight line. The diagrams show this for the graph $y = x^2 - 2$.

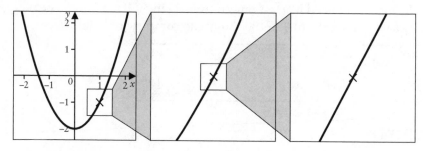

2   (a) What would you expect to see if you zoomed in at $(0, -2)$ on the graph $y = x^2 - 2$?

(b) Check your answer on the graph plotter.

3   Investigate the local straightness of the following graphs.

(a) $y = |x|$ ($|x|$ is entered on some graph plotters as ABS(x).)

(b) $y = 100x^2$ (c) $y = \text{Int}(x)$ (d) $y = |x^2 - 4|$

If a curve appears to be a straight line when you zoom in at a point, then it is 'locally straight' at that point.

When you zoomed in on some of the graphs in the work above, you found that some functions, such as $y = |x|$, were not 'locally straight' everywhere. For example, the graph of $y = |x^2 - 4|$ is locally straight at all points *except* $(2, 0)$ and $(-2, 0)$.

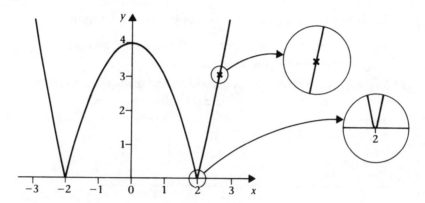

However, the cubic graph *was* locally straight everywhere. In fact, so are *all* polynomial graphs.

A straight line like AB which just touches a locally straight curve at a certain point P is called a **tangent** to the curve at P.

As you zoom in on P the curve increasingly resembles the tangent.

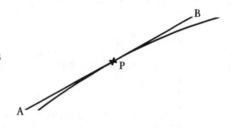

> The gradient of a curve at a point is defined as the gradient of the tangent to the curve at that point.

Finding the value of a gradient

You can already state gradients of linear graphs *exactly*. For example,

$y = 5x + 4 \implies \dfrac{dy}{dx} = 5$ and this is true for the entire graph.

For non-linear graphs the notation $\dfrac{dy}{dx}$ is still used, but now this represents the gradient of the tangent at any particular point.

> The process of obtaining $\dfrac{dy}{dx}$ for a given function y of x is called
>
> **differentiation.**

A practical method for obtaining $\dfrac{dy}{dx}$ at any point on a curve is introduced below.

4D On graph paper, draw accurately the graph of $y = \frac{1}{2}x^2$ for values of x between -3 and 3, using the same scale for both axes.

(a) Draw, as accurately as possible, the tangent at $(1.5, 1.125)$, and hence find the gradient $\dfrac{dy}{dx}$ of the curve at this point.

You can measure the gradient directly without drawing a tangent if you use a gradient measurer.

(b) By repeating this process as necessary, and using the symmetry of the graph, copy and complete the following table.

x		-2	-1.5	-1	0	1	1.5	2
Gradient $\dfrac{dy}{dx}$								

(c) Plot all the points $\left(x, \dfrac{dy}{dx}\right)$ to obtain the gradient graph for

$y = \frac{1}{2}x^2$.

(d) What do these points suggest for the equation of the gradient graph?

Write its equation $\dfrac{dy}{dx} = \cdots$.

5 On graph paper draw accurately the graph of $y = 21 + 4x - x^2$ for values of x between -6 and $+10$ using the same scale for both axes.

(a) Find the gradient of tangents at several points and record your results in a table as in question 4.

(b) Plot the points $\left(x, \dfrac{dy}{dx}\right)$.

(c) Suggest an equation for the gradient graph.

6 On graph paper draw accurately the graph of $y = 0.1x^3 - 2x + 1$ for values of x between -5 and $+5$ using the same scale for both axes.

(a) Find the gradient of tangents at several points and record your results in a table as in question 4.

(b) Plot the points $\left(x, \dfrac{dy}{dx}\right)$ from your table.

(c) What type of equation does the gradient graph appear to have?

In questions 4, 5 and 6 you drew a graph of a function (y) then considered the shape of the gradient graph (the graph of $\dfrac{dy}{dx}$).

Here is a further graph with its gradient graph below it. If you imagine moving from left to right on the top graph, you would experience

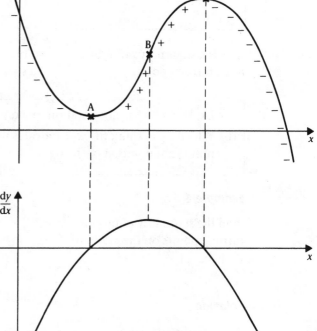

- a numerically large negative gradient which increases to zero at A

- a positive gradient which increases between A and B and then decreases to zero at C

- a gradient which finally decreases through numerically larger and larger negative values.

A, B and C are special points. A and C are the only points where the gradient is zero and B is the point where the gradient reaches its maximum positive value.

Points of a graph where the curve has zero gradient are called **stationary points**.

Points where a graph is locally a maximum or minimum are called **turning points**.

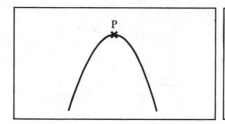 

This **local maximum** is both a stationary point and a turning point.

This is a **local minimum**.

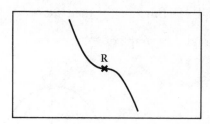

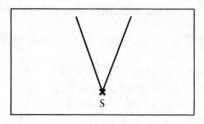

This is a stationary point but not a turning point.

This is a turning point but not a stationary point.

7D

(a) Explain why S is not a stationary point.

(b) Why do you think the word **local** is used for the maximum and minimum points above?

Example 1

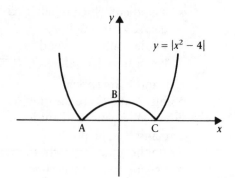

Find the stationary points and/or turning points on the graph of $y = |x^2 - 4|$.

Solution

A and C are turning points (local minima) but are not stationary points. B is both a stationary point and a turning point (a local maximum).

Exercise B (answers p. 183)

1 Copy each of these graphs. Directly beneath each one, sketch the corresponding gradient graph, using the same scale for x.

Mark any points you think are special and state the important features of each graph.

(a)

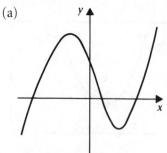

(b)

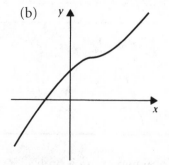

(c)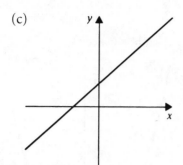

(d)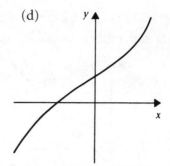

(e)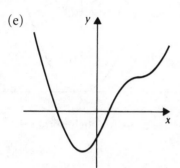

(f)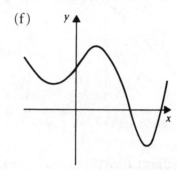

2 Sketch each of these graphs and its gradient graph. Start by deciding what happens to each gradient graph when x is near zero and also when x is numerically large (either positive or negative).

(a)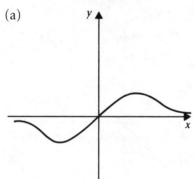

(b)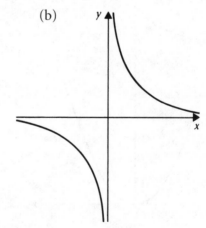

3 Two gradient graphs are sketched below.

(a) For each of them sketch a possible (x, y) graph.

(i)   (ii)

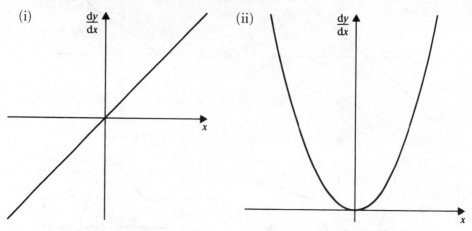

(b) How many other possible (x, y) graphs are there for each of them?

C Gradient functions (answers p. 184)

In Section B (question 4D) you should have found that the graph of
$y = \frac{1}{2}x^2$ has a gradient graph with $\dfrac{dy}{dx} = x$ as its equation.

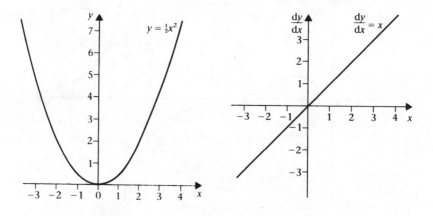

Similarly (question 5) the graph of $y = 21 + 4x - x^2$ has a gradient
graph with $\dfrac{dy}{dx} = 4 - 2x$ as its equation.

In the next question you will investigate the gradient functions of a
range of quadratic functions.

1D   (a) Plot the graph of $y = ax^2 + bx$, using particular values of a and b. You can choose a and b yourself, or perhaps your teacher will allocate their values to you so that everyone in the class has a different pair of values.

(b) Find the value of the gradient for different values of x, either by drawing tangents accurately or by using a gradient measurer. Be careful if you have used different scales for the x- and y-axes: results obtained from a gradient measurer must be multiplied or divided by an appropriate factor.

(c) Draw the gradient graph.

(d) What is the equation of the gradient graph (the **gradient function**)? Does it seem to be related to the values of a and b?

(e) Compare your results with those of students who have used values for a and b that are different from yours. Can you see how in general the gradient function is related to the function $y = ax^2 + bx$?

From the above investigation you should have some justification for the following result.

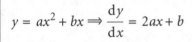

$$y = ax^2 + bx \implies \frac{dy}{dx} = 2ax + b$$

Example 2

Find the gradient of the graph of $y = 3x^2 + x$ when $x = 2$.

Solution

$$y = 3x^2 + x \implies \frac{dy}{dx} = 6x + 1$$

At $x = 2$, the gradient is 13.

Finding gradients numerically

The gradient of a graph at a given point can be obtained very accurately using a computer or calculator.

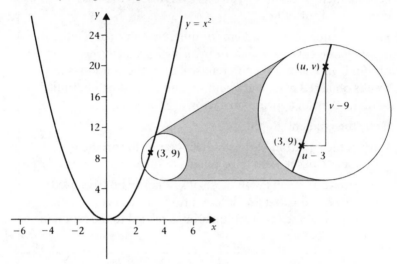

If you zoom in at $(3, 9)$, you know the property of local straightness will mean that the graph looks increasingly like a straight line which becomes more and more like the tangent to the graph at $(3, 9)$. So, to find the gradient of the tangent, you can use the curve itself.

2D
(a) How close should (u, v) be to $(3, 9)$?
(b) Suggest coordinates for (u, v).

Using (u, v) you will get an approximate gradient for $y = x^2$ at $x = 3$ by calculating

$$\text{approximate gradient} = \frac{v - 9}{u - 3}.$$

3D
(a) Why does this give only an approximation?
(b) How could you obtain a better approximation to the actual gradient?

Try your approach using a calculator or computer.

It is often convenient to use function notation when finding gradients numerically.

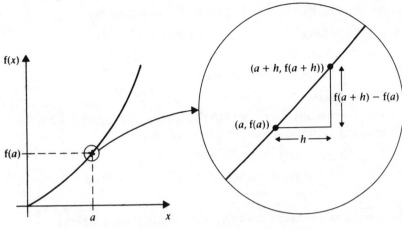

> The gradient of the graph of a function f(x) at a point $(a, f(a))$ is given the symbol f'(a), and can be estimated numerically as
>
> $$f'(a) \approx \frac{f(a+h) - f(a)}{h}$$
>
> where h, the difference in x, is small.

Example 3

Find the gradient of the graph of $f(x) = 2x^3 - 3x^2$ at $(2, 4)$.

Solution

$f(2) = 4$ and $f(2.000\ 01) = 4.000\ 120\ 001 \ldots$

and so the gradient of the graph is approximately

$$f'(2) \approx \frac{4.000\ 120\ 001 - 4}{0.000\ 01} = 12.0001\,.$$

Using smaller differences in x will result in values closer and closer to 12. This limit is the gradient of the graph.

If $f(x) = 2x^3 - 3x^2$ then $f'(2) = 12$.

4   Calculate numerical estimates of the gradients of the functions at the point indicated.

(a) $y = x^3$ at $(2, 8)$ (b) $y = 2x^2 + 3$ at $(3, 21)$

(c) $y = x^2 + 4x$ at $(1, 5)$ (d) $y = x^3 - x^2$ at $(2, 4)$

(e) $y = x^4 + 5x$ at $(1, 6)$

(f) $y = x^2$ at the points with these x-coordinates.

   (i) 3   (ii) 5   (iii) 0   (iv) −2

   Use your results, together with that for $x = 1$, to predict the gradient at the points with these x-coordinates.

   (v) 15   (vi) 3.6

   Confirm these guesses by calculation.

The speed and accuracy of numerical methods, compared with measuring gradients from a graph, enables you to discover many gradient functions.

5   (a) Draw a rough sketch of what you would expect for the gradient graph of $y = x^3$.

(b) Use a numerical method to calculate the gradient at $x = 0$, 1, −2 and 3.

(c) What is the gradient function?

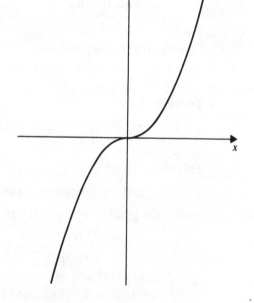

Many graph plotters will calculate gradients numerically for several values of x and plot them on the graph. This gives you an accurate picture of the gradient graph. You can then make a sensible guess at the equation of the gradient graph and check your conjecture by superimposing. Use a graph plotter with this facility to check your answer to question 5(c) and to answer the rest of these questions.

6 For a function of the form

$$y = ax^3$$

what does the gradient function appear to be?

A general polynomial is built up from multiples of simple powers of x. For example, $x + x^2$ is built up as shown below.

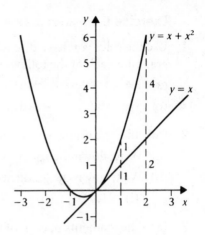

x	0	1	2	3
x^2	0	1	4	9
$x + x^2$	0	2	6	12

When x increases from 1 to 2, x increases by 1, x^2 increases by 3 and $x + x^2$ increases by both amounts, i.e. 4.

7 If $y = ax + bx^2$, check that $\dfrac{dy}{dx} = a + 2bx$ for various values of a and b.

8 If $y = a + bx + cx^2 + dx^3$, find the equation of the gradient graph.

9E If $y = ax^n + bx^m$, find the gradient function.

The work above has provided considerable evidence for the following result.

A polynomial graph with equation of the form

$$y = a + bx + cx^2 + dx^3 \ ...$$

has a gradient graph with equation

$$\frac{dy}{dx} = b + 2cx + 3dx^2 \ ....$$

$\dfrac{dy}{dx}$ is called the **derivative** of y with respect to x and $b + 2cx + 3dx^2$ is called the **derived function**.

Example 4

Find the gradient of the graph of $y = 1 - 3x + 2x^2$ at the point $(2, 3)$.

Solution

$\dfrac{dy}{dx} = -3 + 4x$. At the point $(2, 3)$ $\dfrac{dy}{dx} = -3 + 4 \times 2 = 5$

Exercise C (answers p. 185)

1   Use the rules you have discovered to find the equation of the gradient graph for each of the following.

   (a) $y = 3x^2 + 4$ (b) $v = 5u^3 - 2u^2$

   (c) $y = 6 - x^2$ (d) $s = 4t - t^2$

2   Consider the graph whose equation is $y = 2 + 5x^2$.

   (a) Write down the equation of the gradient graph.

   (b) Write down the gradients of the original graph at these points.

       (i) $(1, 7)$ (ii) $(2, 22)$ (iii) the point where $x = -1$

3   Find the gradients of each of the following graphs at the given points.

   (a) $y = 3 - 2x^3$ at $(0, 3)$ and $(2, -13)$

   (b) $y = 5x - x^2$ at $(2, 6)$ and $(4, 4)$

After working through this chapter you should

1   know that $\dfrac{dy}{dx}$ is the notation for the gradient of a graph of y against x

2   be able to find and apply rates of change in simple problems involving linear functions

3   be able to find gradients of a graph that is locally straight, either by measuring or by using a numerical method

4   be able to sketch the gradient graph for a given graph

5   know that

$$y = a + bx + cx^2 + dx^3 \ldots \implies \frac{dy}{dx} = b + 2cx + 3dx^2 \ldots .$$

7 Using differentiation

The work you have been doing on differentiation is part of the branch of mathematics commonly known as calculus. Calculus was developed by Isaac Newton (1642–1727) and the German mathematician and philosopher Gottlieb Leibniz (1646–1716). Neither of them knew the other was working on the subject and each used a different notation.

Leibniz's notation included $\dfrac{dy}{dx}$, as used in this book.

Calculus is concerned with quantities that change continuously. So it can be applied in many situations – the study of objects moving with varying velocity (a topic you will meet if you opt for mechanics as part of your mathematics AS or A level) as well as in other branches of science and engineering, and in finance and planning. Applying calculus to the dimensions of a manufactured product can lead to an efficient design: you will get a taste of this process in Section B.

A Graph sketching: using gradients (answers p. 185)

Knowing how the gradient of a function behaves can be a great help in sketching the graph of the function.

1 Make a copy of this sketch graph and indicate the following on it.

    (a) The parts of the graph where $\dfrac{dy}{dx}$ is positive

    (b) The parts of the graph where $\dfrac{dy}{dx}$ is negative

    (c) The points on the graph where $\dfrac{dy}{dx}$ is zero

    (d) Any local maxima or minima

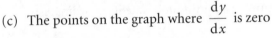

The values and behaviour of $\dfrac{dy}{dx}$ can be used to help sketch graphs.

Knowing the gradient of a graph at a point tells you what the graph is like *near the point* and not just at the point itself.

Finding the stationary points (where $\dfrac{dy}{dx} = 0$) can help you to determine quickly the overall shape of the graph.

At a local minimum,

$$\frac{dy}{dx} = 0$$

 Local minimum

and the sign of $\frac{dy}{dx}$ changes from negative, through zero to positive as x increases *through* the stationary point.

At a local maximum

$$\frac{dy}{dx} = 0$$

 Local maximum

and the sign of $\frac{dy}{dx}$ changes from positive, through zero to negative as x increases *through* the stationary point.

Example 1

(a) Sketch the graph of $y = x^2 - 5x$.

(b) Indicate on your sketch where $\frac{dy}{dx}$ is positive and where it is negative.

(c) For what value of x does $\frac{dy}{dx} = 0$?

(d) Is this point a maximum or a minimum? State its coordinates.

Solution

(a) $y = x^2 - 5x$ or $y = x(x - 5)$

(b) $+$, $-$, as on the graph

(c) $y = x^2 - 5x \Rightarrow \frac{dy}{dx} = 2x - 5$

$$\frac{dy}{dx} = 0 \Rightarrow 2x - 5 = 0 \Rightarrow x = 2.5$$

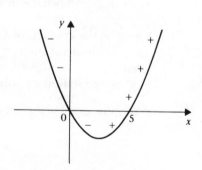

(d) It is clear from the graph that it is a minimum. When $x = 2.5$,
$y = 2.5^2 - 5 \times 2.5 = -6.25$.
The coordinates are $(2.5, -6.25)$.

2 Sketch $y = (x-1)(x-2)(x-4)$. What extra information about the graph could be obtained using calculus? (There is no need to find this extra information!)

3 For $y = x^3 - 12x + 2$, find $\dfrac{dy}{dx}$ and solve the equation $\dfrac{dy}{dx} = 0$.

Hence find the stationary points and sketch the graph.

4 For $u = 3x^2 + 6x + 5$, solve the equation $\dfrac{du}{dx} = 0$.

Hence find the stationary point and sketch the quadratic graph.

5 Use your sketch graph for question 4 to show that $y = x^3 + 3x^2 + 5x + 7$ has no stationary points. Hence sketch the cubic graph.

6 Use a graph plotter to obtain cubic graphs with equations of the form $y = x^3 + ax$ for various values of a. Describe how the value of a affects the shape of the curve.

Relate what you discover to $\dfrac{dy}{dx}$ and stationary points.

The graphs of quadratics and cubics can be sketched rapidly by

1 finding the y-intercept

2 considering the sign of the highest power of x to determine their shape for large positive and negative values of x

3 finding the x-coordinates of any stationary points by solving the equation

$$\frac{dy}{dx} = 0.$$

Example 2

Sketch $y = -x^3 + 27x - 2$.

Solution

When $x = 0$, $y = -2$.

For large x, the graph has roughly the same shape as that of $-x^3$.

At the stationary points,

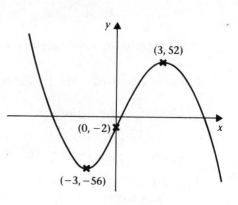

$$\frac{dy}{dx} = 0$$

$$-3x^2 + 27 = 0$$

$$3(9 - x^2) = 0$$

$$x = 3 \text{ or } -3$$

When $x = 3$

$$y = -3^3 + 27 \times 3 - 2 = 52$$

When $x = -3$

$$y = -(-3)^3 + 27 \times (-3) - 2 = -56$$

Exercise A (answers p. 186)

1 Find the stationary points on the graph of $y = x^3 - 12x + 5$. Hence sketch the graph.

2 Repeat question 1 for the graph of $y = 2x^3 - 9x^2 + 12x - 7$.

3 For each function (a) to (f) given below

(i) find all the values of x, if any, for which $\dfrac{dy}{dx} = 0$ and hence find the coordinates of all the stationary points

(ii) sketch carefully the graph of the function and indicate on your sketch the parts of the graph where $\dfrac{dy}{dx}$ is positive and the parts where $\dfrac{dy}{dx}$ is negative

(iii) state whether the stationary points are maximum points or minimum points.

(a) $y = 5x - x^2$ (b) $y = (1 - x)^2$ (c) $y = x^3 - 3x^2 + 5$

(d) $y = 4x - x^2 - 4$ (e) $y = 2x^3 - 9x^2 + 12$ (f) $y = x^4 - 8x^2 + 12$

4 The sketch graphs that follow are those of $y = x^2 - 6x$ and $y = x^3 - 6x^2$.

(a) Find the x-coordinates of A, B and C. Explain the relationship between the x-coordinate of B and the x-coordinates of A and C.

(b) Find the x-coordinates of D, E and F. Does the relationship you noticed in (a) hold for this graph?

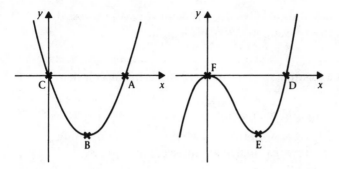

B Optimisation (answers p. 187)

Optimisation means getting the best result. This might mean **minimising** the amount of material used in a design or the amount of pollution caused by an industrial process, or **maximising** the number of customers served in an hour or the number of vaccinations during an epidemic.

Calculus can help with optimisation, as the following examples show.

A circular piece of paper is folded into a cylindrical paper case for a cake. Where should the paper be folded to create the container of greatest volume?

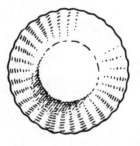 

1D (a) Without doing any calculations, write down what you think happens to the volume of the cylinder as it changes from a tall thin cylinder to a short fat cylinder as shown below.

(b) Draw a rough sketch of a graph which shows these changes in volume.

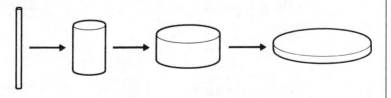

To use calculus methods to solve this problem you can express the volume, V, in terms of a suitable variable length.

2D (a) Construct a formula for the volume V in terms of a chosen variable.

(b) Use calculus to find the maximum volume.

(c) What simplifying assumptions have you made in obtaining your answer? How reasonable are these assumptions?

Example 3

During a promotion drive, an electrical retailer sells a particular make of television at cost price. She finds that, at this price, she sells twenty televisions a week. However, according to a market survey the demand would fall to zero if the price were increased by £40.

By what amount should the retailer increase the price to make the maximum weekly profit?

Solution

For a price increase of £1 you can model the number sold by

$$N = 20 - \tfrac{1}{2}I$$

£I is the increase above cost price and so the profit (in £) is

$$P = NI$$
$$= (20 - \tfrac{1}{2}I)I$$
$$= 20I - \tfrac{1}{2}I^2$$

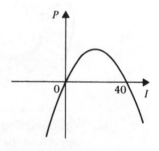

P is maximum when $\dfrac{\mathrm{d}P}{\mathrm{d}I} = 0$.

Since $\dfrac{\mathrm{d}P}{\mathrm{d}I} = 20 - I$, $\dfrac{\mathrm{d}P}{\mathrm{d}I} = 0$ when $I = 20$.

The retailer should increase the price by £20.

3D What has been assumed in the first line of the solution? Can this be justified?

Exercise B (answers p. 188)

1 For a speed of v miles per hour, the fuel consumption, F miles per gallon, of a new car was found to be roughly modelled, for $30 \leqslant v \leqslant 80$, by the formula $F = 25 + v - 0.012v^2$.

(a) Find F and $\dfrac{dF}{dv}$ when $v = 35$ and when $v = 60$. What do these

results indicate about fuel economy?

(b) What speed is most economical for this car?

2 A survey showed that the demand for a product was given approximately by the linear equation $n = 30 - 2P$ where n is the number of items that will be sold (in millions) when the price is £P.

If n million are sold at £P each then the revenue (money taken) will be £R million where

$$R = nP = (30 - 2P)P = 30P - 2P^2.$$

(a) Find $\dfrac{dR}{dP}$ and explain what it means. What is the best selling price?

(b) Calculate the value of $\dfrac{dR}{dP}$ when $P = 5$ and when $P = 10$.

(c) For what range of selling prices would the revenue rise if the price were increased a little?

3 A rectangular strip of plastic of width 20 cm is folded into a length of guttering as shown.

Where should the folds be located to enable the gutter to carry as much water as possible?

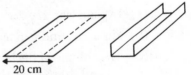

20 cm

4 A new housing estate started with a population of approximately 500 people.

(a) It was planned that it should grow by roughly 100 inhabitants each year.

Find an expression for the intended population P of the estate

t years after its opening. Find $\dfrac{dP}{dt}$ and explain what it represents.

(b) For various reasons, the new estate did not grow as planned and the population was better modelled by the quadratic expression

$$P = 100(5 + t - 0.25t^2).$$

What was the rate of change of the population at the end of the first, second and third years?

What was the maximum population of the estate? What happened to the estate?

5 To find two numbers with the least possible sum and 10 as their product you can take the two numbers to be x and $\dfrac{10}{x}$ and try to minimise $x + \dfrac{10}{x}$.

   (a) Use a graph plotter to sketch $x + \dfrac{10}{x}$.

   (b) From the graph, estimate some possible answers to this minimising problem, depending upon what types of numbers are allowed.

6

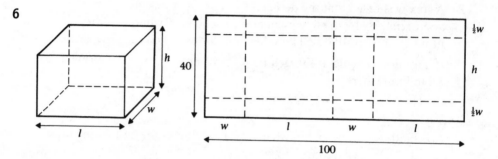

A cardboard box is to be made from a rectangular piece of card, 100 cm by 40 cm, by cutting and folding as necessary along the dashed lines shown in the right-hand diagram. The problem is to find the values of l, w and h which maximise the volume, $V \text{ cm}^3$.

   (a) Explain why $2l + 2w = 100$. Hence express l in terms of w.

   (b) Similarly, find h in terms of w.

   (c) The volume of the box is given by $V = whl$. Use your answers to (a) and (b) to show that $V = w(40 - w)(50 - w)$.

   (d) Find the value of w corresponding to the maximum possible volume. What dimensions will the box then have?

7 Small open-topped boxes are to be made out of sheet steel. Each box is to be made from a 6 cm by 4 cm rectangular piece of steel. A square will be cut from each corner, as shown in the diagram, and the remainder made into the box by bending along the dashed lines and welding.

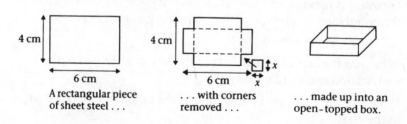

A rectangular piece of sheet steel . . .

. . . with corners removed . . .

. . . made up into an open-topped box.

(a) If the squares cut out have side x cm, show that the volume of the box is V cm^3, where $V = x(4-2x)(6-2x)$.

(b) What should be the dimensions if the volume of the box is to be as large as possible?

8   A farmer has 60 m of fencing. She wants to use it for three sides of a rectangular sheep pen with an existing hedge used for the fourth side.

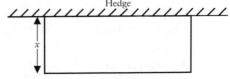

(a) Let x metres be the length of the side shown. Write an expression for the area of the pen in terms of x.

(b) Calculate the value of x that gives the maximum area.

(c) Calculate the maximum area.

9   A box with a lid has a square base of side x cm and height h cm. If its total surface area is 2040 cm^2 write down a formula for its volume V cm^3 and eliminate h to show that $V = 510x - \frac{1}{2}x^3$. Hence find the dimensions giving the maximum possible volume, and calculate this volume.

10E A bicycle manufacturer has designed a new model and wishes to fix the price so that profits are maximised. After an initial cost of £50 000 to set up the production line, it will cost £85 in labour, raw materials and components to produce each bike. Market research suggests that the firm can hope to sell 5000 bikes if the price is fixed at £100, but they can only expect to sell 1000 if the price is £200 per bike. They assume the relationship between price and demand is linear between these two extremes.

How many bikes would you advise the company to manufacture and at what price should they be sold?

11E The farmer in question 8 decides to use the hedge and her 60 m of fencing to make a pen consisting of a rectangle and a semicircle.

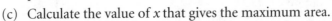

(a) Write an expression for the diameter of the semicircle in terms of x.

(b) Write an expression for the total area of the pen.

(c) Calculate the value of x that gives the maximum area.

(d) Calculate the maximum area.

After working through this chapter you should be able to

1 use differentiation as an aid in graph-sketching

2 use sketches and differentiation in solving optimisation problems.

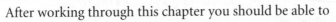

8 Areas under graphs

A Rate graphs (answers p. 190)

Suppose that water flows from a tap into
a bath at a constant rate of 15 litres per
minute.
This can be represented graphically.

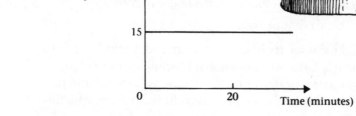

1D	What total volume of water flows from the tap in 20 minutes?
	How is this amount represented on the graph?

Understanding the meaning that can be given to the area under some
graphs is very important.

You probably know that the area under a (time, speed) graph gives the
distance travelled. Speed is the *rate* at which distance is being covered.

The graph above shows the *rate* at which the volume of water in the
bath increases. The area under this graph gives the volume of water in
the bath.

So it seems that the area under a graph showing the 'rate at which
some measure changes' gives the measure in question.

The units labelling the axes of such graphs
also give a clue. The rate of water flow
above is measured in litres per minute, or
number of litres divided by number of
minutes, which can be written as

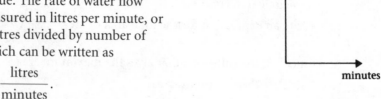

$$\frac{\text{litres}}{\text{minutes}}.$$

Area is calculated by multiplying a height by a width, so the units of
the area under the graph are

$$\frac{\text{litres}}{\text{minutes}} \times \text{minutes} = \text{litres}.$$

Similarly, the meaning of the area under a speed graph could be checked by considering

$$\frac{\text{metres}}{\text{minutes}} \times \text{minutes} = \text{metres}.$$

2   For each of these, what units would be used for the quantity represented by the area under the graph?

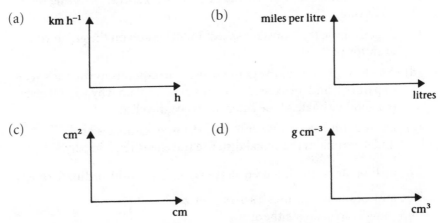

(a) km h⁻¹ ... h

(b) miles per litre ... litres

(c) cm² ... cm

(d) g cm⁻³ ... cm³

Having considered the meaning of the area under a graph, you now need to be able to estimate the area.

3

Suppose the driver of a car leaving the motorway allows the car to decrease in speed gradually over a 60-second time period. The speed is recorded at 10-second intervals to give the table below.

Time (s)	5	15	25	35	45	55
Speed (m s⁻¹)	29.9	23.1	19.2	17.0	15.7	15.0

(a) Plot the (time, speed) coordinates from the table on graph paper and draw the graph for times ranging from 0 to 60 seconds. What does the area under the graph represent?

You need to use the information in the table to estimate the distance the car travels during the 60 seconds. Although common sense may tell you that the speed of the car is continuously changing with time, you can approximate the motion in the following way. Suppose the car travels at a constant 29.9 m s^{-1} during the time interval $0 \rightarrow 10$ seconds, then instantly changes speed and travels at 23.1 m s^{-1} during the time interval $10 \rightarrow 20$ seconds, and so on (call this the 'constant speed' model).

(b) Use this model to estimate the distance the car travels during the 60 seconds.

(c) Superimpose the 'constant speed' model graph on the graph you drew for part (a).

(d) Shade in the area of the graph which corresponds to your answer to part (b), and, by considering this area, explain why your answer is a good estimate of the actual distance travelled.

(e) Do you think your answer to part (b) over-estimates or under-estimates the actual distance travelled? Explain why.

The method of estimation used above is called the **mid-ordinate rule**.

The mid-ordinate rule uses a series of rectangles to estimate the area under a graph. The height of each rectangle is determined by the height of the curve at the mid-point of the interval.

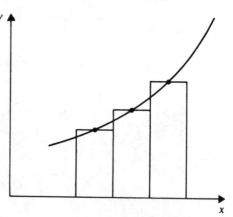

The diagram illustrates the mid-ordinate rule with three strips. It is customary to keep all strip widths the same. This makes the calculation of the area much simpler.

Example 1

These are the fuel consumption results for a test car driven at steadily increasing speed.

Distance driven (km)	0	1	2	3	4	5	6	7	8
Fuel consumption (cm^3 km^{-1})	95	70	62	57	55	60	72	87	109

(a) Sketch the graph, explain briefly the characteristics of the graph and state what the area under the graph represents.

(b) Calculate the area under the graph using the mid-ordinate rule with four strips.

Solution

(a)

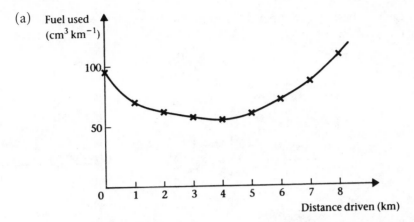

At low speed and at high speed the engine is less economical. As the speed increases from the start, the fuel consumption, in $cm^3\ km^{-1}$, decreases until the most economical speed is reached (after about 4 km); then the fuel consumption increases again.

The area under the graph represents the volume of fuel, in cm^3, used during the 8 km circuit.

(b)

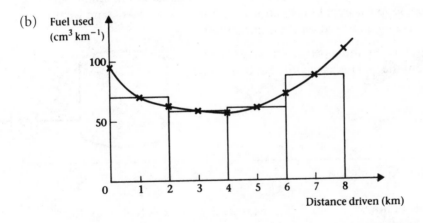

$$Area = 2 \times 70 + 2 \times 57 + 2 \times 60 + 2 \times 87$$
$$= 548$$
$$Fuel\ used = 548\ cm^3$$

Exercise A (answers p. 190)

1   For each of these, say whether the area under the graph represents distance, volume or mass.

(a)

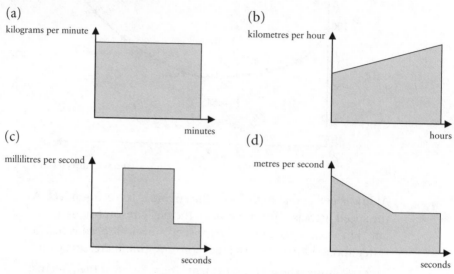

(b)

(c)

(d)

2   The area under a certain graph represents population in millions of people. What might the quantities on the axes represent, and what units might be used for these quantities?

3   Over a 20-minute period, the rate of flow from the oil tank is recorded at two-minute intervals.

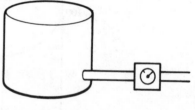

Time (minutes)	1	3	5	7	9	11	13	15	17	19
Rate of flow (litres per minute)	46.3	39.7	34.0	29.2	25.0	21.4	18.4	15.8	13.5	11.6

Use the mid-ordinate rule with 10 strips to calculate an estimate of the volume drained from the tank in the 20-minute period.

B Integration (answers p. 190)

You have already seen that to solve some problems it is necessary to find areas under curves.

The *precise* value of the area under an (x, y) graph from $x = a$ to $x = b$ is denoted by

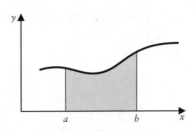

$$\int_a^b y \, dx$$

The notation was introduced by Leibniz.

The symbol $\int$ is an old-fashioned form of the letter 's' and indicates that Leibniz thought of the area under a curve as being obtained by $\int$ umming areas of lots of very thin rectangles.

The area under the graph of $y = x^2 + 4$ is shown in the diagram. The *precise* value of this area is written as

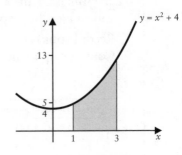

$$\int_1^3 (x^2 + 4) \, dx$$

The process of finding the area under a graph is called **integration** because it is, in essence, a process of combining many small parts to form a whole.

The symbol $\int_a^b f(x) \, dx$ denotes the *precise* value of the area underneath the graph of $y = f(x)$, between $x = a$ and $x = b$.

It is known as the **integral** of y with respect to x over the interval from a to b.

The integral can be found *approximately* by various numerical methods.

---

1   Draw the graph of $y = x$ and shade the area represented by the integral $\int_0^3 x \, dx$. Find the precise value of this integral.

2   Sketch a graph and shade the area under it represented by each of these integrals. Calculate the exact area represented by each integral.

(a) $\int_1^4 x \, dx$ (b) $\int_1^3 5 \, dx$ (c) $\int_1^4 (2x + 3) \, dx$

3D   (a)   Explain why
$$\int_0^u x\,dx = \tfrac{1}{2}u^2 .$$

(b)   Use this formula to evaluate the integral
$$\int_3^7 x\,dx.$$

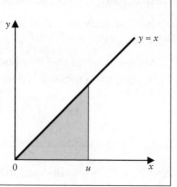

4D   (a)   Use the mid-ordinate rule to calculate an estimate of the area of strips 1 unit wide under the graph of $y = x^2$.

Record your results in a table like this. Continue up to the 5–6 strip.

Strip	Height of mid-ordinate	Area
0 – 1	0.25	0.25
1 – 2	2.25	2.25
2 – 3	6.25	
3 – 4		

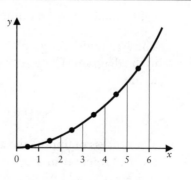

(b)   Let $A(u) = \int_0^u x^2\,dx$.

Use your results from part (a) to complete this table.

u	Estimate of $A(u)$
1	0.25
2	2.50
3	

(For example A(2) is the sum of the areas of the first two strips, A(3) is the sum of the areas of the first three strips, and so on.)

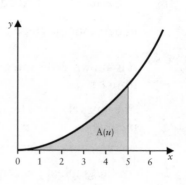

(c)   Will your results in part (b) be an overestimate or an underestimate of the true value of A(u)? Give a reason for your answer.

(d)   Use the completed table from part (b) to draw a graph of A(u) against u. Bearing in mind your answer to part (c), suggest a formula for A(u) in terms of (u).

You may wish to repeat the investigation in question 4D for the function $y = x^3$ and for the function $y = x^4$.

For areas measured from $x = 0$ you have found that

$$f(x) = x \implies A(x) = \tfrac{1}{2}x^2.$$

You have some numerical evidence for the result that

$$f(x) = x^2 \implies A(x) = \tfrac{1}{3}x^3.$$

This result, although true, has *not* of course been *proved* here, only suggested.

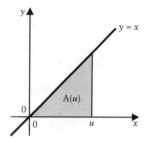

You can now use these area functions, called **integral functions**, to evaluate integrals precisely and easily.

Example 2

Sketch the graph of $y = x^2$. Calculate the area given by

$$\int_{2.5}^{4} x^2 \, dx.$$

Solution

For $f(x) = x^2$, $A(x) = \tfrac{1}{3}x^3$.

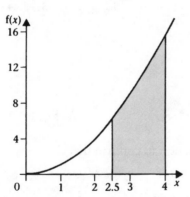

So
$$\int_{2.5}^{4} x^2 \, dx = A(4) - A(2.5)$$
$$= \tfrac{1}{3} \times 4^3 - \tfrac{1}{3} \times 2.5^3$$
$$= 16.125$$

A special notation is used when writing out the evaluation of integrals. For example,

$$\int_{2.5}^{4} x^2 \, dx = \left[\tfrac{1}{3}x^3 \right]_{2.5}^{4}$$

where the new notation on the right-hand side shows the integral function, $\tfrac{1}{3}x^3$, and also shows the limits, 2.5 and 4. The full solution to example 2 would therefore be written

$$\int_{2.5}^{4} x^2 \, dx = \left[\tfrac{1}{3}x^3 \right]_{2.5}^{4} = \tfrac{1}{3} \times 4^3 - \tfrac{1}{3} \times 2.5^3 = 16.125$$

5 Using this new notation, evaluate $\displaystyle\int_{2}^{5} x^2 \, dx$.

On a sketch of $y = x^2$, shade the area you have found.

Example 3

An object starts from rest and its speed v m s^{-1} at time t seconds is given by $v = t^2$. Calculate the distance travelled in the third second of its motion.

Solution

The (time, speed) graph shows that the distance travelled in the third second, as represented by the shaded area, will be given by

$$\int_{2}^{3} t^2 \, dt = \left[\tfrac{1}{3} t^3\right]_{2}^{3}$$

$$= \tfrac{27}{3} - \tfrac{8}{3}$$

$$= \tfrac{19}{3}$$

The distance travelled is $6\tfrac{1}{3}$ m.

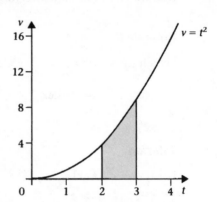

Exercise B (answers p. 192)

1 (a) Sketch the graph of $y = x^2$.

   (b) Explain why

$$\int_{2}^{4} x^2 \, dx = \int_{-4}^{-2} x^2 \, dx.$$

   (c) Use the formula for the integral function to confirm that

$$\int_{2}^{4} x^2 \, dx = \int_{-4}^{-2} x^2 \, dx.$$

2 (a) Using the integral function, evaluate these.

   (i) $\displaystyle\int_{-3}^{-1.5} x^2 \, dx$ (ii) $\displaystyle\int_{-1.5}^{1.5} x^2 \, dx$ (iii) $\displaystyle\int_{1.5}^{3} x^2 \, dx$ (iv) $\displaystyle\int_{-1.5}^{3} x^2 \, dx$

   (b) Write down any relationships which connect two or more of these integrals. Explain, with the aid of a sketch graph, why these relationships are true.

3 (a)

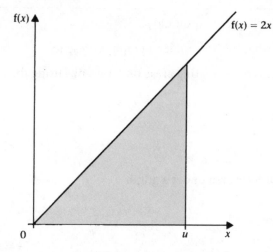

Calculate the shaded area in terms of u.

(b) What is the formula for the integral function?

4 Consider the function $f(v) = 3v$.

(a) Sketch and shade the area between the graph and the horizontal axis, between the limits $v = 0$ and $v = u$.

(b) Calculate the shaded area in terms of u.

5 Repeat question 4 using the following functions.

(i) $f(x) = 2$ (ii) $g(t) = -3$
(iii) $f(t) = 2t$ (iv) $g(v) = -3v$

6 Write down the integral function for these functions when m is any constant and areas are measured from $x = 0$.

(a) $f(x) = m$ (b) $g(x) = mx$

After working through this chapter you should

1   be able to recognise what the area under a graph represents

2   understand the process of estimating areas under graphs using the mid-ordinate rule

3   understand the notation

$$\int_a^b y \, dx$$

used to denote the **precise** area under a graph

4   know that

$$\int_a^b mx \, dx = \left[\tfrac{1}{2} mx^2 \right]_a^b = \tfrac{1}{2} mb^2 - \tfrac{1}{2} ma^2$$

$$\int_a^b x^2 \, dx = \left[\tfrac{1}{3} x^3 \right]_a^b = \tfrac{1}{3} b^3 - \tfrac{1}{3} a^3 .$$

9 Using integration

A Integrals of polynomials (answers p. 193)

So far, you have met the following integral functions:
(a) If $f(x) = m$, then $A(x) = mx$.
(b) If $f(x) = mx$, then $A(x) = \frac{1}{2}mx^2$.
(c) If $f(x) = x^2$, then $A(x) = \frac{1}{3}x^3$.

1D What do you think the integral functions are for these?
(a) $f(x) = x^3$ (b) $f(x) = 2x^2$ (c) $f(x) = x^2 - 3x$
Check your conjectures using the 'area' option on a graph plotter.

2 (a) Sketch the graphs of $y = x^2$ and $y = 2x^2$.

(b) Shade the areas represented by these integrals.

$$\int_0^5 x^2 \, dx \qquad \text{and} \qquad \int_0^5 2x^2 \, dx$$

(c) What simple geometrical transformation connects the two regions?

(d) What will be the connection between $\displaystyle\int_a^b kx^2 \, dx$ and $\displaystyle\int_a^b x^2 \, dx$?

3 (a) Explain, with the aid of a copy of the graph of $y = 2x + 3$, and considering the areas A_1 and A_2, why

$$\int_0^u (2x + 3) \, dx = \left[x^2 + 3x \right]_0^u.$$

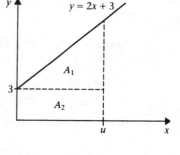

(b) Sketch the graph of $y = x^2 + 4$ and use it to explain, by considering suitable areas, why

$$\int_0^u (x^2 + 4) \, dx = \left[\tfrac{1}{3}x^3 + 4x \right]_0^u.$$

4 Choose two functions of the form $ax^2 + bx + c$, where a, b and c are constants. (Do not always choose positive values for a, b and c.) Write down probable integral functions and check these with a graph plotter.

5 Suggest a general formula for the integral function of any quadratic.

6 Repeat question 4 for a function of the form $ax^3 + bx^2 + cx + d$.

7 Suggest a general formula for the integral function of any cubic.

You now have the following rule for integrating.

A polynomial function of the form $f(x) = a + bx + cx^2 + dx^3$ has integral function $A(x) = ax + \frac{1}{2}bx^2 + \frac{1}{3}cx^3 + \frac{1}{4}dx^4$.

Example 1

Evaluate the integral $\int_2^3 (x+3)(x+2)(x-1)\,dx$.

Solution

$$\int_2^3 (x+3)(x+2)(x-1)\,dx = \int_2^3 (x^3 + 4x^2 + x - 6)\,dx$$

$$= \left[\frac{x^4}{4} + \frac{4x^3}{3} + \frac{x^2}{2} - 6x\right]_2^3$$

$$= 42\tfrac{3}{4} - 4\tfrac{2}{3} = 38\tfrac{1}{12}$$

Exercise A (answers p. 193)

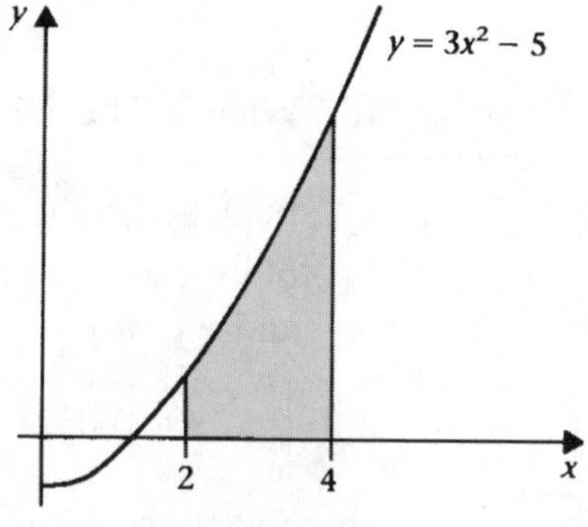

1 (a) Write down the integral which represents the shaded area.

(b) Calculate this area.

2 Evaluate $\int_1^3 (t^3 + t^2 + t + 1)\,dt$.

3 (a) Sketch the graph of $-x^2 + 4x - 3$, showing clearly where the curve cuts the x-axis.

(b) Calculate the area enclosed by the curve and the x-axis.

4 Evaluate these integrals.

(a) $\int_0^1 (x - x^3)\,dx$ (b) $\int_2^4 (x+1)\,dx$ (c) $\int_{-2}^{-1} x^2\,dx$

(d) $\int_0^1 (x^2 - 2x + 1)\,dx$ (e) $\int_0^1 (x+1)(x+2)\,dx$

5 Find the value of a for which $\int_1^a (2x+3)\,dx = 24$.

(Graph at right: $y = 3x^2 - 5$, with shaded area and x-axis markings at 2 and 4.)

6 (a) Explain why the shaded area is given by

$$A = \int_0^a x^2 \, dx + \int_a^b (8 - x^2) \, dx$$

where a and b are to be found.

(b) Find the shaded area A.

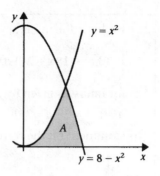

7 Find the shaded areas.

(a)

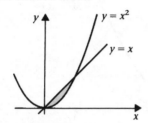

(b)

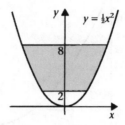

B 'Negative' areas (answers p. 194)

As in the following example, areas below the x-axis often have a special significance.

Current balance of payments falls back after good recovery

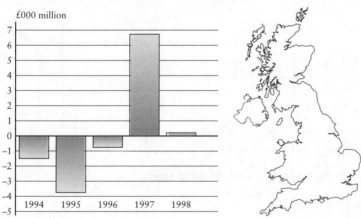

1D Use the graph above to estimate the total current balance of payments from 1994 to 1998.

2D

(a) Evaluate the integral

$$\int_a^b (3x^2 - 18x + 24)\, dx$$

for intervals given by

$a = 1, b = 2;\ a = 2, b = 4;\ a = 1, b = 4$.

(b) Comment on the results by reference to this graph.

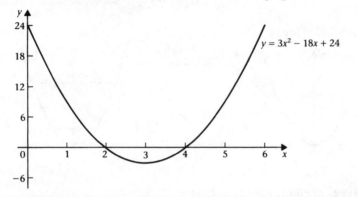

$y = 3x^2 - 18x + 24$

Integrating can be thought of as summing the areas of lots of very thin rectangular strips. Each strip has area yh where h is the width of the strip. y is positive or negative, depending on whether the graph is above or below the x-axis.

yh is positive
if y is positive.

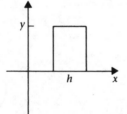

yh is negative
if y is negative.

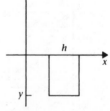

So the integral $\int_a^b y\, dx$ gives positive values to areas above the x-axis and negative values to areas below the x-axis.

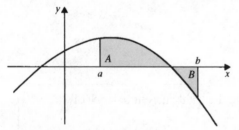

$$\int_a^b y\, dx = A - B$$

Note that the areas A and B are treated as positive. If you were asked to find the total area between the graph and the x-axis over the interval a to b, you would need to find the two areas separately by integration and *add* them, treating B as positive.

3 An alloy casting is in the form of a prism with cross-sectional area as shown.

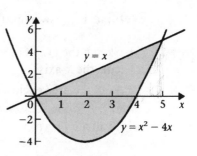

Evaluate $\displaystyle\int_0^5 x\,dx$, $\displaystyle\int_0^4 (x^2 - 4x)\,dx$ and

$\displaystyle\int_4^5 (x^2 - 4x)\,dx$.

Explain how you can use these integrals to evaluate the shaded area.

4 An alternative 'profile' for the prism in question 3 is obtained by translating the graphs up 5 units, so that they become the graphs of

$$y = x + 5 \qquad \text{and} \qquad y = x^2 - 4x + 5.$$

(a) Sketch the graphs of these two functions on the same axes and shade in the area representing the cross-section of the alloy casting.

(b) Evaluate $\displaystyle\int_0^5 (x + 5)\,dx$ and $\displaystyle\int_0^5 (x^2 - 4x + 5)\,dx$, and use your answers to calculate the shaded area, confirming your answer to question 3.

5 In a balanced aquarium, the rate of change of the amount of carbon dioxide dissolved in a litre of water is found to have the following daily pattern.

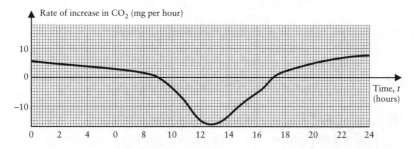

(a) State what **area** represents in the above graph and explain the significant difference between 'positive' and 'negative' area in this situation.

(b) During what part of the day is the amount of carbon dioxide dissolved in the aquarium water increasing? Estimate the total increase during this part of the day.

(c) Estimate the increase in the amount of carbon dioxide dissolved during a full 24-hour cycle.

Exercise B (answers p. 195)

1 (a) Sketch the graph of $y = x^2 - x - 2$, showing clearly where the curve cuts the x-axis.

   (b) Find the area enclosed between the graph and the x-axis.

2 (a) Evaluate $\displaystyle\int_{-2}^{1} (t^3 + 2t^2 - 3)\,dt$.

   (b) Using a suitable sketch, explain why your answer is negative.

3 (a) Sketch the graph of $y = x^3 - 2x^2 - 5x + 6$, showing clearly where the curve cuts the x-axis.

   (b) Calculate the total area enclosed by the curve and the x-axis.

4 A stone is projected vertically upwards such that its speed (v m s^{-1}) after t seconds is given by

   $$v = 25 - 10t.$$

   (a) How far does the stone travel in the first two seconds?

   (b) After how many seconds does it reach its maximum height?

   (c) Calculate the maximum height the stone will reach.

5 Evaluate these.

   (a) $\displaystyle\int_{0}^{1} (x^3 - x)\,dx$ (b) $\displaystyle\int_{-4}^{2} (x + 1)\,dx$ (c) $\displaystyle\int_{1}^{2} (x^3 - 2x + 1)\,dx$

6 Sketch the graph of $y = 3x - x^2$, and then find the total area between the graph and the x-axis over the interval $[0, 5]$.

7 Find the values of a for which $\displaystyle\int_{1}^{a} (5 - 2x)\,dx = 0$.

8 The velocity, in m s^{-1}, after t seconds of a particle is given by $v = 4t - t^2$. Find the total distance travelled in the first 6 seconds.

9 Find the shaded area.

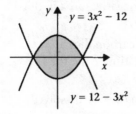

$y = 3x^2 - 12$

$y = 12 - 3x^2$

10 Find *c* if the shaded area is 6 square units.

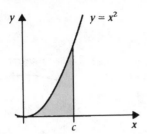

11E

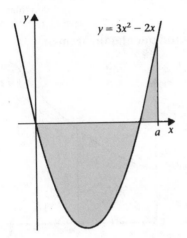

Find *a* such that
$$\int_0^a (3x^2 - 2x)\, \mathrm{d}x = 0.$$

C The fundamental theorem of calculus (answers p. 196)

You have been able to calculate some integrals precisely by first finding an integral function. For example, $x^3 + x$ is an integral function for $3x^2 + 1$ and so

$$\int_3^5 (3x^2 + 1)\, \mathrm{d}x = \left[x^3 + x\right]_3^5.$$

1D What simple relationship is there between a function and its integral function? The table below may help you to spot the connection.

$f(x)$	1	x	$3x^2$	$3x^2 + 1$
$A(x)$	x	$\frac{1}{2}x^2$	x^3	$x^3 + x$

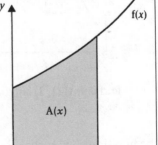

It is clear that if you differentiate the integral function, you obtain the function you are integrating, that is,

$$\frac{d}{dx}(A(x)) = f(x).$$

The process of differentiation (e.g. finding gradients) is an inverse process to that of integration (e.g. finding areas).

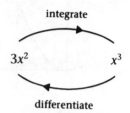

This remarkable relationship is called the **fundamental theorem of calculus.**

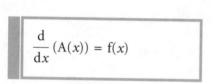

$$\frac{d}{dx}(A(x)) = f(x)$$

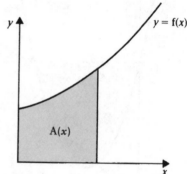

The graphs of all differentiable functions are locally straight, so it is sensible to investigate the connection between differentiation and integration by first considering linear functions.

The gradient of a line segment joining two points is constant.

For example

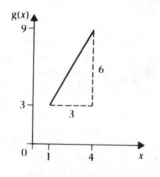

End points (1, 3) and (4, 9)

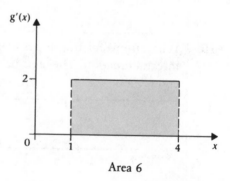

Area 6

(The notation g′(x) means the derived function – the function you get when you differentiate g(x).)

2   Draw diagrams for line segments joining these points.

    (a) $(1, 2), (5, 6)$ (b) $(4, 8), (6, 2)$ (c) $(3, 5), (6, 5)$

    Can you spot a connection between the y-coordinates of the end points of the function and the area under the graph of the derived function?

    Explain this connection by considering the definition of the gradient of a straight line.

    When the graph of $g(x)$ is a *series* of connected line segments, the diagrams obtained are like those below.

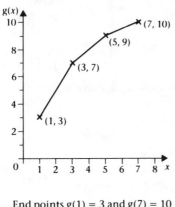
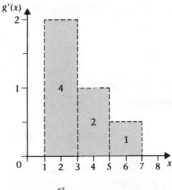

    End points $g(1) = 3$ and $g(7) = 10$ Area $\displaystyle\int_1^7 g'(x)\,\mathrm{d}x = 4 + 2 + 1 = 7$

3   The following diagrams show two further ways of joining the end points $(1, 3)$ and $(7, 10)$ with three line segments.

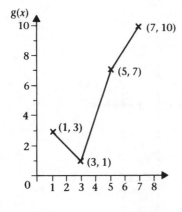

    Sketch the graph of the function $g'(x)$ for each of the examples shown above, or any two similar examples of your own invention.

    In each case, find $\displaystyle\int_1^7 g'(x)\,\mathrm{d}x$. Is it always true that

$$\int_1^7 g'(x)\,\mathrm{d}x = g(7) - g(1)\,?$$

4 Is it always true that $\displaystyle\int_a^b g'(x)\,dx = g(b) - g(a)$? Test this conjecture with *any* similar type of function of your own choice consisting of several line segments.

5E (a) The graph shows a derived function $g'(x)$. Construct a possible graph of the original function $g(x)$.

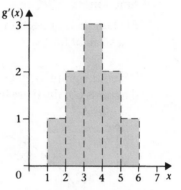

(b) Explain why your answer to part (a) is not unique. Construct another possible graph of $g(x)$.

(c) In each case, check that

$$\int_1^6 g'(x)\,dx = g(6) - g(1).$$

You have seen that, for a graph made up of connected straight-line segments,

$$\int_a^b g'(x)\,dx = g(b) - g(a).$$

Any differentiable function g is locally straight and so can be approximated by a series of straight-line segments.

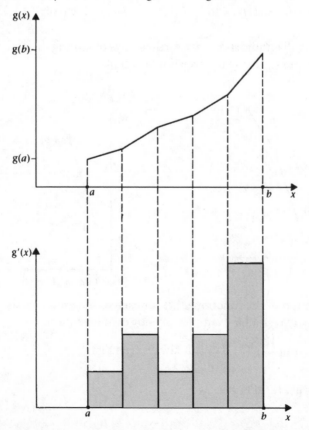

The gradient function g′ can then be approximated by a step-graph. This does not *prove* the fundamental theorem of calculus but at least indicates why

for any differentiable function f,

$$\int_a^b f'(x)\, dx = f(b) - f(a).$$

The fact that integration and differentiation are inverse operations should not come as a surprise when you think about the way in which (time, speed) and (time, distance) graphs are related. Given a (time, distance) function you differentiate to find speed, and given a (time, speed) function you integrate to find distance.

The fundamental theorem gives a clear objective when integrating. You must find a function which, when differentiated, gives the function you wish to integrate!

Exercise C (answers p. 197)

1 (a) Evaluate these.

(i) $\displaystyle\int_{-1}^{1} (x^3 - 3x^2 - x + 3)\ dx$ (ii) $\displaystyle\int_{-1}^{3} (x^3 - 3x^2 - x + 3)\, dx$

(b) Sketch the graph of $y = x^3 - 3x^2 - x + 3$. Hence explain the connection between your answers to (a) and the value of

$$\int_1^3 (x^3 - 3x^2 - x + 3)\ dx.$$

2 (a) If $\displaystyle\int_c^d g(x)\, dx = \left[5x^2 + 3x\right]_c^d$, write down $g(x)$.

(b) If $\displaystyle\int_a^b h(t)\, dt = \left[2t^3 - 7\right]_a^b$, write down $h(t)$.

D The indefinite integral (answers p. 197)

Since $\dfrac{d(x^2 + 5x)}{dx} = 2x + 5$ you know that

$$\int_1^2 (2x + 5)\, dx = \left[x^2 + 5x\right]_1^2 = 8.$$

1D Differentiate each of these.

$$x^2 + 5x + 1, \qquad x^2 + 5x + 4, \qquad x^2 + 5x - 3$$

Explain why each of these functions could be used as an integral function for $2x + 5$ and why each gives the same answer for

$$\int_1^2 (2x + 5)\, dx.$$

To evaluate an integral such as $\displaystyle\int_3^5 (2x)\, dx$ you can use *any* integral function of the form $x^2 + c$

where c is a constant, known as the **constant of integration**.

A general integral function such as $x^2 + c$ is called an **indefinite integral**.

An integral sign without any limits is used to denote indefinite integrals. A constant term '$+c$' should always be included, for example

$$\int (2x)\, dx = x^2 + c,$$

$$\int x^2\, dx = \tfrac{1}{3}x^3 + c.$$

Integrals between limits, for example

$$\int_3^5 (2x)\, dx = 16$$

are called **definite integrals**. A definite integral has a (definite) numerical value.

For definite integrals, there is no need to include the constant of integration because it cancels out as shown in the following example.

$$\int_1^3 x^2\, dx = \left[\tfrac{1}{3}x^3 + c \right]_1^3$$

$$= (9 + c) - (\tfrac{1}{3} + c)$$

$$= 8\tfrac{2}{3} \quad \text{(irrespective of the value of } c)$$

You can therefore simply write

$$\int_1^3 x^2\, dx = \left[\tfrac{1}{3}x^3 \right]_1^3 = 9 - \tfrac{1}{3} = 8\tfrac{2}{3}.$$

Example 2

Find y as a function of x given that $y = 10$ when $x = 1$ and that

$$\frac{dy}{dx} = (3x - 1)(x + 3).$$

Solution

$$y = \int (3x - 1)(x + 3) \, dx$$

$$= \int (3x^2 + 8x - 3) \, dx$$

$$= x^3 + 4x^2 - 3x + c$$

But $y = 10$ when $x = 1$

$\Rightarrow$ $\qquad\qquad 10 = 1 + 4 - 3 + c$

$\Rightarrow$ $\qquad\qquad c = 8$

$\Rightarrow$ $\qquad\qquad y = x^3 + 4x^2 - 3x + 8$

Exercise D (answers p. 197)

1 Find the following integrals.

(a) $\displaystyle\int (x^3 - 1) \, dx$ (b) $\displaystyle\int_1^3 (x + 1)(x - 2) \, dx$

2 Find y as a function of x for these.

(a) $\dfrac{dy}{dx} = x - 4$ (b) $\dfrac{dy}{dx} = 3x^2 + x$

(c) $\dfrac{dy}{dx} = x^2 + x + 1$ (d) $\dfrac{dy}{dx} = (x + 1)(x - 2)$

3 Express y as a function of x for these.

(a) $\dfrac{dy}{dx} = 3x^2 + 4x$ and the (x, y) graph passes through $(1, 5)$

(b) $\dfrac{dy}{dx} = x^2 + x + 1$ and the (x, y) graph passes through $(0, 3)$

4 (a) If $\displaystyle\int_a^b (3x^2 - 2x + 5) \, dx = \left[f(x) \right]_a^b$, write down a possible f(x).

(b) If $\displaystyle\int_c^d (2t + 1)(t - 4) \, dt = \left[k(t) \right]_c^d$, find a suitable k($t$).

After working through this chapter you should

1 be able to integrate polynomial functions algebraically and know that

$$\int (a\,\mathrm{f}(x) + b\mathrm{g}(x))\,\mathrm{d}x = a\int \mathrm{f}(x)\,\mathrm{d}x + b\int \mathrm{g}(x)\,\mathrm{d}x$$

2 be able to find areas by using combinations of appropriate integrals

3 understand why areas below the x-axis are calculated as being negative and areas above the x-axis are positive

4 understand what is meant by a definite integral

5 understand what is meant by an indefinite integral and the need for a constant of integration

6 be able to integrate algebraically by using the fact that integration is the inverse process of differentiation

$$\int_{a}^{b} \mathrm{f}'(x)\,\mathrm{d}x = \mathrm{f}(b) - \mathrm{f}(a).$$

10 Summarising data

A Introduction

The collection of data can be considered to have had a long history. The Domesday Book of William the Conqueror is an early example of a good attempt to collect information about a population. The Bible provides evidence of earlier examples, like the following from the New Testament:

> In those days a decree was issued by the emperor Augustus for a census to be taken throughout the Roman world.
>
> Luke 2:1

or this extract from the Old Testament:

> ... as the Lord had commanded Moses. He drew up the lists ... in the wilderness of Sinai. The total number of Israelites aged 20 years and upwards fit for service, recorded in the lists of fathers' families, was 603 550.
>
> Numbers 1:19, 45–46

A national census of the population is conducted in the United Kingdom every ten years. The ready availability of statistics of this kind helps to keep us informed of trends and changes in society. It is important to be able to 'read' statistical information, for example about the dangers of smoking or about the association of heart disease with certain life styles, and to make informed judgements upon it. Your study of statistics should help you to do this.

One of the early statisticians was Florence Nightingale (1820–1910). As part of her efforts to improve conditions for patients, she collected data in various hospitals on the causes of death and illness. She realised that it was always necessary to *use* and *interpret* information after it had been collected.

> The War Office has some of the finest statistics in the world. What comes of them? Little or nothing. Why? Because the Heads do not know how to make anything of them ... What we want is not so much an accumulation of facts, as to teach the men who are to govern the country the use of statistical facts.
>
> Florence Nightingale

Statistics is not the aimless collection of data for its own sake, or simply for general interest. The collection of data is normally made in response to a problem that needs to be investigated or to a hypothesis that is to be tested. It is the **collection** and **analysis** of data, followed by the making of **judgements**, **decisions** or **inferences**, which form the subject-matter of statistics. This can be summarised in the following way:

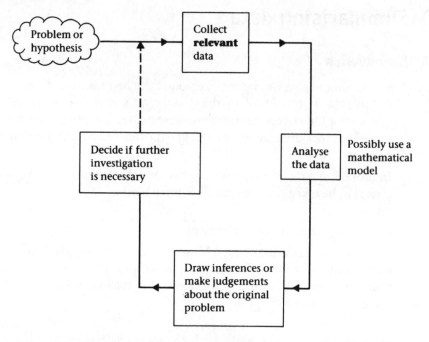

A study of statistics will involve a consideration of each of the areas mentioned in the diagram.

Exercise A (answers p. 197)

The following diagrams are based on statistics from the government publication *Regional Trends* (1996).

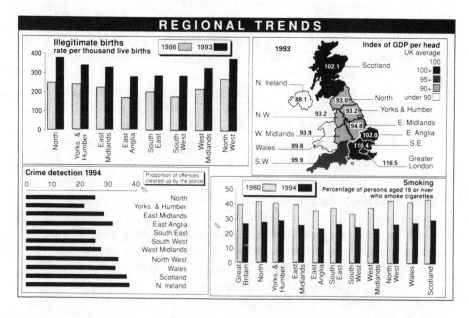

Study the diagrams and then answer the questions based on this material.

1 In 1986, approximately what percentage of all births in the East Midlands were described (in the diagram) as illegitimate?

   What is the corresponding figure for 1993?

   In 1993, which English region registered the greatest and which the least percentage of illegitimate births?

2 The average gross domestic product (GDP) for the UK is fixed at 100. Figures for the regions are given in relation to this figure.

   (a) What is the average GDP for those living in these areas.

        (i)   Greater London
        (ii) Northern Ireland

   (b) Comment on any regional differences in GDP.

3 In 1994, Yorkshire and Humberside had the worst 'clearance' rate for criminal offences.

   (a) What percentage of crimes were cleared up by the police in these areas.

        (i)   the South East
        (ii)   Scotland
        (iii) the North

   (b) Does the table give you any information about the numbers of crimes committed in these regions?

   (c) How do you think data could be collected on these?

        (i)   The clear up rate
        (ii) The number of crimes

        Do you see any problems?

4 The government decides to launch a new anti-smoking campaign.

   (a) Is there any evidence in the table for directing the advertising to particular regions?

   (b) What other information on smoking habits might be useful in advising the government on how to conduct its campaign?

B Types of average

Sometimes it is important to condense a large data set into a few numbers which give an impression of the original set. It is useful to have a single number as the *average* of the data, and you already know three possible such numbers – the **mean**, the **median** and the **mode**.

> Reminder
>
> The mode is the *most frequently* occurring value.
>
> The median is the *middle value* when the data are ranked in decreasing (or increasing) order of magnitude.
>
> The mean is the sum of the data values divided by the number of observations.

For example, in a group of five families, the number of people in each family is 2, 5, 6, 5 and 4. For this data set,

the mean family size is $\frac{1}{5}(2 + 5 + 6 + 5 + 4) = \frac{22}{5} = 4.4$,

the median family size is 5,

the modal family size is also 5.

The three commonly used 'averages' are each appropriate in different circumstances and for different purposes.

Some desirable properties of a number which is used as a 'representative' number for data are:

- it should use all the data values
- it should not be too influenced by 'wayward' values
- it should be easy to calculate.

The **mode** is often used in situations where there are no numerical values; for example, the most common eye colour in a class or the university subject which attracts most students.

The **mean** is influenced equally by all the data values.

The **median** is usually very easy to calculate and has the advantage that it tends to be little affected by a few abnormal items of data – it is said to be 'more robust' than the mean. In finding the median you *have* to use ranked data, that is data which are placed in order.

Exercise B (answers p. 198)

1   In an aptitude test, twenty people were asked to do a jigsaw puzzle and the time taken by each was recorded, with the following results:

Time (seconds)
13 34 40 43 45 46 48 49 51 52
52 53 58 63 72 75 76 78 104

As can be seen, only nineteen people completed the jigsaw.

(a) Calculate the mean and median of these data and decide which is the most appropriate measure of average, giving your reasons.

(b) The twentieth person gave up after 148 seconds. Should this information have been included in your calculations? Give reasons for your answer, stating how the observation would affect the mean and the median.

2 The distribution of the ages of the inhabitants of a south coast seaside town has this shape.

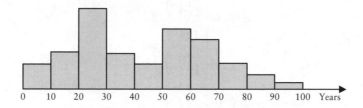

Comment on the shape of the distribution and how well a single value could 'represent' the ages of the inhabitants of this town.

C Stem and leaf diagrams (answers p. 198)

This table shows the hours of sunshine each day in two seaside resorts in the month of July.

Bournemouth

10.1	10.6	13.3	14.1	15.4	11.8	11.0	13.6	13.1	6.9	8.7
14.0	1.6	8.0	2.6	0.5	2.7	0.0	0.2	0.2	0.0	8.7
2.8	3.2	3.9	4.4							

Torquay

10.0	7.8	13.7	14.5	15.1	12.3	11.5	11.5	8.8	0.0	6.9
13.5	0.7	7.8	2.3	1.6	3.8	2.2	0.5	2.0	3.0	5.5
4.6	5.1	5.1	7.6							

The 'stem and leaf diagram' on p. 114 provides a way of organising the data so that you can spot patterns and make comparisons easily. The stem (the column of figures in the middle) shows the units and the leaves (the rows on each side) show the decimal.

1 Describe any general differences in the distributions of hours of sunshine for the two resorts.

Notice that the numbers are placed on the leaves in order of size, smallest closest to the stem. When you make your own stem and leaf diagram you may need to do a rough diagram first, writing the leaf values in the order you meet them, then produce a finished diagram with the leaf numbers in order.

A diagram comparing two sets of values, like the one on p. 114, is called a back-to-back stem and leaf diagram. A stem and leaf diagram can be drawn for a single set of values, usually with the leaves on the right.

```
      Bournemouth          Torquay
                  4 | 15 | 1
                1 0 | 14 | 5
              6 3 1 | 13 | 5 7
                    | 12 | 3
                8 0 | 11 | 5 5
                6 1 | 10 | 0
                    |  9 |
              7 7 0 |  8 | 8
                    |  7 | 6 8 8
                  9 |  6 | 9
                    |  5 | 1 1 5
                  4 |  4 | 6
                9 2 |  3 | 0 8
              8 7 6 |  2 | 0 2 3
                  6 |  1 | 6
          5 2 2 0 0 |  0 | 0 5 7
```

2   The following diagram compares the speeds of two different types of bullet. Twenty speed measurements were made for each bullet type.

```
          Type A              Type B
                  6 | 51 | 0 2
                    | 50 | 1 3 3 8
          8 7 3 3 1 | 49 | 0 5 5 7 8
      9 7 7 5 2 1 1 0 | 48 | 1 2 2 6 9
          8 5 5 1 1 | 47 | 0 4 8
                  4 | 46 | 3
```

$$8 \mid 47 \mid \text{means } 478 \text{ ms}^{-1}$$

$$\mid 49 \mid 5 \text{ means } 495 \text{ ms}^{-1}$$

What conclusions can you draw from this diagram?

The size of the 'class interval' represented by each value in the stem (units, tens, ...) is chosen to give a usable diagram. But the class intervals for a particular diagram must all be the same size.

3 The table gives the heights (in centimetres) of twenty adult females and twenty adult males.

Females	Males
159	180
162	165
142	161
159	173
158	174
139	173
170	173
155	179
156	184
154	177
159	178
163	175
158	168
161	171
152	171
171	175
143	173
158	182
164	164
156	174

(a) By considering the range of each set of heights, say which of the two sets of heights seems more variable.

(b) (i) Draw stem and leaf diagrams for the heights of the females and males separately.

   (ii) Which set of heights is more variable?

   (iii) Find the median in each case.

   (iv) Which has the higher median?

(c) Consider the data as a set of the heights of 40 adults and draw a 'combined' stem and leaf plot. Comment on its shape.

(d) If the group of adults is representative of the population, which of the distributions below is most likely to represent that of adults' height? Explain your choice.

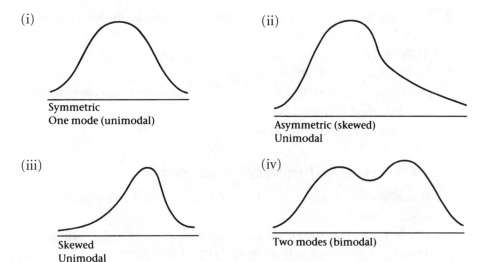

(i)

Symmetric
One mode (unimodal)

(ii)

Asymmetric (skewed)
Unimodal

(iii)

Skewed
Unimodal

(iv)

Two modes (bimodal)

Keep your answers to this question for use in Section E.

A stem and leaf diagram gives an impression of

- the average of the data
- the variability of the data
- the general shape of the distribution.

Exercise C (answers p. 199)

1   Use a stem and leaf diagram to compare the examination marks of two classes.

Class 1   80   62   53   76   76   31   59   78   84
          66   71   50   79   69   87   64   56   65
          58   78   75   60   51

Class 2   71   68   56   79   73   51   48   83   64
          58   75   45   91   80   59   34   55   73
          81   62   64   69

   (a) Which class has performed better in the examination?
   (b) Which class appears to be less variable in terms of pupil attainment?

   Keep your answers for use in Section E.

2   These are the starting salaries for a group of graduates in thousands of pounds.

   30, 22, 9, 24, 15, 16, 20, 32, 22, 24, 20, 18, 20, 28, 19, 26, 17, 16, 17, 24, 22, 18, 22, 14, 20, 26

   Draw a stem and leaf diagram for the data. Comment on its shape. Is it what you would have expected?

   Keep your answers for use in Section E.

D Using cumulative frequency (answers p. 199)

The **cumulative frequency** is the total frequency up to a particular value, or class boundary.

340 sunflower plants were measured six weeks after planting. From the frequency table it is easy to draw up a cumulative frequency table as shown.

Height (cm)	Frequency	Height (cm)	Cumulative frequency
3–6	10	up to 6	10
7–10	21	up to 10	$10 + 21 = 31$
11–14	114	up to 14	$31 + 114 = 145$
15–18	105	up to 18	$145 + 105 = 250$
19–20	54	up to 22	$250 + 54 = 304$
23–26	36	up to 26	$304 + 36 = 340$

It can be helpful to plot cumulative frequencies on a cumulative frequency diagram.

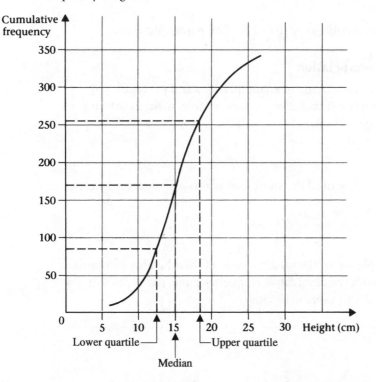

Using the cumulative frequency diagram, the median can be estimated quite easily. For 340 plants, the median height will be approximately that of the 170th plant. By finding 170 on the cumulative frequency axis you can read off the corresponding height on the horizontal axis. The median height is 15 cm.

The lower quartile can be found by reading off the height for the 85th plant. The upper quartile can be found by reading off the height of the 255th plant.

1 (a) Find the values of the lower and upper quartiles.
   (b) Give the interquartile range.

> The xth percentile of a distribution is the value $x\%$ of the way through the distribution.

The 30th percentile will be the height of the plant 30% of the way through the plants placed in order. So for 340 plants this will be the height of the $\frac{30}{100} \times 340$th plant (approximately the 102nd plant).

2   Read off the 30th percentile from the cumulative frequency curve above.

3   Estimate the following from the cumulative frequency curve for the sunflower plants.

   (a) The 60th percentile   (b) The 90th percentile

Using linear interpolation

It is possible to estimate the median, quartiles and percentiles by calculation from the cumulative frequency table, without drawing a cumulative frequency curve.

Example 1

Find the median height of the sunflower plants above, using linear interpolation.

Solution

There are 340 plants, so the median value of their heights will be the 170th value. From the cumulative frequency table, the 145th value is 14 cm and the 250th value is 18 cm.

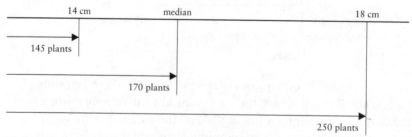

This gives us the following numbers of plants *between* the heights.

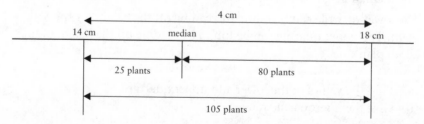

From the second diagram, an estimate of the median, in cm, is

$$14 + \frac{25}{105} \times 4$$

$$= 15.0 \text{ cm to 1 d.p.}$$

4D Use a similar method to calculate an estimate of each of the quartiles from the sunflower plant data.

Exercise D (answers p. 199)

1 A gardener collected 150 worms from her garden and recorded their lengths to the nearest millimetre. The results are given below.

Length (mm)	95–109	110–124	125–139	140–154	155–169	170–184	185–199	200–214
No. of worms	4	10	19	36	43	26	9	3

(a) Write down the cumulative frequency table and draw a cumulative frequency curve to illustrate this information.

(b) Use the curve to estimate the median and interquartile range.

(c) Use the curve to estimate the following.

    (i)   The 15th percentile   (ii)   The 40th percentile

    (iii) The 65th percentile   (iv) The 90th percentile

2 This table shows the lengths of stay in a hospital after a heart attack for 149 males and 48 females.

Length of stay, days	Number of males	Number of females
0–5	40	16
5–10	58	16
10–15	39	7
15–20	6	3
20–25	4	3
25–30	2	3

(a) Produce cumulative frequency tables for the male and the female data.

(b) Draw a cumulative frequency graph for the male length of stay.

(c) Use your graph to obtain these.

　　(i)　The median length of stay for the males

　　(ii)　The interquartile range for the male length of stay

　　(iii)　The 17th percentile for the male length of stay

　　(iv)　The 83rd percentile for the male length of stay

(d) Use linear interpolation on the female data to calculate estimates of these to 1 d.p.

　　(i)　The median length of stay for the females

　　(ii)　The lower quartile for the female length of stay

　　(iii)　The upper quartile for the female length of stay

　　(iv)　Hence the interquartile range for the female length of stay

　　(v)　The 17th percentile for the female length of stay

　　(vi)　The 83rd percentile for the female length of stay

E Box and whisker diagrams (answers p. 200)

A **box plot** or **box and whisker diagram** is a pictorial representation of data based upon five numbers: top of range, upper quartile, median, lower quartile and bottom of range. These are illustrated in the box plot of times for reaction to a stimulus (in hundredths of a second) shown below.

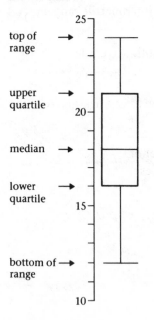

A quarter of the values lie between 12 and 16, a quarter between 16 and 18, a quarter between 18 and 21 and a quarter between 21 and 24 (hundredths of a second).

The middle 50% of the values lie within the box.

25% of the values lie in the upper part of the box.

25% of the values lie in the lower part of the box.

The length of the box (the **interquartile range**) is a measure of the variability or spread of the data.

The box plot for a perfectly symmetric distribution would look something like the one drawn below.

The whiskers are of equal length.

The median is in the middle of the box.

If the distribution had most of its values at the lower end of the range the box plot might be as shown in the second diagram. Since 25% of the values are in the shaded box, this indicates that there is a considerable 'peak' in this part of the distribution.

From a stem and leaf diagram with the 'leaves' written in numerical order it is easy to extract the values of the median and quartiles, although it is important to note carefully the *direction* in which the numbers follow on. It may help to imagine the values written out on a single line. The following example shows the approach.

Adult reaction times

Females ($n = 19$)		Males ($n = 20$)
4 4	2	
3 3 3 3 2 2	2	2 2 2 2 2 3
1 1 0 0	2	0 1
8	1	8 8 8 9 9
7 7 7	1	6 7 7
4 4	1	4 4 5
	1	
	1	
	0	8

| 1 | 4 means 14 hundreths of a second

Median   There are 20 reaction times for males. The two middle values are the 10th and 11th (18 and 19 hundredths of a second) and so the median is 0.185 second.

Lower quartile   There are 10 values below the median. The middle values are the 5th and 6th (16 and 17 hundredths of a second) and so the lower quartile is 0.165 second.

1   Find the median for females and the remaining quartiles for both sets
    of reaction times given above.

2   These box plots summarise the bullet data
    on p. 114.
    What can be deduced from the box plots
    without referring back to the original data?

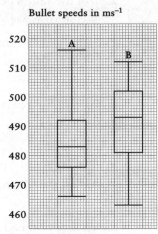

Bullet speeds in ms⁻¹

3   Find the stem and leaf diagrams that you produced for question 3 on
    p. 115 (heights of males and females).

    (a) Use them to find the median and quartiles for females and males
        separately.

    (b) On graph paper draw box and whisker diagrams side by side for
        the female heights and male heights.

Exercise E (answers p. 201)

1   Use the stem and leaf diagrams that you produced for Exercise C
    question 1 (examination marks for two classes).

    Find the medians and quartiles, and on graph paper draw two box and
    whisker diagrams side by side, one for each class.

2   Use the stem and leaf diagrams that you produced for Exercise C
    question 2 (graduate salaries) to draw a box and whisker diagram.

3   Box plots for the maximum daily temperatures during one month, for
    London and Copenhagen, are as shown.

    (a) Which city had the highest
        recorded temperature?
        Which city was generally
        hotter? Carefully justify
        your answer.

    (b) Which city had the greater
        range of maximum
        temperature? Which city
        would you consider to
        have had the more variable
        temperature? Carefully
        justify your answer.

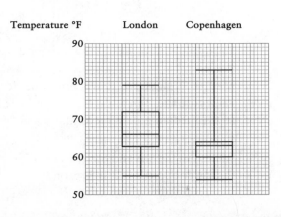

4 The back-to-back stem and leaf plot drawn below gives the daily hours of sunshine measured at the Weston Park Meteorological Station in Sheffield.

January		July
	13	6
	12	0
	11	1 5
	10	1
	9	7
	8	
	7	0 3 6 7 9
2	6	2 6
8 7	5	5 6 7 8 8
	4	3 8 8
3 0	3	1 3
4 3 1	2	5 6
9 7 5	1	6
8 7 5 5 4 3 1 0 0 0 0 0 0 0 0 0 0 0 0 0 0 0	0	0 0 1 6 8

| 6 | 2 means 6.2 hours

(a) What conclusions can you draw directly from the stem and leaf plot?

(b) For each month, find these.
  (i)   The median
  (ii) The lower quartile
  (iii) The upper quartile

(c) Using a common scale, draw box plots for the daily hours of sunshine for January and July.

(d) What are your conclusions from the box plots?

5 Box plots for the alterations in marks for samples of scripts from each member of a team of examiners are as shown.

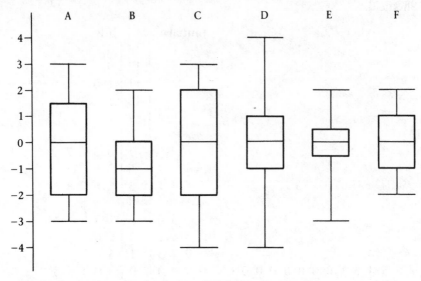

(a) Which examiner is the most reliable marker? Justify your answer.

(b) The examination board only requires a team of five for the following year's examinations. Which examiner would you drop from the team?
Give reasons for your answer.

(c) What would you advise the board to do with the other scripts marked by examiner B? (Other than re-marking all of them!)

F Histograms (answers p. 202)

The lengths of 20 screws were measured. The results are shown below in this frequency table and this diagram.

Length (mm)	Frequency
0–20	5
20–25	5
25–30	8
30–35	2

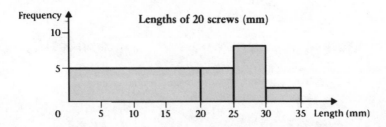

1D	Does the diagram provide a good representation of the data? Justify your answer.

Consider a further data set. The frequency distribution shown is for the length of each of 160 rods.

Length mm	5–7.5	7.5–10	10–12.5	12.5–15	15–17.5	17.5–20	20–22.5	22.5-25	25–27.5	27.5–30
Frequency	4	1	0	10	30	54	28	20	12	1

2D	Draw a frequency diagram for the data as presented.
	Re-group the data into the intervals: 5–15, 15–17.5, 17.5–20, 20–22.5, 22.5–30 and redraw the diagram.
	Comment on whether this sort of diagram provides a good representation of the data.

Representing the frequency by the height of the block creates a misleading impression of the distribution when the data are grouped into *unequal* group intervals. It is the actual size or *area* of the block which is needed to represent the frequency.

Frequency = area of block = width of interval × height of block

$$\text{Height of block} = \frac{\text{frequency}}{\text{width of interval}} = \textbf{frequency density}$$

Applying this idea to the distribution of screw lengths, the following frequency densities are obtained.

Length (mm)	Interval width	Frequency	Frequency density
0–20	20	5	$\frac{5}{20} = 0.25$
20–25	5	5	$\frac{5}{5} = 1.00$
25–30	5	8	$\frac{8}{5} = 1.60$
30–35	5	2	$\frac{2}{5} = 0.40$

This is the diagram that results.

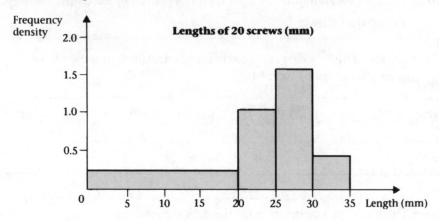

3D | Does this represent the distribution better than the previous diagram?
Explain why.

A diagram where the frequency is represented by area is called a **histogram**. Note that there are *no gaps* between the groups and the vertical axis represents frequency density, *not* frequency.

When handling quantitative data you need to be aware of the existence of two distinct types of data – **continuous** and **discrete**.

Continuous data can, theoretically, be any values within a continuous range. Discrete data can only take *certain* values within a range. Examples of measurements which would produce continuous data are height, weight, and time. Examples of discrete measurements are marks on a test (0, 1, 2, ...) or numbers in a family (1, 2, 3, ...).

It is *always* important to consider the nature of the data, especially when drawing histograms. In the last section you saw how to draw a histogram for continuous measurements. The next example shows how to handle discrete data and also illustrates how to deal with the common problem of a group for which the interval is not fully defined.

Example 2

In a traffic survey, the number of cars passing a point in a one-minute interval was recorded over 120 successive intervals. The results were as follows:

Number of cars (N)	0–9	10–14	15–19	20–29	30+
Frequency (f)	18	46	35	13	12

Draw a histogram for these data.

Solution

To avoid gaps in the histogram the intervals are re-defined in a convenient way. This is illustrated in the sketch below for the 10–14 range (possible values 10, 11, 12, 13 and 14 only).

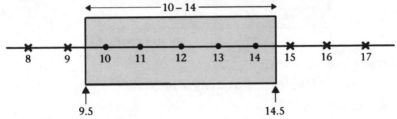

The first interval would therefore be re-defined as −0.5–9.5 to include all ten discrete data values from 0 to 9.

The frequency table becomes:

Class interval	−0.5–9.5	9.5–14.5	14.5–19.5	19.5–29.5	29.5–49.5
Frequency	18	46	35	13	12
Frequency density	$\frac{18}{10} = 1.80$	$\frac{46}{5} = 9.20$	$\frac{35}{5} = 7.00$	$\frac{13}{10} = 1.30$	$\frac{12}{20} = 0.60$

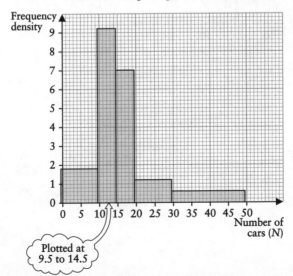

Number of cars passing in a one-minute interval

Plotted at 9.5 to 14.5

Notice that in the above solution the last group (30+) has been defined to be of width 20, twice the width of the 20–29 group.

4D | Is this a reasonable decision?

Exercise F (answers p. 202)

1

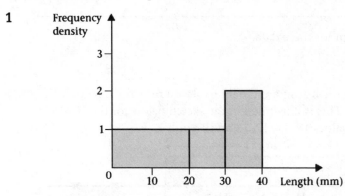

Study the histogram shown.

(a) How many of the lengths are in these intervals?

(i) 20–30 mm   (ii) 30–40 mm   (iii) 0–20 mm

(b) What is the total frequency?

2 For the histogram shown, find the total frequency.

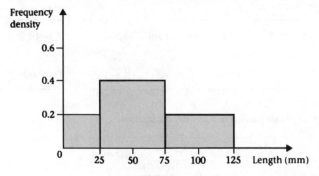

3 Construct histograms for the following data sets.

(a) Volume (cm^3)	f
0–5	5
5–10	5
10–20	10
20–30	20
30–40	10
40–60	5

(b) Number of cars per hour	f
50–59	10
60–79	30
80–99	20
100–139	10

4 Rainfall data are provided below for 50 weather stations in the north of England and 50 in the south. Each figure represents total rainfall (in mm) for June.

(a) Decide on a sensible grouping, which should be the same for the north and south. (Consider using unequal widths if this is sensible.)

(b) Construct frequency tables based on your choice of group size.

(c) Draw histograms for both data sets separately.

(d) Comment briefly on the two distributions.

Northern weather stations (mm of rain)

59	106	109	74	104	115	94	225	140	217
146	149	140	121	132	78	114	86	87	126
120	101	125	108	105	112	97	83	77	88
106	123	95	113	105	144	117	107	174	176
108	87	110	95	78	103	87	83	87	80

Southern weather stations (mm of rain)

89	89	111	93	73	121	103	80	108	88
75	79	103	107	70	82	97	59	90	53
67	46	43	65	112	115	99	217	83	61
98	90	95	87	86	77	96	70	111	74
81	70	72	87	68	85	100	67	54	109

After working through this chapter you should

1   be able to read from statistical graphs and charts

2   be able to obtain the mode, mean or median for a given data set

3   be able to construct a stem and leaf diagram from data and use such diagrams to compare sets of data

4   understand the terms symmetric, skewed, unimodal and bimodal as applied to distributions

5   be able to find the median, quartiles and percentiles of a distribution using a cumulative frequency graph and by linear interpolation

6   be able to draw and interpret box and whisker diagrams

7   be able to draw histograms for discrete and continuous data.

11 Variance and standard deviation

A Averages and spread (answers p. 203)

You have seen that the mean, median and mode are all measures of the 'average' value of a set of data. The mean is particularly important in statistical work and a special symbol is introduced for it.

Suppose the observed values are $x_1, x_2, x_3, ..., x_r, ..., x_n$.

$$\text{Mean} = \frac{\text{Sum of observed values}}{\text{Number of observations}}$$

'x bar' – for the mean of the values

$$\bar{x} = \frac{\text{Sum }(x_1, x_2, ..., x_n)}{n}$$

$$\bar{x} = \frac{1}{n} \sum x$$

Sigma x – for the sum of the observed values

Keys for $\boxed{\bar{x}}$ and $\boxed{\sum x}$ are on your calculator.

Check that you can use *your* calculator to obtain $\sum x$ and $\bar{x}$ for a set of values.

The following are the scores awarded to two gymnasts in a competition.

First gymnast	9.7	9.5	9.7	9.8	9.9	9.6
Second gymnast	8.8	9.2	8.8	9.8	9.4	9.8

The scores can be shown along a number line as follows.

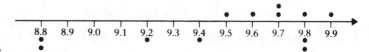

The scores of the second gymnast are much more spread out. It is useful to have a *number* to represent **spread**: for this you need to define a reference point and consider how spread out the observations are about the reference point.

The obvious points about which to measure spread would seem to be the median and the mean, as they represent 'average' values for the data.

You have already met one measure of spread – the interquartile range. It has the disadvantage of being insensitive to changes in the 'outer' 50% of the data. A possible measure of spread around the mean is

the sum of the differences from the mean, i.e. $\sum (x - \bar{x})$

With this, however, positive and negative differences cancel each other out and the result is *always* zero. This problem with negative differences can be solved in two ways, by considering either

the sum of the absolute value of the differences $\sum |x - \bar{x}|$

or the sum of the squares of the differences $\sum (x - \bar{x})^2$

Also, a measure of spread should not be dependent on the number of values in the sample, so an 'average' needs to be taken. The first approach, therefore, gives the mean of the deviations from the mean, or the mean absolute deviation. The second approach gives the *mean of the squared deviations from the mean*. This is the **variance**, and it is an important measure in statistics.

Example 1

Calculate the mean and variance of the ages of seven children at a holiday playgroup. These ages are 1, 2, 2, 3, 5, 6 and 9 years.

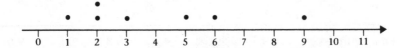

Solution

For these data,

$$\bar{x} = \tfrac{1}{7}(1 + 2 + 2 + 3 + 5 + 6 + 9) = 4$$

The sum of the squared deviations of the points from the mean is

$$(1 - 4)^2 + (2 - 4)^2 + (2 - 4)^2 + (3 - 4)^2 + (5 - 4)^2 + (6 - 4)^2$$
$$+ (9 - 4)^2 = 48$$

The mean squared deviation from the mean is $\tfrac{48}{7} = 6.86$.

So, for the data given, the mean age is 4 years and the variance is 6.86 years^2.

Statisticians use the variance *and* the *square root of the variance*, called the **standard deviation**, to measure spread.

> The mean of the sum of the squared deviations from the mean is called the variance. It is conventional to use the square root of the variance as a measure of spread around the mean. This is called the standard deviation.
>
> $$\text{Standard deviation} = \sqrt{\text{variance}}$$

1 Find the mean and standard deviation of the scores for each gymnast given on p. 131.

2 Obtain by direct calculation the standard deviation for each data set below and comment on how well the standard deviation seems to measure spread.

   (a) 5, 5, 5, 5, 5, 5, 5   (b) 1, 2, 3, 4, 5
   (c) 1, 2, 3, 4, 5, 6   (d) 2, 4, 6, 8, 10

3 Investigate, by considering a number of data sets, what happens to the mean and the standard deviation in these situations.

   (a) All the values in the data set are increased by the same value, for example 2, 5, 7 becomes 12, 15, 17.
   (b) All the values are multiplied by the same number, for example 2, 5, 7 becomes 6, 15, 21.

   Write down your conclusions.

You should have observed the following results for the mean and standard deviation.

> When all data values are multiplied by a constant a, then the new mean and the new standard deviation are a times the original mean and standard deviation.
>
> When a constant value, b, is added to all data values, then the mean is also increased by b. However, the standard deviation does not change.

If you think about data points on the number line, it should be clear that adding a constant to each simply moves each point along the line, the points do not become more spread out. So the mean increases by the constant while the standard deviation does not change.

When you multiply by a constant (for example, a), then the distance between each point increases by a factor of a; the points are more spread out and the spread is a times as great. The mean and standard deviation increase by a factor of a.

The phrase 'standard deviation' is often abbreviated to s.d. and the symbol used to denote standard deviation is, by convention, the letter s. The result above can then be expressed as

Original data values $x_1, x_2, ..., x_n$		mean $= \bar{x}$	s.d. $= s$
Data values if multiplied by a	$ax_1, ax_2, ..., ax_n$	mean $= a\bar{x}$	s.d. $= as$
Data values if b is added	$x_1 + b, x_2 + b, ..., x_n + b$	mean $= \bar{x} + b$	s.d. $= s$

Exercise A (answers p. 204)

1   A student measures the resistance of a piece of wire, repeating the experiment six times to check her results. Her results are:

Resistance (ohms)   54.2   53.7   55.0   53.7   54.0   54.6

(a) Find the mean and standard deviation of the readings.

(b) She discovers that each reading in the table is 10% too high, because of faulty equipment. Write down the new mean and standard deviation.

2   A teacher's class has 32 pupils, having a mean age of 14.0 years and a standard deviation of 0.25 years. Write down the mean and standard deviation of the ages of the same 32 pupils two years later.

3   The temperature is recorded at 12 weather stations in and around London on a given day. The mean recorded temperature is 12 °C, with a standard deviation of 0.5 °C.

The formula for F, the temperature in degrees Fahrenheit, in terms of C, the temperature in degrees Celsius, is

$$F = 1.8C + 32.$$

Write down the mean temperature and the standard deviation in degrees Fahrenheit.

4   A set of numbers has mean 28 and standard deviation 4. A second set of numbers is generated by subtracting x from each number in the first set and then dividing by 2. What are the mean and standard deviation of the second set of numbers?

5   The marks in a test have mean 68 and standard deviation 5.5. They are to be scaled linearly using the formula $y = 2x - 6$, where x is a given mark in the test and y is the corresponding scaled mark. What are the mean and standard deviation of the scaled marks?

6 A set of numbers has mean $\bar{x}$ and standard deviation s. A second set of numbers is generated by subtracting $\bar{x}$ from each number in the first set and then dividing by s. What are the mean and standard deviation of the second set of numbers?

7 The marks in a test have mean 33 and standard deviation 4.2. They are to be scaled linearly using the formula $y = ax + b$, where x is a given mark in the test and y is the corresponding scaled mark, so that the scaled marks have a mean of 50 and a standard deviation of 10.

(a) Find a and b.

(b) Peter gets 40 marks in the test. What is his scaled mark?

B Formulas for variance and standard deviation (answers p. 204)

Sometimes it is necessary to have a formula for the variance. This is important not simply in *calculating* a variance; it can also be useful in general mathematical work, for example to see how the variance relates to other measures. You can obtain a formula as follows.

Suppose a set of data values is $x_1, x_2, x_3, ..., x_n$, having a mean value of $\bar{x}$.

The squared deviations from the mean are:

$(x_1 - \bar{x})^2, (x_2 - \bar{x})^2, ..., (x_n - \bar{x})^2$.

The total of these squared deviations is $\sum (x - \bar{x})^2$.

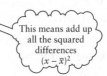

This means add up all the squared differences $(x - \bar{x})^2$

So the mean of the squared deviation is $\dfrac{\sum (x - \bar{x})^2}{n}$.

$$\text{Variance} = \frac{\sum (x - \bar{x})^2}{n}$$

$$\text{Standard deviation} = \sqrt{\left(\frac{\sum (x - \bar{x})^2}{n}\right)}$$

The algorithm on p. 136 is for direct calculation of the variance using this result.

1 Use this algorithm to calculate the variance of the following values.

(a) 2.1, 3.8, 3.9, 6.2

(b) 30, 29, 47

2 Comment on any difficulties in obtaining the variance using this algorithm.

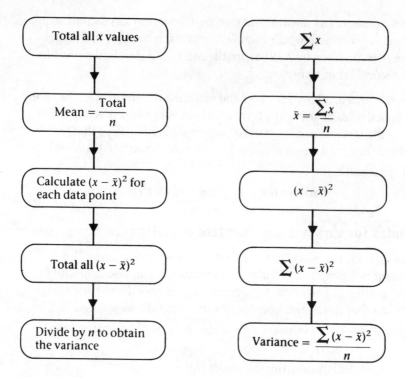

The algorithm above is not efficient and you might look for an alternative expression.

Having an algebraic form for the variance means that it is possible, by some manipulation, to find another way of expressing the result, as follows.

$$\text{Variance} = \frac{\sum (x - \bar{x})^2}{n} = \frac{1}{n} \sum (x - \bar{x})(x - \bar{x})$$

$$= \frac{1}{n} \sum (x^2 - 2x\bar{x} + (\bar{x})^2)$$

$$= \frac{\sum x^2}{n} - \frac{\sum 2x\bar{x}}{n} + \frac{\sum (\bar{x})^2}{n} \tag{1}$$

Since $\bar{x}$ is a constant, it may be taken out of the sum in the second term as a factor.

$$\frac{\sum 2x\bar{x}}{n} = 2\bar{x}\frac{\sum x}{n} = 2\bar{x}\bar{x} = 2(\bar{x})^2$$

Consider the term $\dfrac{\sum (\bar{x})^2}{n}$. This is simply $(\bar{x})^2$, a constant, added to itself n times and the result divided by n, so

$$\frac{\sum (\bar{x})^2}{n} = \frac{n(\bar{x})^2}{n} = (\bar{x})^2$$

With these simplifications, expression (1) for the variance becomes

$$\text{Variance} = \frac{\sum x^2}{n} - 2(\bar{x})^2 + (\bar{x})^2$$

$$= \frac{\sum x^2}{n} - (\bar{x})^2$$

This is a very useful form and saves a great deal of work when evaluating the variance by direct calculation.

$$\text{Variance} = \frac{\sum (x - \bar{x})^2}{n} = \frac{\sum x^2}{n} - \bar{x}^2$$

Example 2

The weights (in kilograms) of the eight forwards in a school rugby team are 65, 60, 70, 58, 61, 52, 72 and 70.

Calculate the mean weight and the standard deviation of the weights.

Solution

$\text{Mean} = \frac{1}{8}(65 + 60 + \cdots + 70) = \frac{508}{8} = 63.5 \text{ kg}$

$\text{Variance} = \frac{1}{8}(65^2 + 60^2 + 70^2 + 58^2 + 61^2 + 52^2 + 72^2 + 70^2) - 63.5^2$

$\qquad = \frac{32\,598}{8} - (63.5)^2$

$\qquad = 42.5$

$\text{Standard deviation} = \sqrt{42.5} = 6.52 \text{ kg}$

Exercise B (answers p. 204)

1 The ages of the children at a party were 2, 3, 3, 4, 5, 5, 5, 6, 7, 8, 8, 9, 9 and 10 years. Find the mean and standard deviation.

2 15 sacks of potatoes were taken from a lorry and weighed. The masses were 49, 52, 47, 53, 55, 48, 50, 50, 54, 52, 51, 52, 49, 50 and 53 kg, to the nearest kilogram.

Calculate the mean and standard deviation of these masses.

3 Five people in a lift have a mean weight $\bar{w} = 70$ kg. The standard deviation of their weights is 10 kg.
   (a) Find their total weight, $\sum w$, and find $\sum w^2$.
   (b) A man weighing 80 kg leaves the lift. Calculate the mean and standard deviation of the weight of those remaining.

4   30 pears in a tray have a mean mass of 105 g and a standard deviation of 6.1 g.
Calculate the total of the squared deviations from the mean of their masses.

If another tray contains 20 pears with mean mass 105 g and standard deviation 8.4 g, find the total of the squared deviations from the mean for all 50 pears in the two trays, and deduce their standard deviation.

C   Variance for frequency distributions (answers p. 204)

In a frequency distribution there may be many different occurrences of the same value. A simple example would be the data set:

14.3, 14.4, 14.5, 14.4, 14.4.

Observation	Frequency
14.3	1
14.4	3
14.5	1

1   Calculate the mean and variance of this data set.

If a data value x_1 occurs, say, f_1 times, then the term $(x_1 - \bar{x})^2$ will need to be added into the total squared deviation f_1 times.

i.e. total squared deviation for the f_1 data values $= (x_1 - \bar{x})^2 \times f_1$

2D   Show that for a frequency distribution
$$\bar{x} = \frac{\Sigma\, xf}{\Sigma f}, \text{ variance} = \frac{\Sigma\, (x - \bar{x})^2 f}{\Sigma f}.$$

It is clear that, with increasingly large data sets and frequency distributions, the calculations will become very tedious. Fortunately, as the variance (and standard deviation) are so important, calculators with statistical functions can obtain the required values easily, provided that the data is entered correctly.

3D   Find out how to use your calculator to obtain the mean, variance and standard deviation of a frequency distribution.

Grouped data

The table shows the number of shots played in each of fifty rallies between two tennis players before and after a coaching session. Only the grouped data for the length of each of the fifty rallies are recorded, not the original results.

Number of shots in rally	Number of rallies	
	Before coaching	After coaching
1–10	32	5
11–20	12	20
21–30	3	15
31–40	2	3
41–50	1	5
51–60	–	2
Total	50	50

Using the **mid-interval value** as representative of the length of rally in the group, the 'before coaching' table becomes

Before coaching

Group	Mid-point	Frequency
1–10	5.5	32
11–20	15.5	12
21–30	25.5	3
31–40	35.5	2
41–50	45.5	1

$\frac{41+50}{2}=45.5$

Taking each of the rallies in the 1–10 group as having 5.5 shots, the total number of shots played for these 32 rallies is *estimated* to be $32 \times 5.5 = 176$.

The data can now be entered into a calculator as

32 rallies of 5.5,
12 rallies of 15.5, and so on.

4D Find out how to use your calculator to obtain means, variances and standard deviations for grouped data.

Enter the 'before coaching' data in your calculator to find the mean and standard deviation of the rally length.

For direct calculations, the formula for the variance for grouped frequency distributions would be obtained as follows.

Let the group mid-value be x. Let the number of data values in a group be f.

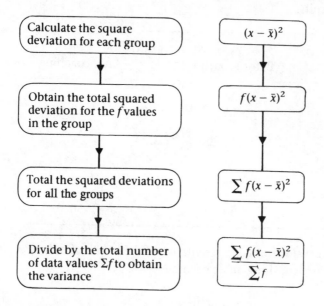

| Variance $= \dfrac{\sum f(x - \bar{x})^2}{\sum f}$ |

An alternative form (equivalent to that obtained on p. 137), which is more useful in calculations is

| Variance $= \dfrac{\sum fx^2}{\sum f} - \bar{x}^2$ |

Exercise C (answers p. 205)

You should use the statistical functions on your calculator for this exercise.

1 (a) For the tennis data on p. 139, calculate the mean and standard deviation of the length of rallies after coaching.

   (b) Has the coaching made a difference? Justify your answer.

2 The projected population distribution of England and Wales for the year 2025 is given below.

   (a) Calculate the total population.

   (b) Calculate the mean and standard deviation of the age of the population.

Age group (years)	Frequency (thousands)
0–14	9 928
15–29	9 953
30–44	10 075
45–59	9 808
60–74	8 989
75–89	4 289
90–99	469

> Be careful with age calculations!
>
> This group has people from 15 to *just* below 30
>
> The midpoint will be
>
> $\frac{15 + 30}{2} = 22.5$ yrs

3 The age distribution of the population of England and Wales in 1986 is given below.

Age group (years)	Mid-value x (years)	Frequency (thousands)
0–14	7.5	9 410
15–29	22.5	11 835
30–44	37.5	10 202
45–59	52.5	8 147
60–74	67.5	7 171
75–89	82.5	3 114
90+	95	184

> Take the group for 90+ to be 90–99 years old

   (a) Why is it reasonable to take the last group to be 90–99 years?

   (b) Calculate the mean and standard deviation of the population in 1986.

   (c) Using your answers to questions 2 and 3(b), comment on what is expected to happen to the age distribution in England and Wales as the years pass.

4 In a statistical investigation of the works of Charles Dickens, a student records the lengths of a number of randomly chosen sentences taken from one of his novels. The results are indicated below.

Sentence length (number of words)	Frequency
1–5	2
6–10	7
11–20	46
21–30	27
31–40	19
41–50	7
50 +	2
Total	110

Choose a suitable upper value for the last group and calculate estimates for the mean and standard deviation of the number of words per sentence of this work.

Give two reasons why the estimates might be inaccurate.

After working through this chapter you should

1 know that the variance is the mean of all the squared deviations from the mean

2 know that the standard deviation is another measure of spread and is equal to the square root of the variance

3 be familiar with these results

For raw data

$$\bar{x} = \frac{\Sigma x}{n}$$

$$\text{variance} = \frac{\Sigma (x - \bar{x})^2}{n}$$

or

$$\frac{\Sigma x^2}{n} - \bar{x}^2$$

For frequency distributions

$$\bar{x} = \frac{\Sigma fx}{\Sigma f}$$

$$\text{variance} = \frac{\Sigma f(x - \bar{x})^2}{\Sigma f}$$

or

$$\frac{\Sigma fx^2}{\Sigma f} - \bar{x}^2$$

4 know these facts

(a) if each value is multiplied by a constant a, then the standard deviation and the mean are also multiplied by a

(b) if each value is increased by adding on a constant b, then the standard deviation is unchanged, but the mean is increased by b.

12 Probability

A Introduction (answers p. 205)

Our modern ideas of probability emerged around 1660, when they were used to analyse games of chance including those on which bets had been placed.

In the nineteenth century, James Clerk Maxwell (in Cambridge) and Ludwig Boltzmann (in Austria) first introduced the ideas of randomness and chance events into the laws of physics with the kinetic theory of gases. They pictured a gas as a vast collection of individual molecules, rushing around chaotically in different directions and at different speeds, colliding with each other and with the walls of the container.

A simple experiment on gases which involves basic ideas of probability is to take a jar containing two gases which are distinguishable (for example by colour). The gases are initially separated by a barrier.

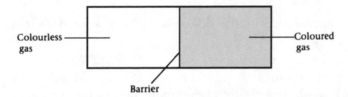

The barrier is removed and the gases mix freely. There will soon be molecules of each gas in each half of the jar. To understand why this happens consider a simplified situation in which there are only four molecules.

Each molecule moves around the jar in a random fashion; sometimes it will be in the left half of the jar and sometimes in the right. The possible distributions are shown in the following table.

No. of molecules on left	No. of molecules on right
4	0
3	1
2	2
1	3
0	4

To assess the probabilities of the five possible distributions it is helpful to 'label' the molecules. There is only one distribution with all molecules on the left:

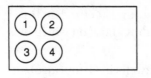

> You are not interested in the exact position of a molecule, only in whether it is on the left or the right

whereas there are four cases of a 1 : 3 split.

1   Illustrate the four cases of the 1 : 3 split.

2   How many cases are there for a 2 : 2 split?

3   With four molecules, how many different cases are there altogether?

4   Write down the probabilities for these cases.
   (a) A 1 : 3 split
   (b) All four molecules on one side of the box and none in the other
   (c) A 2 : 2 split

Though the 2 : 2 split is the most likely, you can see that each of the others is possible. In a real experiment with a very large number of molecules, although all conceivable states are possible, you can show by a similar argument that each side is likely to contain roughly equal numbers of each type of molecule.

Despite the continuous motion of each molecule, the overall state remains roughly constant. The system is said to be in **dynamic equilibrium**.

The use of ideas of chance in basic theories of physics continued in the twentieth century with the development of quantum mechanics.

Ideas of probability and statistics are now firmly embedded in all kinds of scientific study. In turn, some of the greatest scientists, by applying these ideas, have furthered our understanding of probability and statistics.

B   Compound events (answers p. 205)

In using probability ideas it is often necessary to consider outcomes of events which are combinations of simpler events.

For example, for a darts player to score 180 with three darts requires the combination of the events of scoring 60 with each dart.

1D Suppose that a darts player who is aiming for treble 20 succeeds with one dart in five on average.

What is the probability of her scoring 180 with three darts?

Comment on any assumptions you have made.

If two events are such that *the occurrence of one does not affect the probability of the other occurring*, they are called **independent events**.

The probability of two independent events *both* occurring can be found by multiplying their individual probabilities.

Example 1

Three coins are tossed. What is the probability of obtaining three tails?

Solution

The tosses are independent events and so

$$P(T\,T\,T) = P(T) \times P(T) \times P(T)$$
$$= 0.5 \times 0.5 \times 0.5$$
$$= 0.125$$

Example 2

Suppose that 20% of cars fail the MOT test on steering and 30% on brakes. What is the probability of a randomly chosen car passing on both counts?

Solution

Assuming the events 'failing on steering' and 'failing on brakes' are independent, then

$$P(\text{passing on brakes } and \text{ on steering}) = 0.8 \times 0.7$$
$$= 0.56$$

In practice, you might expect the events not to be independent. It is likely that of those cars that fail the brake test, a higher proportion than average also fail the steering test. If this is true, the answer calculated on the assumption of independence will be an underestimate.

In the examples above you looked at the compound event '*A and B*'. If *A* and *B* are independent events then $P(A \text{ } and \text{ } B) = P(A) \times P(B)$. In many situations you might be interested in the event that '*A or B*' happens. This arises in the example on p. 146.

Two people are playing 'snap' with two special packs of cards. One has a yellow pack (16 ones, 12 twos, 8 threes and 4 fours) and one has a red pack (10 each of ones, twos, threes and fours). The packs are well shuffled and each plays the top card simultaneously.

2 There are 40 cards in each pack. What is the total number of pairs of cards which could be played?

3 (a) How many of these are 'double ones', that is a one from the yellow pack and a one from the red pack?

(b) How many are the following pairs?

    (i) double twos   (ii) double threes   (iii) double fours

(c) How many are doubles (i.e. double anything)?

For equally likely outcomes, the probability of an event is

$$\frac{\text{the number of outcomes which correspond to the event}}{\text{the total number of possible outcomes}}$$

So the probability of a double one is

$$\frac{\text{the number of possible 'double ones'}}{\text{the total number of pairs}}$$

4 Use this principle and your answers from question 3 to work out the probability of these pairs.

(a) a double one   (b) a double two   (c) a double

The probability distributions for the two packs are as follows.

Yellow pack				
Number	1	2	3	4
Probability	0.4	0.3	0.2	0.1

Red pack				
Number	1	2	3	4
Probability	0.25	0.25	0.25	0.25

5 Work out the probabilities in question 4 directly from the probability distributions.

6 A blue pack has 10 ones, 20 twos, 10 threes and no fours. Working directly from the probability distributions, calculate the probability of a 'snap' if a yellow pack is played against a blue pack.

The following example is solved by counting cases and demonstrates a general rule for adding probabilities in such cases.

Example 3

A card is selected from an ordinary pack. What is the probability that the card is either an ace or a diamond?

Solution

There are 52 possible cards that could be chosen; 4 of these are aces, 13 are diamonds.

There are only 16 cards which are either aces or diamonds because the ace of diamonds is counted in both the 4 aces and the 13 diamonds.

$$P(\text{ace } or \text{ diamond}) = \frac{4 + 13 - 1}{52} = \frac{4}{13}$$

This solution can be written as

$$P(\text{ace } or \text{ diamond}) = \frac{4}{52} + \frac{13}{52} - \frac{1}{52}$$
$$= P(\text{ace}) + P(\text{diamond}) - P(\text{both ace } and \text{ diamond}).$$

This is a particular example of the **addition law**.

> For any two events A and B, the probability of either A or B or both occurring is
>
> $$P(A \text{ or } B) = P(A) + P(B) - P(A \text{ and } B).$$
>
> Sometimes the notation $A \cup B$ is used for 'A or B or both' and $\cap$ is used for 'and'.
>
> So the addition law is written
>
> $$P(A \cup B) = P(A) + P(B) - P(A \cap B).$$

As a further illustration, consider the MOT test of Example 2. A car fails the test if it fails on *either* brakes *or* steering *or* both.

$$P(\text{fails on brakes or steering}) = 0.3 + 0.2 - 0.3 \times 0.2$$
$$= 0.44$$

The addition law is especially simple when events A and B are **mutually exclusive**, i.e. both cannot occur, because then $P(A \text{ and } B) = 0$.

7 Consider whether the following pairs of events are mutually exclusive and whether they are independent.

(a) I am dealt the ace of spades; you are dealt the ace of spades.

(b) I cut an ace; you cut a king.

(c) Dan's Delight wins next Saturday's 2:30 race at Newbury; Andy's Nag wins next Saturday's 2:30 race at Newbury.

(d) Dan's Delight wins next Saturday's 2:30 race at Newbury; Andy's Nag wins next Saturday's 3:15 race at Newbury.

(e) Mrs Smith has toothache today; Mr Smith has toothache today.

(f) Mrs Smith has a cold today; Mr Smith has a cold today.

You can use the addition law to find out the probability of an event *not* occurring from the probability of its occurring. In the example of the MOT test considered earlier, the probability of a pass on steering and brakes was found to be 0.56, and the probability of a fail was shown to be 0.44. The events 'pass MOT test' and 'fail MOT test' are mutually exclusive: since one of the events *must* occur, the sum of their probabilities must be 1. So

$$P(\text{fail test}) = 1 - P(\text{pass test})$$
$$= 1 - 0.56$$
$$= 0.44$$

In general,

$P(A') = 1 - P(A)$

where $P(A')$ is the probability that A does *not* occur.

This often provides a useful short cut; if you cannot work out the probability of an event simply, see if you can work out the probability of it *not* happening, then subtract this from 1.

Example 4

Three coins are tossed. What is the probability of at least one head?

Solution

There are lots of ways of getting at least one head. But the only way of getting the opposite event, namely no head at all, is to toss three tails.

$$P(T\ T\ T) = 0.5 \times 0.5 \times 0.5 = 0.125$$
$$P(\text{at least 1 head}) = 1 - P(\text{no head})$$
$$= 1 - P(T\ T\ T) = 0.875$$

Example 5

I travel by bus and train on my journey to work. The probability that the bus is late is 0.1 and (independently) the probability that the train is late is 0.05.

Calculate these probabilities.

(a) The bus and train are late.

(b) Either the bus or the train is late.

Solution

(a) P(bus and train late) = P(bus late) × P(train late)
$$= 0.1 \times 0.05 = 0.005$$

(b) P(bus or train late) = 1 − P(bus and train on time)
$$= 1 - 0.9 \times 0.95 = 0.145$$

Exercise B (answers p. 206)

1 In a board game two dice are rolled. Work out the probabilities of these being rolled.

   (a) A double six   (b) At least one six   (c) Only one six

2 A card is selected from a pack of ordinary playing cards. What are the probabilities of these being selected?

   (a) A red ace   (b) A six or a seven   (c) Either an ace or a queen

3 A card is selected from an ordinary pack of 52 cards. What are the probabilities of these being selected?

   (a) A heart or a six   (b) A heart or a spade

4 In a small factory, there are two machines for doing the same job. One is under repair for 10% of the time and the other for 5%. What is the probability of both being out of action at the same time? (Assume independence.)

5 A car manufacturer sends 50 cars of a new model on a test run. The following petrol consumptions are recorded.

Litres km^{-1}	0.120–0.124	0.124–0.128	0.128–0.132	0.132–0.136	0.136–0.140
No. of cars	5	11	16	12	6

   A consumer organisation buys two cars of this type and tests them under similar conditions. Estimate the probability that both use more than 0.136 litres km^{-1}. (State any assumptions you make.)

6 Each packet of a breakfast cereal contains a plastic soldier. Equal numbers of 12 different models are used. What is the probability of buying two packets in a supermarket and finding Hannibal, one of the 12, in both? (State any assumptions you make.)

7 Under normal working, 8% of the articles being mass-produced in a factory are substandard. If a sample of 2 is checked every half hour, what proportions of the samples would you expect to consist of these

   (a) 2 good articles   (b) 2 substandard articles

   (State any assumptions you make.)

C Tree diagrams (answers p. 206)

When analysing the probabilities of a combination of events, a **tree diagram** often helps.

Example 6

A student's assessment consists of three tests, of which he must pass at least two to continue with the course. He estimates that the probabilities of passing the tests are 0.7, 0.8 and 0.9 respectively. Calculate the probability that he will be able to stay on the course.

Solution

You can represent the situation with a tree diagram (see below).

Assume independence at each test (i.e. the probability of passing the test is not influenced by what happens at the previous test). To find the probability of a particular sequence of events, you *multiply* the probabilities on the branches.

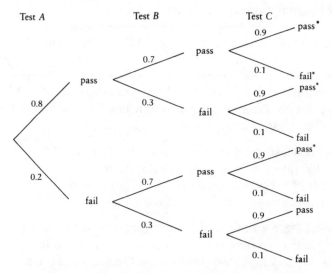

For example, P(passes A, fails B, passes C) = $0.8 \times 0.3 \times 0.9$

$$= 0.216.$$

To obtain the probability of continuing with the course, you should *add* the probabilities on the routes representing 'one or no failed tests'. These are marked with a star on the tree diagram. The answer required is therefore

$$0.8 \times 0.7 \times 0.9 + 0.8 \times 0.7 \times 0.1 + 0.8 \times 0.3 \times 0.9 + 0.2 \times 0.7 \times 0.9$$

$$= 0.902$$

The probabilities can be added here because the combined events are mutually exclusive and cannot occur together.

1 Trish selects a card at random from a pack of playing cards, and
   replaces it. She repeats this three times.

   (a) Draw a tree diagram and calculate the probability of her getting
       these.

   (i) Three hearts   (ii) Three cards of the same suit

   (b) Suppose she selects the three cards without replacement. Draw a
       new tree diagram and re-calculate the probabilities for (a).

Exercise C (answers p. 206)

1 Assuming that the probability of a female birth is approximately 0.49,
   construct a tree diagram to show the possible outcomes of the sexes of
   children in a family with three children. Hence find the probability of
   these.

   (a) Exactly one girl

   (b) At least one girl

   (c) At least one child of each sex

2 A company has four external telephone lines. Assuming the
   probability is $\frac{2}{3}$ that any one is in use at any instant, calculate the
   probabilities of these happening.

   (a) At least one line is free

   (b) At least two lines are free

   Have you assumed independence? If so, is this justified?

3 A bag contains 5 white and 7 black beads; another contains 3 white
   and 9 black beads. One bead is taken from the first bag and placed in
   the second. After thorough mixing, one bead is then taken from the
   second bag and placed in the first bag. What is the probability that
   there are 5 white beads in the first bag at the end?

D Conditional probability (answers p. 206)

The most common kind of colour blindness involves difficulty in
distinguishing between colours in the red/yellow/green range. The
probability of a member of the population, chosen at random,
suffering from this defect is 0.03. However, given that the person
chosen is male, the probability of his being colour blind is 0.05.

Can the incidence of colour blindness among females be calculated
from these figures? One approach is to imagine a population of 1000
'typical' people, 500 of them male and 500 female.

1 (a) How many of the 1000 people would you expect to be colour blind?

   (b) How many males would you expect to be colour blind?

   (c) From these results, how many females would you expect to be colour blind?

   (d) Given that a person chosen at random is female, what is the probability that she is colour blind?

The value you have found in question (d) is called the conditional probability of colour blindness given that the subject is female. We can use the symbolism $P(C|F)$ to represent this.

2 State what each of these probabilities represents and give its value.

   (a) $P(C|M)$ (b) $P(C'|F)$ (c) $P(C'|M)$

Conditional probabilities can be worked out more formally using a tree diagram. This one has been completed for the colour blindness figures.

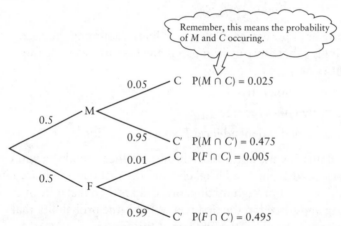

Remember, this means the probability of M and C occuring.

The probabilities on the right hand set of branches are conditional probabilities. For example the 0.05 on the top right branch is $P(C|M)$. (Check that you understand what the probabilities on the other three right-hand branches represent and that their values agree with those you just obtained.)

The tree diagram should help you understand the difference between these two statements.

$P(C|M) = 0.05$ (given that the person chosen is male, the probability of him being colour blind is 0.05)

$P(C \cap M) = 0.025$ (the probability of selecting someone who is male and colour blind is 0.025).

Multiplying in the usual way along the top branches we get

$P(M) \times P(C|M) = P(M \cap C)$

$(0.5 \ \times \ 0.05 \ \ = 0.025)$

3 Write corresponding equations for the other three routes through the tree.

> In general,
> $$P(A)P(B|A) = P(A \cap B)$$
> (We omit the multiplication sign as this is a type of algebra.)
>
> Dividing both sides by $P(A)$ we obtain a useful formula for conditional probability.
> $$P(B|A) = \frac{P(A \cap B)}{P(A)}$$

Most problems in conditional probability can be solved by listing equally likely possibilities, by using the above formula or by deducing values from a tree diagram.

Example 7

A fair spinner has the numbers 1 to 20 on it. What is the conditional probability that, given that it stops on an odd number, it stops on a multiple of 3?

Solution

1 2 **3** 4 5 **6** 7 8 **9** 10 **11** <u>12</u> 13 14 **<u>15</u>** 16 17 <u>18</u> **19** 20

There are 10 odd numbers (bold). Of these, 3 are multiples of 3 (underlined). So the the required probability is $\frac{3}{10}$.

Example 8

Given that a card picked at random from a pack of 52 playing cards is a club, find the probability that it is a picture card.

Solution

From the formula,
$$P(\text{picture card}|\text{club}) = \frac{P(\text{club} \cap \text{picture card})}{P(\text{club})}$$

$$P(\text{picture card}|\text{club}) = \frac{\frac{3}{52}}{\frac{13}{52}}$$

$$= \frac{3}{13}$$

Example 9

The events A and B are such that $P(A) = \frac{1}{2}$, $P(A'|B) = \frac{1}{3}$ and $P(A \cup B) = \frac{3}{5}$. Find $P(B)$.

Solution

$P(A \cup B)$ means the probability of A occurring or B occurring or both.

Hence $P(A \cup B) = p + q + r$, where p, q and r are the probabilities marked on the tips of the tree diagram.

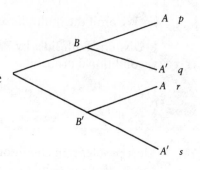

From the information given,

$$p + q + r = \tfrac{3}{5},$$
$$p + r = \tfrac{1}{2},$$
$$q = \tfrac{3}{5} - \tfrac{1}{2} = \tfrac{1}{10}.$$

So $P(B) \times \frac{1}{3} = \frac{1}{10}$ and hence $P(B) = \frac{3}{10}$.

Conditional probability provides an alternative definition of independence of events. A and B are independent if the probability of B occurring does not depend on whether A occurs.

> When events A and B are independent,
> $P(B\,|\,A) = P(B\,|\,A') = P(B)$.

Example 10

The events A and B are independent, $P(A \cup B) = \frac{5}{8}$ and $P(A \cap B') = \frac{7}{24}$.

Calculate   (a) $P(B)$ (b) $P(A)$ (c) $P(A \cap B)$

Solution

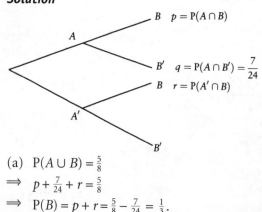

(a) $P(A \cup B) = \frac{5}{8}$

$\Rightarrow p + \frac{7}{24} + r = \frac{5}{8}$

$\Rightarrow P(B) = p + r = \frac{5}{8} - \frac{7}{24} = \frac{1}{3}.$

Because of the independence of A and B, $P(B|A) = P(B|A')$
$= P(B)$. The branches of the tree may be labelled as shown.

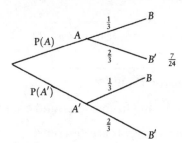

(b) $P(A) \times \frac{2}{3} = \frac{7}{24}$
$\Rightarrow P(A) = \frac{7}{16}$

(c) $P(A \cap B) = P(A)P(B) = \frac{7}{16} \times \frac{1}{3} = \frac{7}{48}$

Exercise D (answers p. 206)

1   Cards are picked one at a time at random from an ordinary pack of
52 cards and then replaced.

(a) Given that a diamond is picked, state the probability that it is an
ace.

(b) Given that an ace is picked, state the probability that it is a
diamond.

(c) Given that a picture card is picked (jack, queen or king), state the
probability that it is a black card (clubs or spades).

(d) Given that a black card is picked, state the probability that it is a
picture card.

2   An ordinary dice is thrown. What is the probability of throwing a
multiple of 2, given that the number thrown is not prime?

3   A bag contains 10 balls, 7 of them red and 3 green. A ball is picked at
random and not replaced. A second ball is then picked.

(a) Find the probability that the second ball is red, given that the first
ball is red.

(b) Find the probability that the second ball is green, given that the
first ball is green.

4   A and B are two events such that $P(A) = 0.6$, $P(B|A) = 0.5$,
$P(A|B) = 0.75$. Find

(a) $P(A \cap B)$ (b) $P(B)$ (c) $P(A \cup B)$

5   X and Y are two independent events such that $P(X \cap Y) = 0.1$ and
$P(Y|X) = 0.25$. Find

(a) $P(Y)$ (b) $P(X)$ (c) $P(X' \cap Y')$

6 Two events A and B are such that

$$P(A) = \tfrac{1}{2}, \qquad P(B) = \tfrac{1}{3}, \qquad P(A|B) = \tfrac{1}{4}.$$

Evaluate these.

(a) $P(A \cap B)$ (b) $P(A \cup B)$ (c) $P(A' \cap B')$

After working through this chapter you should

1 be able to calculate probabilities arising from compound events

2 understand what is meant when two events are described as independent and know that when two events are independent,

$$P(B|A) = P(B|A') = P(B)$$

3 be able to use tree diagrams

4 understand and be able to use the following formulas.

$$P(A \cup B) = P(A) + P(B) - P(A \cap B)$$
$$P(A') = 1 - P(A)$$

5 understand how to use conditional probabilities including the formula

$$P(A)P(B|A) = P(A \cap B).$$

13 Probability distributions

A Random variables (answers p. 207)

The outcome of statistical enquiries or experiments often produces numerical data. For example, when a die is thrown, the outcome is a number from 1 to 6; a traffic survey produces a number of vehicles per minute; weather data produce the number of millimetres of rainfall per day; a survey of family size might be used to investigate the number of children per family, or annual income. In all these cases, the outcome is a variable which has a set of possible values.

The value which the variable takes for any particular throw of a die, or vehicle count, or day's rainfall, and so on, is essentially random: you cannot predict with certainty what its value will be. These variables are therefore called **random variables**.

Random variable	Set of possible values
Score on a die	1, 2, 3, 4, 5, 6
Number of vehicles per minute	0, 1, 2, ...
Rainfall in millimetres	Any positive real number
etc. ...	...

It is useful to denote a random variable by a capital letter, for example X, and the particular values it can take by lower case letters, for example $x_1, x_2, x_3, \ldots, x_n$. So if a random variable, S, is the score on a die, the particular values it can take are $s = 1, 2, 3, 4, 5, 6$.

Example 1

Two dice are thrown and the number of sixes counted. Calculate and list the probabilities of obtaining 0, 1 and 2 sixes.

Solution

Assume the dice are fair $\Longrightarrow$ P(six thrown on one dice) $= \frac{1}{6}$.
Let X be the number of sixes ($x = 0$, 1 or 2) when two dice are thrown.
$$P(x = 0) = \left(\tfrac{5}{6}\right)^2 = \tfrac{25}{36}$$
Two possible outcomes occur for one six: (six, no six) or (no six, six):
$$P(x = 1) = \tfrac{1}{6} \times \tfrac{5}{6} + \tfrac{5}{6} \times \tfrac{1}{6} = \tfrac{10}{36}$$
Only one outcome leads to $x = 2$ (two sixes):
$$P(x = 2) = P(\text{six, six}) = \left(\tfrac{1}{6}\right)^2 = \tfrac{1}{36}$$

x	0	1	2
$P(X = x)$	$\frac{25}{36}$	$\frac{10}{36}$	$\frac{1}{36}$

The list or table above is called the **probability distribution** for the random variable X. In general, the probability distribution for a random variable is a statement (or table) which assigns probabilities to the possible values of the variable.

Sometimes probabilities are assigned by arguing that the possible outcomes are equally likely. But in other cases, you may need to estimate the probabilities from relative frequencies, or from past experience.

Note that, since the probability distribution gives the probability of every possible outcome, the sum of the probabilities must be 1 (one of the events *must* happen).

> For any probability distribution, the sum of the probabilities must equal 1.

Example 2

A family with two children is chosen at random. The random variable X stands for the number of boys. Assume each child is equally likely to be a boy or girl.

(a) Write down the probability distribution for the random variable.

(b) Draw a graph of the probability distribution.

Solution

(a) Considering the sex of the children (younger followed by elder) gives a set of four equally likely outcomes
{(B, B) (B, G) (G, B) (G, G)}
Only one of the four possible outcomes gives two boys, so
$$P(x = 2) = \tfrac{1}{4}$$
Two possible outcomes result in just one boy in the family, so
$$P(x = 1) = \tfrac{2}{4}$$
By a similar argument
$$P(x = 0) = \tfrac{1}{4}$$

x	0	1	2
$P(X = x)$	0.25	0.5	0.25

Notice that the three possible values for X are *not* equally likely and that the sum of the probabilities equals 1. The most likely number of boys is 1.

(b) As X can only take discrete values, the most appropriate form of graph is a **stick graph**.

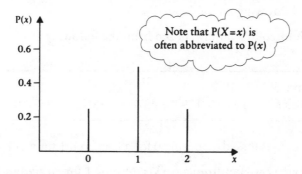

There are two fundamentally different types of distribution of quantitative data: continuous and discrete. Similarly, there are the same two types of probability model.

The time taken for a telephone call is a **continuous** random variable. The duration of a call can theoretically take any real number value (within reasonable limits for telephone calls). On the other hand, many variables are discrete. They cannot be said to vary continuously. For example, the number of children in a family must be a whole number.

1 Say whether each of the following random variables is continuous or discrete.

(a) The number of children in a family
(b) The number of cracked eggs in a box of 6
(c) The weight of cows in a herd
(d) The height of fully-grown sunflower plants
(e) The number of kittens in a litter
(f) A motorist's reaction time

The rest of the work in this chapter will be restricted to discrete random variables.

Exercise A (answers p. 207)

For each of the following random variables, either calculate its probability distribution or estimate it using relative frequencies calculated from the data given. Check also that the sum of the probabilities in each distribution is 1.

1 $S =$ score obtained throwing an unbiased die.

2 $X =$ number of children in a family chosen from the following population.

Number of children x	0	1	2	3	4 or over
Number of families f	123	179	457	88	45

3 $S =$ score when a coin is tossed, counting 0 for a head and 1 for a tail.

4 $Y =$ value of a playing card cut from a pack, counting 1 for an ace, and 10 for a ten, jack, queen or king.

5 $X =$ positive difference of the scores showing on two dice (so that $(6, 2)$ would score 4, as would $(2, 6)$).

6 $H =$ the number of heads when three coins are thrown.

B The mean and variance of a random variable (answers p. 207)

In Chapter 10 you used the *mean* as a representative value for a set of data. For a sample of values of a variable X you calculated this using the formula

$$\bar{x} = \frac{\Sigma\, fx}{n}$$

Σ stands for 'the sum of'

where f is the frequency of the value x, and n is the total number of values. As the frequency f divided by the total number of values n is the relative frequency, you can rewrite this formula using relative frequencies.

$$\bar{x} = \Sigma \left(\frac{f}{n}\right) x$$

So to calculate the mean, you multiply the values of x by their relative frequencies, and sum over all values of x.

Example 3

Using relative frequencies, calculate the mean of the following data set:
1, 1, 2, 3, 3, 3, 3, 3, 4, 4.

Solution

x	1	2	3	4	
f	2	1	5	2	$n = 10$
$\dfrac{f}{n}$	0.2	0.1	0.5	0.2	

$$\text{Mean} = \sum \left(\frac{f}{n}\right)x$$
$$= 0.2 \times 1 + 0.1 \times 2 + 0.5 \times 3 + 0.2 \times 4$$
$$= 2.7$$

Suppose you are to be 'banker' in the following game. You ask the player to select a card at random from a special yellow pack. You pay out £y, where y is the number on the card selected. The full pack is reshuffled after each game. The mean winnings per game is given by the formula

$$\bar{y} = \sum \left(\frac{f}{n}\right)y$$

There are 40 yellow cards in the pack and the constitution of the pack is as follows.

Score on card (y)	1	2	3	4
Number of cards (f)	16	12	8	4

1 You play the game 400 times. How much would you expect to pay out? What would be a reasonable amount to charge for each game?

2 Out of 1000 games, you would expect, 'on average', 400 £1 payouts, 300 £2 payouts, 200 £3 payouts and 100 £4 payouts.

y	1	2	3	4	
f	400	300	200	100	$n = 1000$
$\dfrac{f}{n}$	0.4	0.3	0.2	0.1	

Achieving this precise result is, of course, unlikely, but it is the distribution you might 'expect' from the probability distribution. Work out the mean of these winnings.

The 'expected relative frequencies' are simply the probabilities. So this mean value is the sum of the values of Y multiplied by their probabilities.

$$\text{Mean} = \sum yP(y)$$

The mean represents the average winnings from a game. It is called the **mean of the random variable Y**, and is often denoted by the Greek letter μ ('mu').

To break even in the long run, you should charge this amount per game.

3 A pack of blue cards is made up as follows.

Score on card	1	2	3	4
Number of cards	10	20	10	0

(a) Write down the probability distribution for B, the score on a card selected from this pack.

(b) Calculate the mean μ of the random variable B.

For any discrete random variable X, the mean is defined as

$$\mu = \sum xP(x)$$

This means that to find the mean of a discrete random variable, you multiply the values of X by their probabilities, and add. Compare the formulas for sample distributions and probability distributions.

Real world	Mathematical model
Sample distributions	Probability distributions
$\bar{x} = \sum \left(\dfrac{f}{n}\right)x$	$\mu = \sum xP(x)$

For probability distributions, the relative frequencies are replaced by the probabilities. For large samples, relative frequency and probability are likely to be close, and get closer as the sample size gets larger.

The ideas used to calculate the mean of a random variable from its probability distribution can also be applied to the variance.

The variance of a frequency distribution can be redefined in terms of relative frequency.

$$\text{Variance} = \frac{\sum fx^2}{n} - \bar{x}^2$$

$$= \sum \left(\frac{f}{n}\right)x^2 - \bar{x}^2$$

Replacing relative frequency with probability gives a formula for the variance of the random variable. The symbol σ^2 ('sigma squared') is used to denote this variance to distinguish it from the sample variance which is given the symbol s^2. So the *standard deviation* of the population is σ and of a sample is s.

Real world	Mathematical model
Sample distributions	Probability distributions
$s^2 = \sum\left(\dfrac{f}{n}\right)x^2 - \bar{x}^2$	$\sigma^2 = \sum x^2 P(x) - \mu^2$

Example 4

For the number of boys in a family of two children, calculate these.

(a) The mean   (b) The standard deviation

Solution

(a) The mean

n	0	1	2
P(n)	0.25	0.5	0.25

$$\mu = \sum nP(n)$$
$$= 0 \times 0.25 + 1 \times 0.5 + 2 \times 0.25$$
$$= 1$$

Using this probability model, you can predict that for a large sample of families with two children, the mean number of boys per family will be approximately 1.

(b) The standard deviation

$$\sigma^2 = \sum n^2 P(n) - \mu^2$$
$$= (0^2 \times 0.25 + 1^2 \times 0.5 + 2^2 \times 0.25) - 1^2$$
$$= 1.5 - 1 = 0.5$$
$$\sigma = 0.707$$

According to this probability model, you can predict that for a large sample of families with two children, the standard deviation of the number of boys will be approximately 0.707.

Example 5

At a fund-raising charity event a game consists of rolling three regular six-sided dice. Each die has two yellow, two blue and two red faces. If all three faces show the same colour then you pay out a prize of £1. If two faces are the same colour, you pay 10p. How much should you charge per turn so that you can expect to make a profit for the charity?

Solution

If a single die is rolled, $P(\text{red}) = P(\text{blue}) = P(\text{yellow}) = \frac{1}{3}$
If three dice are rolled,
$P(\text{all the same colour}) = P(\text{all red}) + P(\text{all blue}) + P(\text{all yellow})$
$= (\frac{1}{3})^3 + (\frac{1}{3})^3 + (\frac{1}{3})^3 = \frac{1}{9}$
$P(\text{two the same colour}) = P(\text{two reds}) + P(\text{two blues}) + P(\text{two yellows})$
Two reds can be obtained as follows:

$$\text{RR(Y or B)} \quad \text{or} \quad \text{R(Y or B)R} \quad \text{or} \quad \text{(Y or B)RR}$$

So, $P(\text{two reds}) = 3 \times \frac{1}{3} \times \frac{1}{3} \times \frac{2}{3} = \frac{2}{9}$
Similarly, $P(\text{two yellows}) = P(\text{two blues}) = \frac{2}{9}$
So $P(\text{two the same colour}) = \frac{6}{9}$
Let $X =$ amount paid out per game (in pence). X takes values in the set $\{0, 10, 100\}$.

x	0	10	100
$P(x)$	$\frac{2}{9}$	$\frac{6}{9}$	$\frac{1}{9}$

Mean of $X = 0 \times \frac{2}{9} + 10 \times \frac{6}{9} + 100 \times \frac{1}{9}$
$= \frac{160}{9} = 17\frac{7}{9}$ pence

Since on average you would pay out $17\frac{7}{9}$ pence per game, if you charge anything greater than this you can expect to make a profit. If you charged 20p a game you would make an average profit of $2\frac{2}{9}$ per game.

Working through calculations for mean and variance a few times should give you a 'feel' for the meaning of these important statistical formulas. However, to save time spent on laborious 'number-crunching', you may already have been tempted to see if the statistical function keys of your calculator will work out means and variances for random variables, just as they did for data. The answer is that they can! All that is required is for probabilities to be entered instead of frequencies.

Exercise B (answers p. 207)

For questions 1, 2, 3 in this exercise you should calculate the mean and variance *without* using the statistical functions on your calculator.

1 The random variable *D* has the value obtained from a single roll of an unbiased die. Write down the probability distribution for *D*, and calculate the mean and the variance.

2 There are five coins in a bag, one 50p coin, two 20p coins and two 10p coins. One coin is withdrawn at random. Calculate the mean value of the amount withdrawn and the variance.

3 Calculate the mean and variance of the score for each of the spinners shown below.

(a) 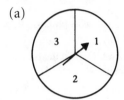 (b) 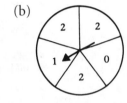 (c)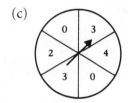

4 A card is withdrawn at random from a pack of playing cards. Counting 1 for an ace and 10 for a jack, queen or king, calculate the mean and variance of the value of the card withdrawn.

5 A certain slot machine returns cash prizes according to the following probability distribution.

Prize (pence)	0	10	20	50
Probability	0.1	0.4	0.4	0.1

   (a) Work out the expected prize from the machine.
   (b) Suggest a value of coin to operate the machine so that the machine owner makes a profit, while allowing the player to believe there may be a chance of beating the machine.

After working through this chapter you should

1 understand the terms **random variable** and **probability distribution**

2 appreciate the difference between **discrete** and **continuous** random variables

3 be able to calculate the **mean** and **variance** of a discrete random variable and understand their significance.

Answers

1 Linear and other graphs

A Introduction (p. 1)

1 (a)

Profit (£) per radio	0	1	2	3	4	5	6
Number of radios sold	60	50	40	30	20	10	0
Total profit (£) from sales	0	50	80	90	80	50	0

(b)

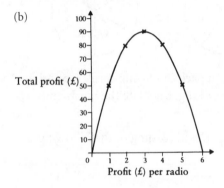

(c) She should choose a profit per radio of £3, giving a total profit of £90.

2 (a) Number of radios sold = $60 - 10x$ or $10(6 - x)$

(b) The table was completed by multiplying 'profit per radio' × 'number of radios sold'.

The answer given in part (a) leads to

$x \times (60 - 10x) = x(60 - 10x)$

$= 60x - 10x^2$

or any equivalent expression.

(c) The graph on p. 1 shows the number of radios sold at a given profit per radio. If y stands for the number of radios sold, then (a) gives

$y = 60 - 10x$

This is the equation of the first graph.

The graph that you have drawn for 1(b) shows the total profit for a given profit per radio. If t stands for the total profit, then (b) gives

$t = x(60 - 10x)$

This is the equation of the second graph.

3 For each graph, you might consider:
- general impression of shape;
- whether or not it passes through the origin;
- steepness of the graph in different places;
- symmetries – reflection, rotation, translation;
- values of x for which the function is undefined;
- what happens when x is close to the undefined values;
- what happens when x is very large (positive or negative);
- whether or not there are any restrictions on the values of y;
- similarities to graphs of other functions;
- how the functions might be classified.

The list is not exhaustive, nor is it necessary to record all features at this stage.

$|x|$ is called the absolute value of x. It is sometimes written as abs(x) or as mod(x), which is short for the modulus of x. It means the numerical value of x, disregarding its sign.

so $|-4.3| = 4.3$ and $|4.3| = 4.3$.

int(x) means the nearest integer below x (or x itself if x is an integer), for example int(4.3) = 4 but int(−4.3) = −5.

4 The graphs are reflections in the x-axis of the graphs in parts (a) to (d) of question 3.

5 Both pairs of graphs are reflections of one another in the line $y = x$.

6

	No. of days	Distance walked (miles)	Distance from Land's End (miles)
(a)	1	30	770
(b)	2	60	740
(c)	t	$30t$	$800 - 30t$

(d) In the first graph, *s* represents the distance, in miles, walked from John O'Groats, which is 30*t*. Therefore, *s* = 30*t* is the equation of the graph.

In the second graph, *s* represents the distance, in miles, from Land's End, which is 800 − 30*t*. Therefore, *s* = 800 − 30*t* is the equation of the graph.

7D The graph assumes that the walker is moving at a constant speed all the time. However:

- The walker will have to stop overnight, which would introduce steps into the graph.
- It is unlikely that his overnight stops will be exactly 30 miles apart.
- There will probably be short rests throughout the day for refreshments, introducing more steps into the graph.
- He could not maintain a perfectly constant walking speed. This would be affected by hills, terrain, traffic, fatigue and many other factors.

Overall, the true graph might look like this:

 Distance walked

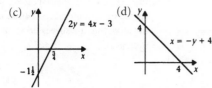

0   1   2

Time (days)

Exercise A (p. 5)

1 (a)   (b)

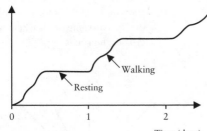

(c)   (d)

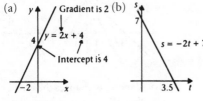

(e)   (f)

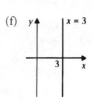

2 (a) $y = 2x + 2$ (b) $y = -2x + 4$

(c) $s = \frac{1}{2}t + 3$ or $2s = t + 6$

(d) $y = \frac{3}{2}x - 2$ or $2y = 3x - 4$

3 (a) $y = 2x + 3$

(b) $\dfrac{y - 6}{x - 2} = 2$ or $\dfrac{y - 4}{x - 1} = 2$

$\Rightarrow y = 2x + 2$ $\Rightarrow y = 2x + 2$

(c) $\dfrac{y - 4}{x - 5} = 3$ or $\dfrac{y - 19}{x - 10} = 3$

Both give $y = 3x - 11$.

(d) $\dfrac{y - 0}{x + 4} = \dfrac{5}{-5} \Rightarrow y = -x - 4$

(e) $\dfrac{y - 2}{x - 1} = \dfrac{1}{3}$ or $\dfrac{y - 1}{x + 2} = \dfrac{1}{3}$

Both give $3y = x + 5$.

(f) $\dfrac{y + 2}{x + 3} = 2$ or $\dfrac{y - 2}{x + 1} = 2$

Both give $y = 2x + 4$.

4 (a) $y = 4x - 14$

(b) $y = 0.25x + 6.25$

(c) $y = -4x - 13$

5 (a) No   (b) Yes   (c) No

(d) Yes   (e) No   (f) Yes

(g) Yes   (h) Yes   (i) Yes

(j) Yes   (k) No   (l) Yes

B Perpendicular and parallel lines (p. 6)

1 The lines are parallel: they all have the same gradient.

2 The lines are parallel, having the same gradient. The value of *c* tells you where the graph crosses the *y*-axis.

3 $y = 3x - 4$, $y = 3x + \frac{1}{2}$ and $y = -\frac{1}{2} + 3x$ are parallel.

$y = 7 - 3x$, $y = -3x + 4$ and $y = -2 - 3x$ are parallel.

$y = 7 - \frac{1}{2}x$ and $y = -\frac{1}{2}x + 2$ are parallel.

4 a and b, d and f, e and i, and h and g are perpendicular pairs (c is not perpendicular to any of the lines).

5 If one of the gradients is m, the other gradient is $\dfrac{-1}{m}$ (or an equivalent rule).

6 $y = 2x + 4$ and $y = -\frac{1}{2}x - 3$ are perpendicular to one another.

$y = \frac{1}{5}x - 2$ and $y = 2 - 5x$ are perpendicular to one another.

$y = 3 - 2x$ and $y = \frac{1}{2}x + 5$ are perpendicular to one another.

7 (i) equation (ii) gradient (iii) intercept

   (a) $y = -3x - 7$ -3 -7

   (b) $y = -\frac{1}{2}x + 4$ $-\frac{1}{2}$ 4

   (c) $y = -\frac{4}{5}x - \frac{1}{5}$ $-\frac{4}{5}$ $-\frac{1}{5}$

   (d) $y = \frac{3}{2}x - 3$ $\frac{3}{2}$ -3

   (e) $y = \frac{7}{2}x - \frac{3}{2}$ $\frac{7}{2}$ $-\frac{3}{2}$

   (f) $y = -\frac{2}{3}x + \frac{3}{2}$ $-\frac{2}{3}$ $\frac{3}{2}$

8 $\dfrac{-a}{b}$

9 (a) $(5, 7)$ (b) $(5, 4.5)$ (c) $(5.5, 3)$

   (d) $(6, 1)$ (e) $(1, 1)$ (f) $(-2.5, 1.5)$

Exercise B (p. 7)

1 $y = 4x + 8$ and $-8x + 2y - 7 = 0$

2 $4x + 6y + 3 = 0$ and $y = -\frac{2}{3}x$

3 $y = -\frac{1}{3}x + 2$ and $x + 3y = 1$

4 $y = 6 - \frac{3}{5}x$ and $-3x - 5y + 1 = 0$

5 (a) $y = 4x - 3$ or $4x - y - 3 = 0$

   (b) $y = -\frac{2}{3}x + 4$ or $2x + 3y - 12 = 0$

   (c) $y = -\frac{1}{7}x$ or $x + 7y = 0$

   (d) $y = 9x - 47$ or $9x - y - 47 = 0$

6 (a) The midpoint of AB is $(3, 8)$, of BC is $(2, 4)$, of CD is $(8, 2)$ and of DA is $(9, 6)$.

(b) Two sides have gradient $-\frac{1}{3}$, while the other two have gradient 4.

(c) Opposite sides are parallel so it is a parallelogram.

7 The mid-point is $(3.5, 3)$.
The gradient of the given line is $\frac{2}{5}$.
So the gradient of the perpendicular is -2.5.
The equation of the perpendicular is $y = -2.5x + 11.75$.

S1.1 The equation of a straight line (p. 8)

1 (a)

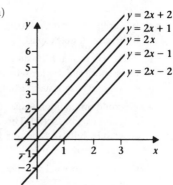

(b) Varying c translates the line up and down. The value of c is where the line crosses the y-axis.

2 (a)

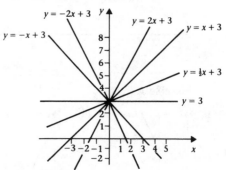

(b) Varying m changes the gradient of the line. When m is positive, the line slopes up as x increases. When m is negative the line slopes down as x increases.

3

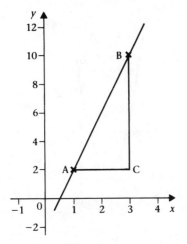

$$\text{Gradient} = \frac{BC}{AC} = \frac{8}{2} = 4$$

4 (a) $\text{Gradient} = \dfrac{11-2}{2+1} = \dfrac{9}{3} = 3$

  (b) $\text{Gradient} = \dfrac{8}{-4} = -2$

  (c) $\text{Gradient} = \dfrac{0}{3} = 0$

5 (a) $\text{Gradient} = \dfrac{4}{2} = 2$

  (b) The line crosses the y-axis at $(0, 1)$ so the y-intercept is 1.

  (c) When $x = 0$ When $x = 2$

   $y = 2 \times 0 + 1$ $y = 2 \times 2 + 1$

   $y = 1$ $y = 5$

  (d) For $y = 2x + 1$

   1 represents the y-intercept.
   2 represents the gradient.

6 (a) Choose any two points on the line, for example $(-1, 2)$ and $(-3, 8)$, which give the gradient -3.

  (b) The line crosses the y-axis at $(0, -1)$, so the y-intercept is -1.

  (c) For any point on the line, substituting the x-coordinate in the equation will give the y-coordinate; for example, take the point $(1, -4)$.

   When $x = 1$

    $y = -3 \times 1 - 1$

    $y = -4$

  (d) For $y = -3x - 1$

   -1 represents the y-intercept.
   -3 represents the gradient.

7 (a) The equation of the line is $y = -2x + 6$

    gradient y-intercept

  (b) The equation of the line is $y = 5x - 2$

    gradient y-intercept

8 (a) $m = -4,\ c = 9$

  (b) $y = 3x + \frac{3}{2} \Rightarrow m = 3,\ c = \frac{3}{2}$

  (c) $y = 2x + \frac{5}{2} \Rightarrow m = 2,\ c = \frac{5}{2}$

  (d) $y = -\frac{3}{5}x - 2 \Rightarrow m = -\frac{3}{5},\ c = -2$

  (e) $y = 5x - 7 \Rightarrow m = 5,\ c = -7$

  (f) $y = -\dfrac{5x}{4} + 5 \Rightarrow m = -\frac{5}{4},\ c = 5$

2 Quadratic graphs and equations

A Quadratic functions (p. 11)

1D The graph is always a parabola. A negative value of a turns the parabola upside down.

2 The graph of $y = x^2 + 3$ is that of $y = x^2$ translated upwards by 3 units.

3 Similarly, the graph of $y = x^2 + q$ is that of $y = x^2$ translated upwards by q units. This is not surprising since to get from $y = x^2$ to $y = x^2 + q$ you simply add q to the y-coordinates.

4 The graph of $y = (x + 4)^2$ is that of $y = x^2$ translated 4 units to the left.

5 The graph of $y = (x + p)^2$ is that of $y = x^2$ translated p units to the left.

6 (a) The graph of $y = (x + 5)^2 + 2$ is that of $y = x^2$ translated 5 units to the left and up 2 units.

  (b) $(-5, 2)$ (c) $x = -5$

7 (a) The graph of $y = x^2$ is moved p units to the left.

  (b) The graph of $y = x^2$ is moved up q units.

  (c) $(-p, q)$ (d) $x = -p$

8 (a) $y = x^2 + 3$ (b) $y = (x - 2)^2$
    (c) $y = x^2 - 4$ (d) $y = (x + 5)^2$
    (e) $y = (x - 2)^2 + 3$ (f) $y = (x + 2)^2 + 5$
    (g) $y = (x - 1)^2 - 1$ (h) $y = (x + 3)^2 - 2$
    (i) $y = -(x - 1)^2 - 1$

9 (a)

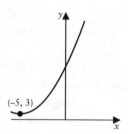

(-5, 3)

    (b) $y = x^2 + 10x + 28$

10 (b) It can be seen from the graph that
$y = x^2 + 2x$ has its vertex at $(-1, -1)$, so

a translation of $\begin{bmatrix} -1 \\ -1 \end{bmatrix}$ maps $y = x^2$ onto

$y = x^2 + 2x$.

Hence $y = x^2 + 2x$ is equivalent to
$y = (x + 1)^2 - 1$.

11 (a) (ii) $\begin{bmatrix} -5 \\ -25 \end{bmatrix}$;

         $x^2 + 10x = (x + 5)^2 - 25$

    (b) (ii) $\begin{bmatrix} 3 \\ -9 \end{bmatrix}$; $x^2 - 6x = (x - 3)^2 - 9$

    (c) (ii) $\begin{bmatrix} -3.5 \\ -12.25 \end{bmatrix}$;

         $x^2 + 7x = (x + 3.5)^2 - 12.25$

12 (a) $x^2 + 4x = (x + 2)^2 - 4$
    (b) $\quad x^2 + 4x = (x + 2)^2 - 4$
      $\Rightarrow x^2 + 4x + 9 = (x + 2)^2 - 4 + 9$
      $\Rightarrow x^2 + 4x + 9 = (x + 2)^2 + 5$

13 (a) (i) $x^2 + 10x + 25$ (ii) $x^2 - 6x + 9$
    (b) (i) $(x + 2)^2$ (ii) $(x + 6)^2$
      (iii) $(x - 5)^2$

14 (a) $(x + 3)^2$ (b) $(x + 3)^2 - 9$
     (c) $(x + 3)^2 - 4$

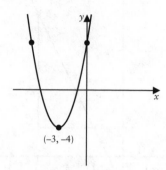

(-3, -4)

15 (a) $(x + 6)^2 - 36$ (b) $(x + 6)^2 - 16$

16 (a) $(x - 7)^2 - 49$ (b) $(x - 7)^2 + 31$

17 (a) $(x + 7)^2 - 47$ (b) $(x - \frac{3}{2})^2 - \frac{5}{4}$
    (c) $(x + 4)^2 - 19$

18 (a) $(x - 1)^2$
    (b) Any value squared is greater than or
      equal to 0. So the smallest value of
      $(x - 1)^2$ is 0 when $x = 1$.

19E (a) $(x + \frac{1}{2}b)^2 + c - \frac{1}{4}b^2$ (b) $(-\frac{1}{2}b, c - \frac{1}{4}b^2)$
    (c) $\qquad c - \frac{1}{4}b^2 > 0$
      $\Rightarrow \quad 4c - b^2 > 0$
      $\Rightarrow \qquad 4c > b^2$

Exercise A (p. 16)

1 (a) $y = x^2 + 6x + 16$
    (b) $y = x^2 - 2x + 5$
    (c) $y = x^2 - 12x + 28$
    (d) $y = x^2 + 8x + 15$

2 (a) (i) $(x + 4)^2 - 11$
      (ii) $x^2 + 8x + 16 - 11$
         $= x^2 + 8x + 5$
      (iii)

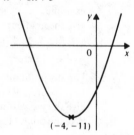

(-4, -11)

(b) (i) $(x-2)^2 - 7$

   (ii) $x^2 - 4x + 4 - 7$
         $= x^2 - 4x - 3$

   (iii)

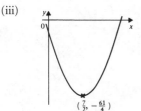

       $(2, -7)$

(c) (i) $(x - \frac{5}{2})^2 - \frac{1}{4}$

   (ii) $x^2 - 5x + \frac{25}{4} - \frac{1}{4}$
         $= x^2 - 5x + 6$

   (iii)

       $(\frac{5}{2}, -\frac{1}{4})$

(d) (i) $(x - \frac{7}{2})^2 - \frac{61}{4}$

   (ii) $x^2 - 7x + \frac{49}{4} - \frac{61}{4} = x^2 - 7x - 3$

   (iii)

       $(\frac{7}{2}, -\frac{61}{4})$

3 (a) (i) $y = (x+2)^2 + 3$

      (ii) $y = (x-2)^2 - 5$

   (b) (i) $y = x^2 + 4x + 7$

      (ii) $y = x^2 - 4x - 1$

4 (a) $(x+2)^2 - 6$

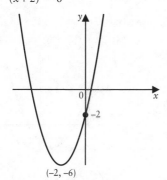

      $(-2, -6)$

(b) $(x - \frac{5}{2})^2 - \frac{13}{4}$

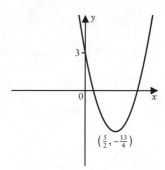

      $(\frac{5}{2}, -\frac{13}{4})$

(c) $(x+6)^2 - 41$

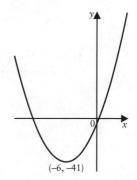

      $(-6, -41)$

5E $d = 2, e = -6, f = 3$

B Zeros of quadratics (p. 17)

1D (a) Either $a = 0$ or $b = 0$ or both a and
        $b = 0$.

   (a) (i) $x + 2 = 0$

          $\Rightarrow x = -2$

      (ii) $x - 1 = 0$

          $\Rightarrow x = 1$

      (iii) $(x-1)(x+2) = 0$

          $\Rightarrow x - 1 = 0$ or $x + 2 = 0$

          $\Rightarrow \qquad x = 1$ or $x = -2$

2 (a) The graph shows that 1 and 5 give the
      points $x = -1$ and $x = -5$ where the
      curve cuts the x-axis. The values are
      also the zeros of the function because

        $(x+1)(x+5) = 0$

      $\Rightarrow x + 1 = 0$ or $x + 5 = 0$

      $\Rightarrow x = -1$ or $x = -5$

(b) When α and β are distinct numbers, the graph will cross the x-axis at two points, irrespective of whether α and β are positive, negative or zero. If α and β are equal then the two crossing points coincide and the graph touches the x-axis. α and β give the points $x = -\alpha$ and $x = -\beta$ where the graph cuts the x-axis. The values $-\alpha$ and $-\beta$ are also the zeros of the function with that graph.

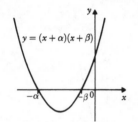

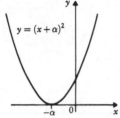

3

$y = -(x+\alpha)(x+\beta)$
is the reflection in the x-axis of
$y = (x+\alpha)(x+\beta)$

4   (a) $y = (x-1)(x-5)$
    (b) $y = (x+3)(x-9)$
    (c) $y = (x+10)(x+2)$
    (d) $y = x(x-4)$
    (e) $y = -(x-1)(x-5)$
    (f) $y = -(x+2)(x-6)$
    (g) $y = -(x+3)(x+0.5)$
    (h) $y = -x(x-2)$
    (i) $y = (x+3)(x-3)$
    (j) $y = -(x-7)^2$
    (k) $y = (x+2)^2$
    (l) $y = -(x+5)(x-5)$

5   (a) $y = (x+2)(x-1)$

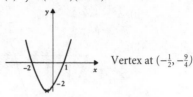

Vertex at $(-\frac{1}{2}, -\frac{9}{4})$

    (b) $y = (x-2)^2$

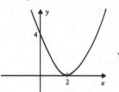

Vertex at $(2, 0)$

    (c) $y = -(x+1)^2$

Vertex at $(-1, 0)$

6   (a) $(x+3)(x+4)$ (b) $(x-3)(x+1)$
    (c) $(x-5)(x-2)$ (d) $(x+2)(x-2)$
    (e) $(x-7)$ (f) $(x-3)^2$
    (g) $(x+1)(x+2)$ (h) $(x+2)^2$
    (i) $(x+7)(x-7)$

7   (a)

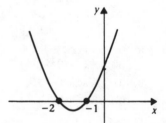

    (i) Zeros at -1 and -2
    (ii) $(x+1)(x+2)$
    (b)

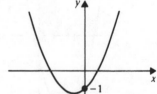

    (i) Zeros at roughly 0.6 and -1.6.
    (ii) There are *no* factors of the form $ax + b$, a and b whole numbers.

(c)

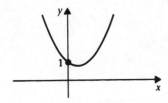

    (i)   There are no zeros.
    (ii) Hence there are no factors.

8   (a) −3 or −2   (b) −5 or −1
    (c) 3 or 5   (d) 2 or 6
    (e) −3 or 3   (f) −5 or 5
    (g) $x = 3$ or −6
    (h) $x = -2$ or 5
    (i) $x = 0$ or 4
    (j) $x = 3$

9   (a) $x^2 + 2x - 15 = 0$, $x = -5$ or 3
    (a) $x^2 + x - 12 = 0$, $x = -4$ or 3
    (c) $x^2 + x - 90 = 0$, $x = -10$ or 9
    (d) $x^2 - 49 = 0$, $x = -7$ or 7
    (e) $x^2 - 9 = 0$, $x = -3$ or 3
    (f) $x^2 - 9 = 0$, $x = -3$ or 3
    (g) $x^2 + 2x - 35 = 0$, $x = -7$ or 5
    (h) $x^2 - 5x = 0$, $x = 0$ or 5
    (i) $x^2 - 1 = 0$, $x = -1$ or 1

10 (a) $(2x + 1)(x + 3)$ (b) $(4x + 1)(x - 7)$
    (c) $(2x + 3)(x + 1)$ (d) $(2x - 1)(x + 3)$
    (e) $x(3x - 1)$ (f) $(2x + 1)(x - 4)$
    (g) $(2x - 1)(3x - 2)$ (h) $(9x + 4)(x + 1)$
    (i) $(2x - 3)(2x + 5)$ (j) $(6x - 1)(x + 12)$
    (k) $(3x + 2)(3x - 4)$

Exercise B (p. 23)

1   (a) −1 or −3 (b) 1 or −9 (c) 1 or $-\frac{3}{2}$
    (d) $\frac{1}{4}$ or −2 (e) $\frac{2}{5}$ or −4 (f) 0 or $\frac{7}{2}$
    (g) $\frac{4}{3}$ or $\frac{1}{2}$ (h) $-\frac{5}{4}$ or $-\frac{3}{2}$

2   (a) −6 or 4 (b) −2 or 8 (c) $\frac{2}{3}$ or 4
    (d) −1 or $\frac{1}{3}$ (e) −2 or $-\frac{1}{2}$
    (f) $-\frac{5}{2}$ or −1

3   (a) $-\frac{1}{2}$ or 3 (b) $\frac{1}{2}$ or −2 (c) $\frac{1}{3}$ or 3
    (d) $-\frac{1}{5}$ or 3 (e) $-\frac{2}{5}$ or 1 (f) $-\frac{2}{5}$ or $\frac{3}{2}$

4 (a)

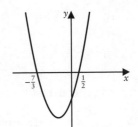

    (b)

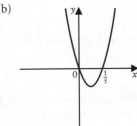

5 $2x^2 - 5x + 3$ or $(x - 1)(2x - 3)$
    $x = 1$, $x = \frac{3}{2}$

6 2 s, 6 s

C Solving quadratic equations by completing the square (p. 24)

1D $x^2 - 4x = (x - 2)^2 - 4$
  $\implies$ $x^2 - 4x - 4 = (x - 2)^2 - 8$
           $x^2 - 4x - 4 = 0$
  $\implies$ $(x - 2)^2 - 8 = 0$
  $\implies$ $(x - 2)^2 = 8$
  $\implies$ $x - 2 = \pm\sqrt{8}$
  $\implies$ $x = 2 \pm \sqrt{8}$

Thus there are two roots (solutions) to the equation. The positive one, 4.83 to 2 d.p. gives the length of one side of the lawn.

2 (a) (i) $\pm\sqrt{5} - 3$
         (ii) −0.76, −5.24
    (b) (i) $\pm\sqrt{\frac{17}{4}} + \frac{3}{2}$
         (ii) 3.56, −0.56
    (c) (i) $\pm\sqrt{\frac{13}{4}} - \frac{5}{2}$
         (ii) −0.70, −4.30

3 (a) (i) $\pm\sqrt{\frac{3}{4}} - \frac{3}{2}$
         (ii) −0.63, −2.37

(b) (i) $\pm \sqrt{\frac{11}{12}} + \frac{1}{2}$

(ii) $1.46, -0.46$

(c) (i) $\pm \sqrt{\frac{5}{16}} - \frac{3}{4}$

(ii) $-0.19, -1.31$

4D (a) All the terms have been divided by a.

(b) $x^2 + \frac{b}{a}x + \frac{b^2}{4a^2} = \left(x + \frac{b}{2a}\right)^2$

$$\Rightarrow x^2 + \frac{b}{a}x = \left(x + \frac{b}{2a}\right)^2 - \frac{b^2}{4a^2}$$

(c) $-\frac{c}{a} = \frac{-4ac}{4a^2}$

This puts all the right-handed side over the same denominator.

(d) The squares of both

$+\sqrt{\frac{b^2 - 4ac}{2a}}$ and $-\sqrt{\frac{b^2 - 4ac}{2a}}$

are equal to $\frac{b^2 - 4ac}{2a}$.

(e) $\sqrt{\frac{9}{16}} = \frac{3}{4}$ because $\left(\frac{3}{4}\right)^2 = \frac{9}{16}$

But $\frac{\sqrt{9}}{\sqrt{16}}$ also equals $\frac{3}{4}$.

5 (a) (i) $\frac{-7 \pm \sqrt{17}}{4}$

(ii) $-0.72, -2.78$

(b) (i) $\frac{9 \pm \sqrt{33}}{6}$

(ii) $2.46, 0.54$

(c) (i) $\frac{-3 \pm \sqrt{29}}{2}$

(ii) $1.19, -4.19$

6 (a) -8, no roots   (b) 44, 2 roots
(c) 0, 1 root   (d) 41, 2 roots
(e) 0, 1 root   (f) -7, no roots

The relationship is described in the panel following the question.

Exercise C (p. 28)

1 (a) (i) $\pm\sqrt{11} - 2$ (ii) $1.32, -5.32$
(b) (i) $\pm\sqrt{11} + 4$ (ii) $7.32, 0.68$
(c) (i) $\pm\sqrt{2} - 3$ (ii) $-1.59, -4.41$
(d) (i) $\pm\sqrt{\frac{21}{4}} + \frac{3}{2}$ (ii) $3.79, -0.79$

2 (a) (i) $\frac{-5 \pm \sqrt{13}}{2}$ (ii) -4.30 or -0.70

(b) (i) $\frac{-6 \pm \sqrt{12}}{6}$ (ii) -1.58 or -0.42

(c) (i) $\frac{-4 \pm \sqrt{28}}{6}$ (ii) -1.55 or 0.22

(d) (i) $\frac{8 \pm \sqrt{84}}{10}$ (ii) -0.12 or 1.72

(e) (i) $\frac{7 \pm \sqrt{57}}{4}$ (ii) -0.14 or 3.64

(f) (i) $\frac{7 \pm \sqrt{73}}{6}$ (ii) 2.59 or -0.26

3 (a) Positive, so 2 solutions
(b) Negative, so no real solutions
(c) Positive, so 2 solutions
(d) Positive, so 2 solutions

4 (a) $x^2 + 2x - 4 = 0 \Rightarrow x = -3.24$ or 1.24
(b) $5x^2 - 3x - 4 = 0 \Rightarrow x = -0.64$ or 1.24
(c) $x^2 - 7x + 8 = 0 \Rightarrow 1.44$ or 5.56
(d) $5x^2 + 3x - 1 = 0 \Rightarrow -0.84$ or 0.24

5 (a) $0, 8$ (b) $-1, 4$ (c) $-1.62, 0.62$
(d) $x = \pm 5$ (e) no solutions   (f) 5

6 (a) Area of path
$= x \times 1 + (3x + 2) \times 1 + x \times 1 = 5x + 2$
Area of lawn $= 3x \times x = 3x^2$
Hence $3x^2 = 5x + 2$.

(b) $3x^2 - 5x - 2 = 0 \Rightarrow x = 2$ since x must be positive.

The dimensions are 2 metres × 6 metres.

7 (a) The numbers are n and $n + 1$.
Therefore $n(n + 1) = 10$.

(b) $n = \frac{-1 \pm \sqrt{41}}{2}$

The two numbers are $\frac{-1 \pm \sqrt{41}}{2}$ and $\frac{1 \pm \sqrt{41}}{2}$.

8 (a) (i) no solutions   (ii) $x = 2$
(iii) $0.76, 5.24$

(b) (i) matches A.
(ii) matches C.
(iii) matches B.

(c) If $b^2 - 4ac < 0$, the equation has no solutions.
If $b^2 - 4ac = 0$, the equation has a single (repeated) solution.
If $b^2 - 4ac > 0$, the equation has two solutions.

9 (a) (i) $\pm\sqrt{\frac{13}{9}} - \frac{1}{3}$

(ii) $0.87, -1.54$

(b) (i) $\pm\sqrt{\frac{17}{16}} + \frac{7}{4}$

(ii) $2.78, 0.72$

(c) (i) $\pm\sqrt{\frac{15}{16}} - \frac{1}{4}, 0.31, -0.81$

S2.1 Multiplying brackets (p. 30)

1 (a) $5x + 15$ (b) $2x - 8$

(c) $16x + 40$ (d) $-2x - 12$

(e) $-4x + 28$ (f) $6x - 12y$

2 (a) $3 + 2x + 6 = 9 + 2x$

(b) $2x - 12$

(c) $a + 40 - 5a = 40 - 4a$

(d) $t - 4 + 4t = 5t - 4$

(e) $p - 1 + 6p - 16 = 7p - 17$

(f) $5 - 30x + 54 = 59 - 30x$

(g) $y - 9y + 18 = 18 - 8y$

(h) $4x - 2x + x^2 = 2x + x^2$

(i) $2 - 3x - 6x^2$

3 (a) $x^2 + 6x + 8$ (b) $x^2 - 2x - 3$

(c) $x^2 + 3x - 4$ (d) $x^2 - 7x + 10$

(e) $x^2 - 2x - 35$ (f) $x^2 + 10x + 16$

(g) $x^2 - 11x + 18$ (h) $x^2 + 3x - 28$

4 (a) (i) $x^2 + 6x + 9$

(ii) $x^2 + 14x + 49$

(iii) $x^2 - 18x + 81$

(iv) $x^2 - 12x + 36$

(b) (i) $b = 2p$

(ii) $c = p^2$

S2.2 Further factorisation (p. 31)

1 (a) (i) $x^2 + 5x + 6$ (ii) $x^2 - 5x + 6$

(iii) $x^2 + 9x + 20$ (iv) $x^2 - 9x + 20$

(b) The constant term c is obtained by multiplying together the numbers in the brackets, together with their signs (+ or −). For example,

$$(x-2)(x+3) = x^2 + x - 6$$

$$-2 \times 3 = -6$$

(c) The coefficient b is obtained by adding together the numbers in the brackets. For example,

$$(x-2)(x+3) = x^2 + x - 6$$

$$-2 + 3 = 1$$

2 (a) $(x+2)(x+7)$ (b) $(x+8)(x+5)$

(c) $(x-2)(x-7)$ (d) $(x+6)^2$

(e) $(x-8)(x+1)$ (f) $(x+7)(x-4)$

(g) $(x-6)(x-2)$ (h) $(x-9)(x+4)$

(i) $(x-8)(x+6)$ (j) $(x+6)(x-4)$

3 (a) $x(x+2)$ (b) $(x+3)(x-3)$

(c) $x(x-8)$ (d) Not possible

(e) $x(x+25)$ (f) $(x+5)(x-5)$

(g) Not possible   (h) $(x+1)(x-1)$

(i) $x(x-1)$

3 Simultaneous equations and inequalities

A Simultaneous equations (p. 33)

Exercise A (p. 34)

1 The algebraic solution of $x = 3, y = 2$ confirms what is shown on the graph.

2 (a) $x = 5, y = 2$ (b) $x = -4, y = 3$

(c) $x = \frac{2}{3}, y = 7$

3 (a) $(2, 6)$ (b) $(4, -\frac{1}{2})$ (c) $(2, \frac{5}{2})$

4 $(4, 9), (7, 4), (2, 3)$

5 $c = 7$ (The point the lines all go through is $(5, 3)$.)

6 (a) $x = 3, y = 1$ (b) $x = 7, y = 3$

(c) $x = -1, y = -2$

7 (a) $x + 2y = 160$; x is the number of £1 articles and y is the number of £2 articles.

(b) $x + y = 117$

(c) $x = 74, y = 43$, so 74 articles at £1 were sold and 43 at £2.

8   Equations like these are needed, where f is the father's age now and s is the son's age now.

$$f = s + 25$$
$$f - 7 = 6(s - 7)$$

The father is 37 and the son 12.

9   (a)   (i)   You soon get to a trivial equation like $0 = 0$.

   (ii)   The two lines are identical, because the equations are equivalent, as you can see by dividing both sides of the second equation by 3.

   (b)   (i)   You get a false equation like $19 = 0$.

   (ii)   The two lines are parallel so there are no solutions.

B   Simultaneous equations, only one linear (p. 35)

1 $(3, 1)$ and $(5, 5)$

2D   It makes the algebra easier to do it that way but both methods give correct values.

Exercise B (p. 37)

1   (a) $x = 0$ and $y = 2$ or $x = 1$ and $y = 5$

   (b) $x = 3$ and $y = 9$ or $x = -\frac{1}{2}$ and $y = -5$

   (c) $x = 2$ and $y = 4$ or $x = -\frac{1}{2}$ and $y = \frac{11}{4}$

2   (a) $x = 4$ and $y = 0$ or $x = -8$ and $y = 12$

   (b) $x = 1$ and $y = 2$ or $x = \frac{2}{3}$ and $y = \frac{19}{9}$

3

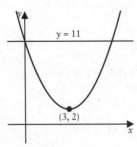

$y = 11$

$(3, 2)$

$(0, 11)$ and $(6, 11)$

4   (a) $(1.24, 7.73)$ or $(-0.64, 2.07)$

   (b) $(5.56, -25.37)$ or $(1.44, -0.63)$

   (c) $(1.19, 3.37)$ or $(-1.69, -2.37)$

5 $x = 0$ and $y = 5$ or $x = 4$ and $y = -3$

6   (a) $x + y = 2$ gives $y = 2 - x$.

   Substituting this into $x^2 + y^2 = 9$ gives
   $$x^2 + (2 - x)^2 = 9$$
   $$\Rightarrow x^2 + 4 - 4x + x^2 = 9$$
   $$\Rightarrow 2x^2 - 4x - 5 = 0$$

   (b) $x = 2.87$ and $y = -0.87$ or $x = -0.87$ and $y = 2.87$

C   Inequalities (p. 38)

1D   Reasoning informally, £73.00 − £11.00 = £62.00 gives the amount that can be paid in hourly wages before National Insurance has to be paid. $62 \div 8 = 7.75$ gives the number of hours that can be worked. A formal approach using inequalities is given in the text.

2D   (a)   From the graph you can see that the curve is 'higher' than the y-axis when
   $$x > 2 \text{ or } x < -1.$$

   (b)   The graph of $y = (x + 1)(x - 2)$ crosses $y = 4$ at $x = -2$ and $x = 3$. So the solution set is
   $$x > 3 \text{ or } x < -2.$$

Exercise C (p. 40)

1   (a) $x < -2$ (b) $-5 < 5x \Rightarrow -1 < x$

   (c) $2x - 6 < 8 \Rightarrow x < 7$

   (d) $3x + 15 < 2x + 3 \Rightarrow x < -12$

   (e) $x > -2$

2   (a) $-3 < x < 1$ (b) $x < -4$ or $x > 2$

   (c) $-2 < x < 2$

3   (a) $x < -5$ or $x > 2$

   (b) $-6 < x < -4$

   (c) $x < 1$ or $x > 7$

   (d) $x < 2$ or $x > 3$

4   The square of any number except 0 is positive. Therefore x may take any value except 2.

5   (a) $-5 < x < 4$

   (b) $x < -\frac{1}{2}$ or $x > 3$

6 (a) $0 < x < 3$ (b) $0 < x < 1$

(c) $-2 < x < 5$

(d) $x < \dfrac{-1 - \sqrt{5}}{2}$ or $x > \dfrac{-1 + \sqrt{5}}{2}$

7 $-\frac{5}{2} < x < 3$

8 (a) $x < -4$ or $x > 2$

(b) $x < -\frac{2}{3}$ or $x > 1$

9 (a)
$$\dfrac{n(n+1)}{2} > 50$$
$$\Rightarrow \quad n(n+1) > 100$$
$$\Rightarrow \quad n^2 + n - 100 > 0$$

Solving $n^2 + n - 100 = 0$ gives $n = 9.51$ or -10.51 to 2 d.p.

A sketch graph shows that $n^2 + n - 100 > 0$ when $n > 9.51$ or $n < -10.51$.

So $n = 10$ gives the first triangle number greater than 50.

(b) 55 (by substituting 10 into the formula for the nth triangle number)

(c) 14

(d) 105

(e) 1035 (from $n = 45$)

S3.1 Linear inequalities (p. 41)

1 All methods should give (or confirm) the result $t > 2$.

2 (a) $p > 5$ (b) $p < 5$

3 (a) $x > 1$ (b) $x > 3$ (c) $x < \frac{8}{3}$

(d) $x > -\frac{13}{5}$ (e) $x < \frac{17}{2}$ (f) $x < -2$

4 $x < -2$

5 (a)
$$5x + 1 < 2x + 7$$
$$\Rightarrow \quad 3x < 6$$
$$\Rightarrow \quad x < 2$$

(b)
$$2x - 1 > 5 - x$$
$$\Rightarrow \quad 3x > 6$$
$$\Rightarrow \quad x > 2$$

(c)
$$1 - 2x < x - 7$$
$$\Rightarrow \quad 8 < 3x$$
$$\Rightarrow \quad \tfrac{8}{3} < x$$
$$\Rightarrow \quad x > \tfrac{8}{3}$$

(d)
$$3 > 1 + 2x$$
$$\Rightarrow \quad 2 > 2x$$
$$\Rightarrow \quad 1 > x$$
$$\Rightarrow \quad x < 1$$

(e)
$$1 - \tfrac{1}{3}x < 4$$
$$\Rightarrow \quad -\tfrac{1}{3}x < 3$$
$$\Rightarrow \quad x > -9$$

(f)
$$3 - 2x > 2 - 3x$$
$$\Rightarrow \quad x > -1$$

(g)
$$3(x + 2) < 11(x - 2)$$
$$3x + 6 < 11x - 22$$
$$-8x < -28$$
$$8x > 28$$
$$x > \tfrac{7}{2}$$

(h)
$$2(5 - x) > 3(x - 10)$$
$$10 - 2x > 3x - 30$$
$$-5x > -40$$
$$5x < 40$$
$$x < 8$$

4 Polynomials

A Factorising (p. 43)

1 The student's expansion of the brackets should give $x^3 + 3x^2 - 6x - 8$.

2D (a) -1, 2 and -4

(b) The result is zero every time.

(c) If a particular number, call it a, is a zero of $P(x)$, then $(x - a)$ is a factor of x. Conversely, if $(x - a)$ is a factor of x, then a is a zero of $P(x)$.

3 (a) (i) -24 (ii) -30 (iii) -24

(iv) 0   (v) 0   (vi) 6

(vii) 0   (viii) -24

(b) $x + 1$, $x + 3$, $x - 4$

(c) $(x + 1)(x + 3)(x - 4)$
$$= (x^2 + 4x + 3)(x - 4)$$
$$= x^3 - 13x - 12$$

4 (a) $a = -2$. The value is chosen so that $x + 2 = 0$.

(b) $P(-2) = 0$, therefore $x + 2$ is a factor of $P(x)$.

5 (a) $P(2) = (2-2)(2^2-2-2) = 0$

(b) $P(a) = (a-a)Q(a) = 0 \times Q(a) = 0$

6 $(x-3)(x-1)(x+1)$ since $P(3) = 0$, $P(1) = 0$, $P(-1) = 0$

7 (a) $x^3 + 2x^2 - 9x - 18$

(b) $x^3 + 5x^2 + 2x - 8$

8 $30 = 5a \Rightarrow a = 6$

9 (a) $P(x) = x^3 - bx^2 + 2x + x^2 - bx + 2$

$\qquad = x^3 + (1-b)x^2 + (2-b)x + 2$

Like terms are gathered together to simplify the expression.

(b) For the two expressions to be equal, the coefficients for each term must be the same. This is clearly true for x^3 and $+2$, also

$\qquad 1 - b = -2 \qquad$ (1) (from x^2 term)

$\qquad 2 - b = -1 \qquad$ (2) (from x term).

The two equations both give $b = 3$.

The process of obtaining equations from equivalent expressions by comparing coefficients is usually referred to as **equating coefficients**.

10 (a) $b = 2$; $(x-1)(x-1)(x+3)$

(b) $b = -2$; $(x-7)(x-4)(x+2)$

11 (a) (i) $a = 1$ ⎫ These are easy to spot

(ii) $c = -4$ ⎬ because only two terms are combined to give the particular term.

(b) $(x+2)(x^2 + bx - 4)$

$\qquad = x^3 + bx^2 - 4x + 2x^2 + 2bx - 8$

$\qquad = x^3 + (2+b)x^2 + (2b-4)x - 8$

Equating coefficients gives

$\qquad 2 + b = -1 \qquad\qquad$ (1)

$\qquad 2b - 4 = -10 \qquad$ (2)

Both equations give $b = -3$.

(c) $P(x) = (x+2)(x^2 - 3x - 4)$

$\qquad P(x) = (x+2)(x-4)(x+1)$

With practice it is possible to complete the stage represented by (b) entirely in your head by doing it in logical steps. For example

1. For the x^2 term,

$\qquad (x+2)(x^2 + bx - 4)$ gives $(2+b)x^2$

2. $2 + b$ has to be -1, hence $b = -3$.

3. Check in the same way that this value gives -10 for the coefficient of x.

12 (a) $(x-2)(x+3)(x+8)$

(b) $(x+1)(x-1)(x+4)$

(c) $(x+1)(x-2)(x-3)$

(d) $(x-1)(x+2)(x-4)$

(e) $(x+1)(x+4)(x+5)$

(f) $(x+1)(x+3)(x-3)$

(g) $(x-2)(x+3)(x+4)$

Exercise A (p. 46)

1 (a) $P(-3) = 0$ (b) $Q(x) = x^2 - 5x + 4$

2 (a) $P(-1) = 0 \Rightarrow x+1$ is a factor

(b) $(x+1)(x-2)(x-4)$

(c) $-1, 2, 4$

3 $1, -3$

4 $(x+2)(x^2 + 2x - 2) = 0$

$\qquad \Rightarrow x = -2, 0.73, -2.73$

5 (a) $x^3 - 8 = (x-2)(x^2 + 2x + 4)$

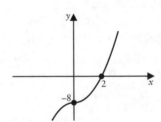

(b) $x^3 - 3x^2 + x - 3 = (x-3)(x^2 + 1)$

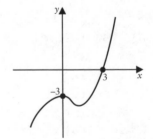

(c) $x^4 - 16 = (x^2 + 4)(x-2)(x+2)$

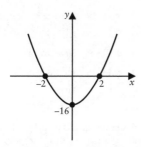

Each linear factor gives a zero. Quadratic factors that cannot be factorised give no further zeros.

6 $(x+2)(x-4)(x-5)$

B   Sketching polynomials (p. 46)

Exercise B (p. 48)

1

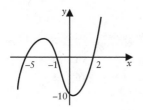

2 (a) The zeros are -2 and 3.

$(x+2)(x-3)(x-3)$

(b)

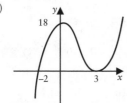

3

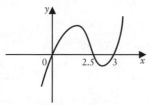

The function is negative when $x<0$ and when $2.5<x<3$.

4

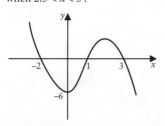

5 (a) Zeros are -2, -1, 1 and 3.

$P(x) = (x-3)(x-1)(x+1)(x+2)$

(b)

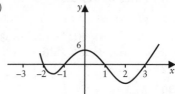

(c) $x<-2$ or $-1<x<1$ or $x>3$

6 (a) $(x+2)(x^2-2x+2)=0$

$\Rightarrow x=-2$

(b)

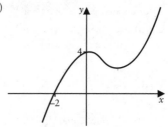

The quadratic equation $x^2-2x+2=0$ has no solutions, hence the cubic equation has only one solution.

S4.1   Expanding brackets (p. 48)

1 (a) $(x+1)(x^2-2x-8)=x^3-x^2-10x-8$

(b) $(x-2)(x^2-7x+12)$

$= x^3-7x^2+12x-2x^2+14x-24$

$= x^3-9x^2+26x-24$

(c) $(x-1)(x^2+6x+5)=x^3+5x^2-x-5$

(d) $(x^2-2x+1)(x+3)$

$= x^3-2x^2+x+3x^2-6x+3$

$= x^3+x^2-5x+3$

2 (a) $(x^2-1)(x^2-4)=x^4-5x^2+4$

(b) $(x^2-4)^2=x^4-8x^2+16$

(c) $(x-1)(x+3)(x^2+6x+9)$

$= (x^2+2x-3)(x^2+6x+9)$

$= x^4+6x^3+9x^2+2x^3+12x^2$

$\quad +18x-3x^2-18x-27$

$= x^4+8x^3+18x^2-27$

(d) $(x+1)(x-2)(x^2-x-12)$

$= (x+1)(x^3-3x^2-10x+24)$

$= x^4-2x^3-13x^2+14x+24$

5 Powers and surds

A Rules of indices (p. 50)

1 (a) (i) 64   (ii) 64   (iii) 64

  (b) (i) 16 384   (ii) 16 384
      (iii) 16 384   (iv) 16 384

2 $3 + 5 = c$

3D $7 - 3 = d$

4 (a) Because

$$a^4 \times a^4 \times a^4 = (a \times a \times a \times a)$$
$$\times (a \times a \times a \times a) \times (a \times a \times a \times a)$$
$$= a^{12},$$

or because $a^4 \times a^4 \times a^4 = a^{(4+4+4)} = a^{12}$.

  (b) (i) a^8 (ii) b^{16}
      (iii) x^{15} (iv) a^{30}

5D (a) $\frac{1}{16}, \frac{1}{8}$

  (b) $\frac{1}{128}$

  (c) 2^{-7}

  (d) 2^{-7} does equal $\frac{1}{128}$.

Exercise A (p. 51)

1 (a) 2^5 (b) 2^{10} (c) 2^5 (d) 2^{15}

2 (a) p^8 (b) p^{12} (c) p^{10} (d) p^3
  (e) p^3 (f) p^5

3 (a) 6   (b) $\frac{1}{9}$ (c) $\frac{1}{1000}$ (d) 27
  (e) 125

4 (a) y^{-2} (b) c^5 (c) x^0 or 1   (d) x^6

5 $(\frac{1}{2})^3 = \frac{1}{2^3} = 2^{-3} = \frac{1}{8}$; 3^{-2} does not equal any of the others.

6 (a) $\frac{1}{16}$ (b) $\frac{1}{27}$ (c) $\frac{1}{4}$ (d) 4
  (e) 1   (f) 16   (g) $\frac{1}{16}$ (h) 1

B Fractional indices and surds (p. 52)

1D (a) 2^1 (b) $\pm \sqrt{2}$
  (c) (i) $\pm \sqrt[3]{2}$ (ii) $\pm \sqrt{3}$
      (iii) $\sqrt[3]{3}$ (iv) $\pm \sqrt{4}$
      (v) $\sqrt[n]{2}$ (vi) $\sqrt[n]{a}$

Your calculator will be using fractional indices to mean square roots, cube roots and so on.

2 (a) ± 3 (b) 2   (c) ± 4 (d) ± 9

3 (a) ± 3 (b) $\pm \frac{1}{5}$ (c) 100   (d) ± 0.1
  (e) ± 0.2

4 (a) (i) ± 8 (ii) ± 8
  (b) (i) 9   (ii) 9
  (c) (i) ± 125 (ii) ± 125

5 (a) (i) ± 343 (ii) ± 343
  (b) (i) 16   (ii) 16
  (c) (i) ± 27 (ii) ± 27

6 The calculator should give 343 also.

7 (b) $8^{\frac{4}{3}}$ (c) $\pm 81^{\frac{3}{4}}$

8 (a) 2   (b) $\pm \frac{1}{2}$ (c) 9
  (d) $\frac{1}{9}$ (e) ± 8 (f) $\frac{1}{10}$
  (g) 1   (h) ± 1000 (i) 16
  (j) 1   (k) 8   (l) 10 000
  (m) ± 27 (n) $\frac{1}{25}$ (o) 100
  (p) ± 1000 (q) $\frac{1}{125}$

9 $\sqrt{2}, \sqrt{3}, \sqrt{4}$

10 (a) $14 + 6\sqrt{5}$ (b) $17 - 4\sqrt{13}$
  (c) $29 - 12\sqrt{5}$

11 (a) (i) ± 6 (ii) ± 6
  (b) (i) $\pm \frac{2}{3}$ (ii) $\pm \frac{2}{3}$

Exercise B (p. 55)

1 (a) 3   (b) ± 32 (c) $\frac{1}{3}$ (d) $\pm \frac{3}{7}$
  (e) $\frac{1}{5}$ (f) ± 1728 (g) $\pm \frac{1}{8}$ (h) $\pm \frac{1}{27}$
  (i) $\pm \frac{8}{729}$ (j) $\frac{4}{9}$

2 (a) $7^{\frac{1}{2}}$ (b) $10^{\frac{1}{3}}$ (c) $5^{\frac{3}{2}}$ (d) $7^{\frac{2}{3}}$
  (e) $10^{-\frac{1}{4}}$ (f) $3^{-\frac{5}{2}}$ (g) $7^{-\frac{3}{2}}$ (h) $3^{-\frac{2}{3}}$

3 (a) ± 0.7 (b) ± 1.25
  (c) ± 0.125 (d) ± 1000

4 (a) $2\sqrt{2}$ (b) $2\sqrt{15}$
  (c) $4\sqrt{2}$ (d) $2\sqrt{2}$

5 (a) $x = \dfrac{-5 \pm \sqrt{21}}{2}$ (b) $x = \dfrac{3 \pm \sqrt{45}}{2}$
  (c) $x = \dfrac{-7 \pm \sqrt{85}}{6}$

6 $\pi r^2 = 50$

$$r^2 = \frac{50}{\pi}$$

$$r = \sqrt{\frac{50}{\pi}} = \sqrt{\frac{25 \times 2}{\pi}} = 5\sqrt{\frac{2}{\pi}}$$

Circumference $= 2\pi r$

$$= 2\pi \times 5\sqrt{\frac{2}{\pi}}$$

$$= 10\pi\sqrt{\frac{2}{\pi}}$$

$$= 10\sqrt{\frac{2\pi^2}{\pi}}$$

$$= 10\sqrt{2\pi}$$

7   (a) $3 \pm \sqrt{3}$ (b) $-4 \pm \sqrt{13}$
    (c) $-2 \pm \sqrt{6}$

8   (a) $9 - \sqrt{3}$ (b) $5 - 2\sqrt{6}$
    (c) $1 + \sqrt{3}$

9   (a) $4 \pm 3\sqrt{2}$ (b) $-4 \pm 2\sqrt{3}$
    (c) $7 \pm 3\sqrt{6}$

10 (a) $\dfrac{\sqrt{3}-1}{2}$ (b) $-\left(\dfrac{1+\sqrt{2}+\sqrt{3}+\sqrt{6}}{2}\right)$

    (c) $\dfrac{\sqrt{10}+\sqrt{15}}{5}$ (d) $\sqrt{10}+4\sqrt{2}-\sqrt{5}-4$

    (e) $\dfrac{2\sqrt{5}-2\sqrt{2}}{3}$

11 $10 - 7\sqrt{2}$

6 Rates of change

A Linear functions (p. 57)

1D (a) From the graph, temperature changes
        of 10, 20, 50 degrees Celsius
        correspond to changes of 18, 36, 90
        degrees Fahrenheit.

    (b) The gradient is $\frac{72}{40} = 1.8$ (or $\frac{9}{5}$), and it
        represents the change in degrees
        Fahrenheit per degree Celsius (i.e. the
        change in degrees Fahrenheit
        corresponding to a change of 1 degree
        Celsius).

    (c) $F = 1.8C + 32$; 32 is the intercept on
        the vertical axis; 1.8 is the gradient,
        derived from the triangle drawn on the
        diagram (or from knowledge of
        boiling points and freezing points).

2   1.8

3D (a)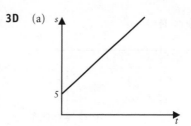

    (b) 4

4   (a) 3   (b) 3

5   (a) Difference in y-coordinates $= -6$;
        difference in x-coordinates $= 2$

    (b) $\dfrac{dy}{dx} = \dfrac{-6}{2} = -3$

6D (a) $\dfrac{dy}{dx} = 3$, (i.e. gradient is 3)

        $\Rightarrow y = 3x + c$.   (1)

        Because c is not known, any of the
        lines shown is a possible line.

        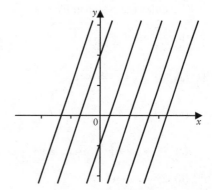

        All such lines are said to form the
        family of straight lines with $\dfrac{dy}{dx} = 3$.

    (b) In the case in question, $(2, 5)$ is a point
        on the line. Substituting in (1),

        $5 = 3 \times 2 + c \Rightarrow c = -1$.

        So the equation is $y = 3x - 1$.

(c)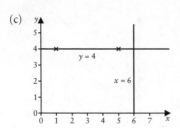

By choosing two points on the line $y = 4$ as shown, the gradient

$$\frac{dy}{dx} = \frac{0}{4} = 0.$$

By choosing any two points on the line $x = 6$, the difference in x-coordinates is shown to be always 0. This leads to division by zero which is not defined.

Exercise A (p. 59)

1   (a) -7 (b) 1   (c) -2 (d) $\frac{1}{2}$

2   (a) Difference in y-coordinates $= -2$;
       difference in x-coordinates $= 4$

   (b) $\dfrac{dy}{dx} = \dfrac{-2}{4} = -\dfrac{1}{2}$

3   (a) $y = \dfrac{1}{2}x + 2 \Rightarrow \dfrac{dy}{dx} = \dfrac{1}{2}$

   (b) $y = -x + 7 \Rightarrow \dfrac{dy}{dx} = -1$

   (c) $-y = -x + 6 \Rightarrow y = x - 6 \Rightarrow \dfrac{dy}{dx} = 1$

   (d) $2y = -x + 4$

$$\Rightarrow y = -\frac{1}{2}x + 2 \Rightarrow \frac{dy}{dx} = -\frac{1}{2}$$

4   (a) $C = 702 + 2.87n$

   (b) $\dfrac{dC}{dn} = 2.87$. This represents the extra cost (change in cost) for each unit used.

5   (a) $\dfrac{ds}{dt} = -8$ (b) $\dfrac{dy}{dt} = 4$

   (c) $\dfrac{dz}{dy} = -1$ (d) $\dfrac{dy}{dx} = 10$

   (e) $y = 12 - 20x \Rightarrow \dfrac{dy}{dx} = -20$

6   (a) $\dfrac{dC}{dr} = 2\pi$. This is how much the circumference increases by when the radius increases by one unit.

   (b) Using the result of (a), an extra $2 \times 2\pi = 4\pi$ metres would be needed (neglecting any deviation of the equator from a perfect circle).

   (c) Surprisingly, this would still be 4π metres.

7   $\dfrac{dy}{dx} = 5$ (gradient)

   So the line has equation $y = 5x + c$.
   $(-1, 2)$ is a point on the line, so

   $2 = 5 \times -1 + c \Rightarrow c = 7$.

   The equation is $y = 5x + 7$.

8   (a) $y = -2x + 8$ (b) $s = \frac{1}{2}t + 1$

   (c) $p = \frac{2}{3}x + 3$

9   $\dfrac{dy}{dx} = \dfrac{6}{3} \Rightarrow \dfrac{dy}{dx} = 2, y = 2x + 3$

10 (a) (i) $C = 5 + 7t$ (ii) $\dfrac{dC}{dt} = 7$

   (b) (i) $\dfrac{dC}{dt} = 6$ (ii) $C = 8 + 6t$

11

Test mark, T	25	26	49	50
Rescaled mark, R	0	4	96	100

   (a) $\dfrac{dR}{dT} = 4$ (b) $R = 4T - 100$

B   Gradients of curves (p. 61)

Your results for the gradients in questions 4D, 5 and 6 may vary slightly from the answers given.

1   With an increasing magnification, the curve looks more and more like a straight line. At $x = 4$ the graph looks more and more like a horizontal straight line.

2   You should expect to see the curve looking more and more like a horizontal straight line.

3 (a) $y=|x|$ is locally straight near all values of x, except $x=0$.

(b) $y=100x^2$ is locally straight everywhere.

(c) $y=\text{Int}(x)$ is locally straight near any value of x which is not an integer but has a discontinuity at each integer value.

(d) $y=|x^2-4|$ is locally straight near all values of x, except $x=\pm 2$.

4D (a) 1.5

(b)

x	-2	-1.5	-1	0	1	1.5	2
$\dfrac{dy}{dx}$	-2	-1.5	-1	0	1	1.5	2

(c)

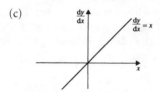

(d) $\dfrac{dy}{dx}=x$

5 (a)

x	-6	-4	-2	0	2	4	6	8	10
$\dfrac{dy}{dx}$	16	12	8	4	0	-4	-8	-12	-16

(b)

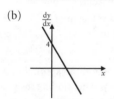

(c) $\dfrac{dy}{dx}=4-2x$

6 (a)

x	-5	-4	-3	-2	-1	0	1	2	3	4	5
$\dfrac{dy}{dx}$	5.5	2.8	0.7	-0.8	-1.7	-2	-1.7	-0.8	0.7	2.8	5.5

(b)

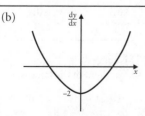

(c) It appears to have a quadratic equation.

7D (a) The graph is not locally straight at S and its gradient at S is therefore undefined. (At a stationary point the gradient must be zero.)

(b) At a **local** maximum the curve is higher than at **nearby** points but not necessarily higher than at all other points on the curve.

Infinitely many points on this curve are higher than the local maximum and infinitely many are lower than the local minimum.

Exercise B (p. 66)

1 Any points where the tangent to the curve is horizontal correspond to a point where the gradient graph meets the x-axis.

(a)

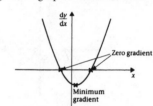

The gradient decreases to zero and becomes negative. The gradient then increases and becomes positive again.

(b)

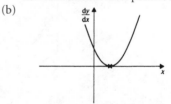

The gradient never becomes negative but there is just one point where it is zero.

(c)

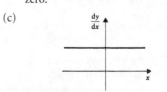

The gradient is constant for all x.

(d)

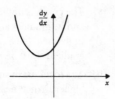

The gradient is always positive for all x. It decreases to a minimum gradient but not to zero (over the range shown).

(e)

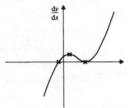

There are two points where the gradient is zero. The right-hand point is a stationary point but not a turning point.

(f)

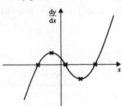

There are three points where the gradient is zero.

2   (a)

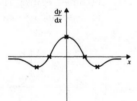

(b)

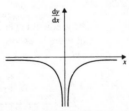

As x becomes numerically large, the gradients tend towards zero. As x tends to zero, the gradient reaches its maximum value in (a), whereas in (b) the gradient becomes very large and negative.

3   (a)   (i)

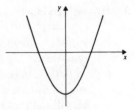

(ii)

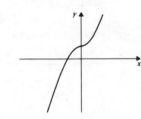

(b)   There are infinitely many possible original graphs – formed by translating the above graphs parallel to the y-axis.

C   Gradient functions (p. 68)

1D   Your investigations should indicate that the gradient function is $2ax + b$.

2D   (a)   The closer you take (u, v) to $(3, 9)$, the better will be the approximation to the gradient of the curve at $(3, 9)$, within the limitations of your calculator.

(b)   Possible values are $(3.1, 3.1^2)$, $(3.01, 3.01^2)$, $(3.001, 3.001^2)$ and so on.

3D   (a)   This gives only an approximation because you are finding the gradient of a line that crosses the curve twice, not a tangent.

(b)   You could use a spreadsheet, giving results like these.

u	gradient
3.1	6.1
3.01	6.01
3.001	6.001

This suggests (but does not prove) that the gradient of the tangent is 6.

4   (a) 12   (b) 12   (c) 6   (d) 8   (e) 9
    (f) (i) 6   (ii) 10   (iii) 0   (iv) −4
        (v) 30   (vi) 7.2

5 (a)

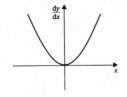

(b)

Value of x	0	1	−2	3
Gradient	0	3	12	27

(c) $\dfrac{dy}{dx} = 3x^2$

6 $\dfrac{dy}{dx} = 3ax^2$

7 Checks for various values of a and b.

8 $\dfrac{dy}{dx} = b + 2cx + 3dx^2$

For example,

$y = 3 + 5x^2 + x^3 \implies \dfrac{dy}{dx} = 10x + 3x^2$.

9E You should have investigated the gradient functions of graphs such as, for example,

$y = 3x^2 + 4x^3, \qquad y = 5x^3 - 3x^4$.

The general conclusion you should have reached is that, if a and b are constants,

$y = ax^n + bx^m$

$\implies \dfrac{dy}{dx} = anx^{n-1} + bmx^{m-1}$.

The gradient of the sum is the sum of the gradients.

Exercise C (p. 74)

1 (a) $\dfrac{dy}{dx} = 6x$ (b) $\dfrac{dv}{du} = 15u^2 - 4u$

   (c) $\dfrac{dy}{dx} = -2x$ (c) $\dfrac{ds}{dt} = 4 - 2t$

2 (a) $\dfrac{dy}{dx} = 10x$

   (b) (i) 10   (ii) 20   (iii) −10

3 (a) $\dfrac{dy}{dx} = -6x^2$

   When $x = 0$, gradient $= 0$.

   When $x = 2$, gradient $= -24$.

   (b) $\dfrac{dy}{dx} = 5 - 2x$

   When $x = 2$, gradient $= 1$.

   When $x = 4$, gradient $= -3$.

7 Using differentiation

A Graph sketching: using gradients (p. 75)

1 The local maxima and minima consist of the three points marked with dots.

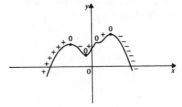

2 $y = (x - 1)(x - 2)(x - 4)$

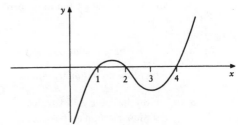

The coordinates of the stationary points could be determined precisely by using calculus.
(Note that the stationary points are *not* at $x = 1.5$ and $x = 3$.)

3 $\dfrac{dy}{dx} = 3x^2 - 12$

$\dfrac{dy}{dx} = 0$ when $x = \pm 2$

At $x = 2$, $y = 2^3 - (12 \times 2) + 2 = -14$
At $x = -2$, $y = (-2)^3 - (12 \times -2) + 2 = 18$

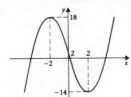

4 $\dfrac{du}{dx} = 6x + 6$

$\dfrac{du}{dx} = 0$ when $x = -1$

$u = 3 \times (-1)^2 + 6 \times (-1) + 5 = 2$

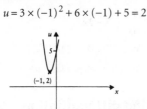

5 $\dfrac{dy}{dx} = 3x^2 + 6x + 5$. From the graph for question 4 you can see that the least value of $\dfrac{dy}{dx}$ is 2 and so the equation $\dfrac{dy}{dx} = 0$ has no solutions.

The (x, y) graph therefore has *no* stationary point and its gradient is minimum when $x = -1$.

6 $a > 0$: $\dfrac{dy}{dx} = 0$ has no solutions, and so there are no stationary points.

$a = 0$: gives the cubic $y = x^3$, with a stationary point at the origin.

$a < 0$: $\dfrac{dy}{dx} = 0$ has two solutions, $x = \pm\sqrt{-\tfrac{1}{3}a}$, and so there are two stationary points.

Exercise A (p. 78)

1 $\dfrac{dy}{dx} = 3x^2 - 12 = 3(x^2 - 4)$

The stationary points occur when $\dfrac{dy}{dx} = 0$, that is when $x = 2$ or -2. The stationary points are $(2, -11)$ and $(-2, 21)$.

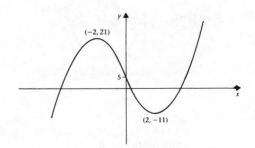

2 $\dfrac{dy}{dx} = 6x^2 - 18x + 12$

$\qquad = 6(x^2 - 3x + 2)$

$\qquad = 6(x - 1)(x - 2)$

$\dfrac{dy}{dx} = 0$ when $x = 1$ or $x = 2$. The stationary points are $(1, -2)$ and $(2, -3)$.

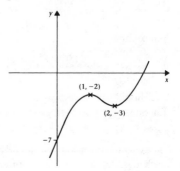

3 (a) (i) $y = 5x - x^2 = x(5 - x)$

$\qquad\qquad \dfrac{dy}{dx} = 0$ for $x = 2.5$

$\qquad\qquad$ Stationary point at $(2.5, 6.25)$

(ii)

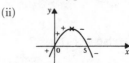

(iii) Maximum at $(2.5, 6.25)$

(b) (i) $y = (1 - x)^2 = 1 - 2x + x^2$

$\qquad\qquad \dfrac{dy}{dx} = 0$ for $x = 1$

$\qquad\qquad$ Stationary point at $(1, 0)$

(ii)

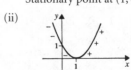

(iii) Minimum at $(1, 0)$

(c) (i) $y = x^3 - 3x^2 + 5$

$\dfrac{dy}{dx} = 0$ for $x = 0$, $x = 2$

Stationary point at $(0, 5)$, $(2, 1)$

(ii)

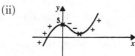

(iii) Maximum at $(0, 5)$,
minimum at $(2, 1)$

(d) (i) $y = 4x - x^2 - 4$

$\dfrac{dy}{dx} = 0$ for $x = 2$

Stationary point at $(2, 0)$

(ii)

(iii) Maximum at $(2, 0)$

(e) (i) $y = 2x^3 - 9x^2 + 12$

$\dfrac{dy}{dx} = 0$ for $x = 0$, $x + 3$

Stationary point at $(0, 12)$,
$(3, -15)$

(ii)

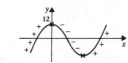

(iii) Maximum at $(0, 12)$,
minimum at $(3, -15)$

(f) (i) $y = x^4 - 8x^2 + 12$

$\dfrac{dy}{dx} = 0$ for $x = 0$, $x = \pm 2$

Stationary points at $(2, -4)$,
$(-2, -4)$, $(0, 12)$

(ii)

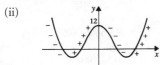

(iii) Maximum at $(0, 12)$,
minima at $(2, -4)$ and $(-2, -4)$

4 (a) $+6, +3, 0$
The quadratic has reflection symmetry
and so B's x-coordinate is $\dfrac{+6 + 0}{2}$.

(b) $+6, +4, 0$. The cubic does *not* have
reflection symmetry.

B　Optimisation (p. 79)

1D (a) The volume will increase, reach a
maximum, then decrease.

(b) In terms of the radius, r, of the
cylinder, you might expect the
volume, V, to vary as in this graph.

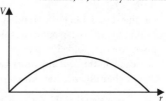

2D (a) Let the fixed radius of the circular
paper be R. The paper folds up to form
a cylinder with radius r and volume V.

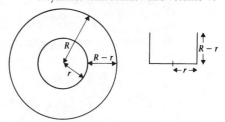

Volume = area of base × height
$$V = \pi r^2 (R - r)$$
$$= \pi R r^2 - \pi r^3$$

(b) $\dfrac{dV}{dr} = 2\pi R r - 3\pi r^2$ (Note that R is fixed
and does not vary
with r.)

$= \pi r(2R - 3r)$

$\dfrac{dV}{dr} = 0$ when $r = 0$ (zero volume) and

when $r = \frac{2}{3}R$ (maximum volume). The
maximum volume is therefore

$$\pi\left(\tfrac{2}{3}R\right)^2\left(R - \tfrac{2}{3}R\right) = \tfrac{4}{27}\pi R^3 .$$

V can, of course, be expressed in terms
of other lengths, for example fixed
diameter D and variable height h. It
could also be expressed in terms of an
area, such as the area of the base of the
cake case. It is important to choose
quantities which make the calculations
reasonably easy.

(c) The main assumption is that a circular piece of paper will fold up to form a cylinder. It will in fact only do this if the sides are fluted, which then means that applying the formula for the volume of a cylinder will not give a correct expression for the volume of the cake case. The error, however, will not be very great. You might like to estimate the error.

Another assumption is that cake cases are cylindrical, when in fact most cake cases have sloping rather than vertical sides.

For this discussion point, it might be helpful to get hold of some actual cake cases. Are they folded so that $r = \frac{2}{3}R$? If not, can you think of any other factors that might influence the chosen shape?

3D It has been assumed that the relationship between I and N is linear. In fact we only know two points, $(0, 20)$ and $(40, 0)$, on the graph of N in terms of I. Joining them with a straight line is reasonable if there is no evidence suggesting we should not.

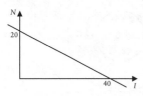

The straight line has the equation $N = 20 - \frac{1}{2}I$.

Exercise B (p. 81)

1 $F = 25 + v - 0.012v^2, \ 30 \leqslant v \leqslant 80$

(a) $\dfrac{\mathrm{d}F}{\mathrm{d}v} = 1 - 0.024v$

v	35	60
F	45.3	41.8
$\dfrac{\mathrm{d}F}{\mathrm{d}v}$	0.16	−0.44

At the higher speed, the number of miles per gallon is lower.

At 35 m.p.h., the number of miles per gallon *increases* with increasing speed. At 60 m.p.h. it *decreases*.

(b) $\dfrac{\mathrm{d}F}{\mathrm{d}v} = 0$ when $v = 41.7$. The most economical speed is 41.7 m.p.h.

2 $n = 30 - 2P, \ R = 30P - 2P^2$

(a) $\dfrac{\mathrm{d}R}{\mathrm{d}P} = 30 - 4P$ gives the rate at which revenue from the items changes with their price. The best selling price is £7.50.

At this price, $\dfrac{\mathrm{d}R}{\mathrm{d}P} = 0$.

(b) When $P = 5, \dfrac{\mathrm{d}R}{\mathrm{d}P} = 10$

When $P = 10, \dfrac{\mathrm{d}R}{\mathrm{d}P} = -10$.

(c) $\dfrac{\mathrm{d}R}{\mathrm{d}P} = 30 - 4P$ must be positive if revenue is to rise with an increase in price and so $P < 7.50$.

3 If h is the variable height of the gutter, then the cross-sectional area A is given by
$$A = (20 - 2h)h = 20h - 2h^2.$$

$$\dfrac{\mathrm{d}A}{\mathrm{d}h} = 20 - 4h$$

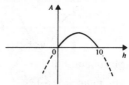

From this and the graph we see that the area is maximised when $h = 5$.

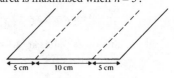

4 (a) $P = 500 + 100t$

$$\dfrac{\mathrm{d}P}{\mathrm{d}t} = 100$$

This represents the rate at which the population is increasing each year.

(b) $P = 100(5 + t - 0.25t^2)$

$$\frac{dP}{dt} = 100 - 50t$$

$t = 1, \dfrac{dP}{dt} = 50; \; t = 2, \dfrac{dP}{dt} = 0;$

$t = 3, \dfrac{dP}{dt} = -50$

The population stopped increasing after 2 years, and then it decreased.

The maximum population occurred when $t = 2$ and was

$100(5 + 2 - 0.25 \times 2^2) = 600$.

The population decreased to zero and so the estate was abandoned.

5 If integers only are permitted, the minimum is 7 when the numbers are 2 and 5.

If all positive numbers are permitted, the minimum is approximately 6.3, when both numbers are just less than 3.2.

If negative numbers are permitted, there is no limit to the minimum value that the sum takes.

6 (a) The length of the net is

$w + l + w + l = 100$.

$2l + 2w = 100$

$l + w = 50$

$l = 50 - w$

(b) The width of the net is

$\frac{1}{2}w + h + \frac{1}{2}w = 40$.

$h + w = 40$

$h = 40 - w$

(c) $V = whl$

$V = w(40 - w)(50 - w)$

(d) $\dfrac{dV}{dw} = 0 \Rightarrow 3w^2 - 180w + 2000 = 0$.

This has two roots, but one, $w = 45.3$, is too large for the card. The other root, $w = 14.7$, gives a box 14.7 cm by 35.3 cm by 25.3 cm.

7 (a) The dimensions of the box are

length $= 6 - 2x$, width $= 4 - 2x$, height $= x$

so the volume is

$V = (4 - 2x)(6 - 2x)x$.

(b) V is maximum when $x \approx 0.8$.
The approximate dimensions are 0.8 cm by 2.4 cm by 4.4 cm.

8 (a) Length of side parallel to hedge $= 60 - 2x$

$\Rightarrow$ Area, $A = x(60 - 2x) = 60x - 2x^2$

(b) $\dfrac{dA}{dx} = 60 - 4x$

When A is a maximum, $60 - 4x = 0$

$\Rightarrow \qquad\qquad\qquad\qquad x = 15$

(c) Maximum area $= 15(60 - 30) = 450 \text{ m}^2$

9 $2x^2 + 4xh = 2040$ \hfill (1)

$V = x^2 h$ \hfill (2)

$h = \dfrac{V}{x^2}$ \hfill (from (2))

$2x^2 + \dfrac{4xV}{x^2} = 2040$ \hfill (substituting into (1))

$\Rightarrow \qquad V = 510x - \frac{1}{2}x^3$

$\Rightarrow \qquad \dfrac{dV}{dx} = 510 - \frac{3}{2}x^2$

When V is a maximum, $\dfrac{dV}{dx} = 0$.

$0 = 510 - \frac{3}{2}x^2$

$x^2 = 340$

$x = \pm 18.44$

Substituting into (1) shows that $h = 18.44$ cm also, in other words the box is a cube of side 18.44 cm. Substituting into (2) gives a volume of 6270 cm^3.

10E Let the price per bike be £P. The number sold drops by 40 for each increase of £1 in the price, and so the number sold is

$$5000 - 40(P - 100) = 9000 - 40P$$

Total revenue = £$(9000 - 40P)P$

Total costs = £50 000 + 85(9000 − 40P)

Profit = revenue − costs

$$= £(-815\,000 + 12\,400P - 40P^2)$$

$$\frac{d(\text{Profit})}{dP} = 0 \text{ when } 12\,400 - 80P = 0, \text{ i.e.}$$

$$P = 155$$

Number sold = 9000 − 40P = 2800

Approximately 2800 should be manufactured and they should be sold at a price of £155 each.

11E (a) Curved length = $60 - 2x$

Circumference of circle = $120 - 4x$

Diameter of circle = $\dfrac{120 - 4x}{\pi}$

(b) Total area, A of pen

$$= \frac{x(120 - 4x)}{\pi} + \frac{\pi}{2}\left(\frac{60 - 2x}{\pi}\right)^2$$

$$= -\frac{2x^2 + 1800}{\pi}$$

$$\frac{dA}{dx} = -\frac{4x}{\pi}$$

(c) When A is a maximum, $\dfrac{8 - 4x}{\pi} = 0$

$$\Rightarrow x = 0$$

(d) Maximum area = $\dfrac{1800}{\pi}$

8 Areas under graphs

A Rate graphs (p. 84)

1D Water flows at a constant 15 litres per minute for 20 minutes. The total volume of water is $15 \times 20 = 300$ litres.

This is represented by the area of the rectangle (shaded on the graph).

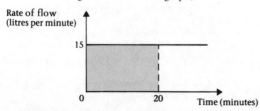

2 (a) km   (b) miles   (c) cm^3 (d) g

3 (a) and (c)

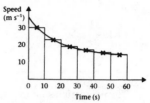

The area under the graph represents the distance travelled in the 60 seconds.

(b) $10 \times (29.9 + 23.1 + \cdots + 15.0)$
$= 10 \times 119.9 \approx 1200$ m

(d) The area under the 'steps' is close to the area under the curve of the graph.

(e)   On each step, area B is smaller than area A. So the step area is an underestimate of the area under the curve.

Exercise A (p. 88)

1 (a) mass   (b) distance
(c) volume (or capacity)   (d) distance

2 There are various possible answers, for example,
'Rate of population increase (millions of people per year)' on the vertical axis and 'Time (years)' on the horizontal axis.

3 Total area = $2 \times (46.3 + 39.7 + \cdots + 11.6)$
$= 2 \times 254.9$

So the volume drained $\approx 510\,\ell$

B Integration (p. 89)

1 The integral represents the area under the graph of $y = x$ between $x = 0$ and $x = 3$.

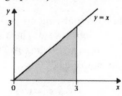

This is the area of a triangle (shaded),
$\frac{1}{2} \times 3 \times 3 = 4.5$.

Thus $\displaystyle\int_0^3 x\,dx = 4.5$

2 (a)

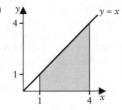

Area of shaded trapezium = 7.5

Thus $\int_1^4 x\,\mathrm{d}x = 7.5$

(b)

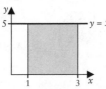

Area of shaded square = 10

Thus $\int_1^3 5\,\mathrm{d}x = 10$

(c)

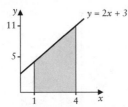

Area of shaded trapezium = 24

Thus $\int_1^4 (2x+3)\,\mathrm{d}x = 24$

3D (a)

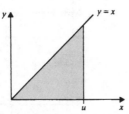

$\int_0^u x\,\mathrm{d}x = $ area of shaded triangle

$= \frac{1}{2} \times$ base $\times$ height

$= \frac{1}{2} \times u \times u$

$= \frac{1}{2}u^2$

(b)

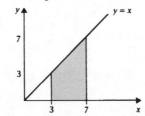

$$\int_3^7 x\,\mathrm{d}x = \int_0^7 x\,\mathrm{d}x - \int_0^3 x\,\mathrm{d}x$$
$$= \tfrac{1}{2} \times 7^2 - \tfrac{1}{2} \times 3^2$$
$$= 24.5 - 4.5$$
$$= 20$$

4D (a)

Strip	Height of mid-ordinate	Area
0–1	0.25	0.25
1–2	2.25	2.25
2–3	6.25	6.25
3–4	12.25	12.25
4–5	20.25	20.25
5–6	30.25	30.25

(b)

u	Estimate of A(u)
1	0.25
2	2.50
3	8.75
4	21.00
5	41.25
6	71.50

(c) The results will be an underestimate because of the curvature of the graph.

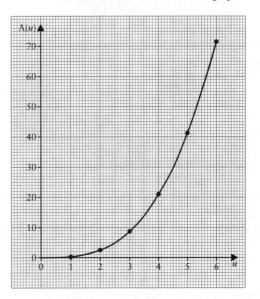

(d) Experimentation shows that these estimates of A(u) are close to $\dfrac{u^3}{3}$.

u	Estimate of A(u)	$\dfrac{u^3}{3}$
1	0.25	0.33
2	2.50	2.67
3	8.75	9.00
4	21.00	21.33
5	41.25	41.67
6	71.50	72.00

If narrower strips are used, results closer to $\dfrac{u^3}{3}$ are obtained.

Repeating the investigation for $y = x^3$ suggest A(u) = $\dfrac{u^4}{4}$.

Repeating it for $y = x^4$ suggests A(u) = $\dfrac{u^5}{5}$.

5 $\displaystyle\int_2^5 x^2\,dx = \left[\tfrac{1}{3}x^3\right]_2^5$
$= (\tfrac{1}{3} \times 5^3) - (\tfrac{1}{3} \times 2^3)$
$= \tfrac{1}{3}(5^3 - 2^3)$
$= 39$

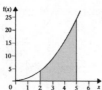

Exercise B (p. 92)

1 (a)

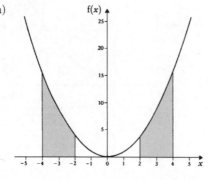

(b) $\displaystyle\int_2^4 x^2\,dx$ and $\displaystyle\int_{-4}^{-2} x^2\,dx$ are the areas of the regions shaded above. By symmetry these are equal.

(c) $\displaystyle\int_2^4 x^2\,dx = \left[\tfrac{1}{3}x^3\right]_2^4 = 18\tfrac{2}{3}$. Similarly,
$\displaystyle\int_{-4}^{-2} x^2\,dx = 18\tfrac{2}{3}$.

2 (a) (i) $\displaystyle\int_{-3}^{-1.5} x^2\,dx = \left[\tfrac{1}{3}x^3\right]_{-3}^{-1.5} = 7.875$

(ii) 2.25 (iii) 7.875 (iv) 10.125

(b) $\displaystyle\int_{-3}^{-1.5} x^2\,dx = \int_{1.5}^{3} x^2\,dx$

$\displaystyle\int_{-1.5}^{1.5} x^2\,dx + \int_{1.5}^{3} x^2\,dx = \int_{-1.5}^{3} x^2\,dx$

3 (a) Shaded area $= \tfrac{1}{2} \times u \times 2u = u^2$

(b) $\displaystyle\int_0^u 2x\,dx = \left[x^2\right]_0^u = u^2$

4 (a)

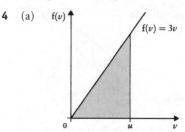

(b) Shaded area $= \tfrac{1}{2} \times u \times 3u = \tfrac{3}{2}u^2$

5 (i) (a)

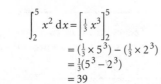

(b) Shaded area $= 2u$

(ii) (a)

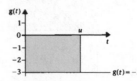

(b) Shaded area $= -3u$

(iii) (a)
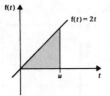

(b) Shaded area = u^2

(iv) (a)
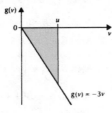

(b) Shaded area = $-\frac{3}{2}u^2$

6   (a) $A(x) = mx$ (b) $A(x) = \frac{1}{2}mx^2$

3   (a)
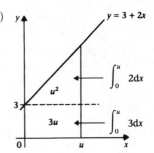

(b)
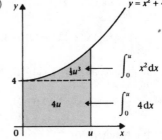

9 Using integration

A Integrals of polynomials (p. 95)

1D   (a) $f(x) = x^3 \Rightarrow A(x) = \dfrac{x^4}{4}$

(b) $f(x) = 2x^2 \Rightarrow A(x) = \dfrac{2x^3}{3}$

(c) $f(x) = x^2 - 3x \Rightarrow A(x) = \dfrac{x^3}{3} - \dfrac{3x^2}{2}$

In this discussion point there is an opportunity to become familiar with the use of the 'area' option before it is needed for questions 4 and 6.

2   (a), (b)

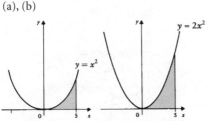

(c) The graph of $y = 2x^2$ is obtained by a one-way stretch × 2 along the y-axis. Areas are therefore increased by a factor of 2.

(d) $\displaystyle\int_a^b kx^2\, dx = k\int_a^b x^2\, dx$

4, 5 $f(x) = ax^2 + bx + c$

$$\Rightarrow A(x) = \frac{ax^3}{3} + \frac{bx^2}{2} + cx$$

6, 7 $f(x) = ax^3 + bx^2 + cx + d$

$$\Rightarrow A(x) = \frac{ax^4}{4} + \frac{bx^3}{3} + \frac{cx^2}{2} + dx$$

Exercise A (p. 96)

1   (a) $\displaystyle\int_2^4 (3x^2 - 5)\, dx$ (b) $\left[x^3 - 5x\right]_2^4 = 46$

2    $\left[\frac{1}{4}t^4 + \frac{1}{3}t^3 + \frac{1}{2}t^2 + t\right]_1^3 = 34\frac{2}{3}$

3   (a) The zeros of the function are 1 and 3.

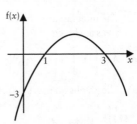

(b) The area required is given by

$$\int_1^3 (-x^2 + 4x - 3)\, dx$$

$$= \left[-\frac{1}{3}x^3 + 2x^2 - 3x\right]_1^3$$

$$= 1\frac{1}{3}$$

4 (a) $\left[\frac{1}{2}x^2 - \frac{1}{4}x^4\right]_0^1 = \frac{1}{4}$

(b) $\left[\frac{1}{2}x^2 + x\right]_2^4 = 8$

(c) $\left[\frac{1}{3}x^3\right]_{-2}^{-1} = 2\frac{1}{3}$

(d) $\left[\frac{1}{3}x^3 - x^2 + x\right]_0^1 = \frac{1}{3}$

(e) $\displaystyle\int_0^1 (x+1)(x+2)\,\mathrm{d}x = \int_0^1 (x^2 + 3x + 2)\,\mathrm{d}x$

$\qquad = \left[\frac{1}{3}x^3 + \frac{3}{2}x^2 + 2x\right]_0^1 = 3\frac{5}{6}$

5 $\displaystyle\int_1^a (2x+3)\,\mathrm{d}x = \left[x^2 + 3x\right]_1^a$

$\qquad = (a^2 + 3a) - (1 + 3)$

$\qquad = a^2 + 3a - 4$

It is required that

$\qquad a^2 + 3a - 4 = 24$

$\Rightarrow a^2 + 3a - 28 = 0$

$\qquad (a+7)(a-4) = 0$

$\qquad\qquad a = -7 \text{ or } 4$

A value greater than 1 is required for a so $a = 4$.

6 (a) The graphs intersect where
$x^2 = 8 - x^2 \Rightarrow x = 2$ (since $x > 0$).
The graph of $y = 8 - x^2$ intersects the
x-axis where $x^2 = 8 \Rightarrow x = \sqrt{8}$.

The integrals arise from splitting the
areas as shown.

(b) $A = \left[\frac{1}{3}x^3\right]_0^2 + \left[8x - \frac{1}{3}x^3\right]_2^{\sqrt{8}} \approx 4.42$

7 (a) The graphs intersect at $(0, 0)$ and $(1, 1)$.

The shaded area is

$\frac{1}{2} \times 1 \times 1 - \displaystyle\int_0^1 x^2\,\mathrm{d}x = \frac{1}{2} - \frac{1}{3} = \frac{1}{6}$

(b)

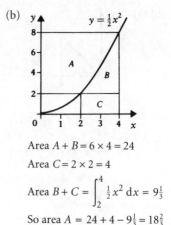

Area $A + B = 6 \times 4 = 24$

Area $C = 2 \times 2 = 4$

Area $B + C = \displaystyle\int_2^4 \frac{1}{2}x^2\,\mathrm{d}x = 9\frac{1}{3}$

So area $A = 24 + 4 - 9\frac{1}{3} = 18\frac{2}{3}$

Required area $= 37\frac{1}{3}$

B   'Negative' areas (p. 97)

1D   £1000 million approximately

2 (a) The integrals are 4, -4, 0 respectively.

(b) In the first case, the area is entirely
above the x-axis. In the second, it is
entirely below. In the third, the areas
above and below the x-axis are equal
and cancel each other out.

3 $\displaystyle\int_0^5 x\,\mathrm{d}x = 12\frac{1}{2}$

$\displaystyle\int_4^5 (x^2 - 4x)\,\mathrm{d}x = 2\frac{1}{3}$.

$\displaystyle\int_0^4 (x^2 - 4x)\,\mathrm{d}x = -10\frac{2}{3}$

Shaded area $= (12\frac{1}{2} - 2\frac{1}{3}) + 10\frac{2}{3}$

$\qquad\qquad = 20\frac{5}{6}$ square units

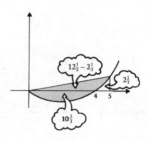

4 (a)

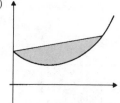

(b) $\int_0^5 (x+5)\,dx = \left(\dfrac{5+10}{2}\right) \times 5 = 37\tfrac{1}{2}$

$\int_0^5 (x^2 - 4x + 5)\ dx = 16\tfrac{2}{3}$

Shaded area = $37\tfrac{1}{2} - 16\tfrac{2}{3}$

$\qquad\qquad = 20\tfrac{5}{6}$ square units

This confirms the value obtained in question 3.

5 (a) Area above an interval on the t-axis represents CO_2 added during that interval.

   Area below an interval represents CO_2 taken away during that interval.

   (b) From 5 p.m. until 9 a.m. The increase is about 70 mg.

   (c) The 'negative' area between $t = 9$ and $t = 17$ is also about 70. So the amount dissolved stays roughly constant.

Exercise B (p. 100)

1 (a)

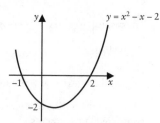

$y = x^2 - x - 2$

   (b) $4\tfrac{1}{2}$ square units

2 (a) $\int_{-2}^1 (t^3 + 2t^2 - 3)\ dt = \left[\tfrac{1}{4}t^4 + \tfrac{2}{3}t^3 - 3t\right]_{-2}^1$

$\qquad\qquad = -6\tfrac{3}{4}$

(b)

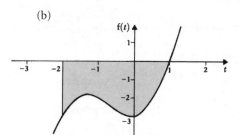

Between $t = -2$ and $t = 1$, the graph lies completely below the t-axis and hence the integral is negative.

3 (a)

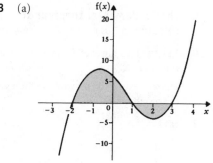

   (b) $\int_{-2}^1 (x^3 - 2x^2 - 5x + 6)\ dx = \tfrac{63}{4}$

$\int_1^3 (x^3 - 2x^2 - 5x + 6)\ dx = -\tfrac{16}{3}$

The total area is $\tfrac{63}{4} + \tfrac{16}{3} = \tfrac{253}{12} \approx 21.08$.

4 (a) 30 m

   (b) $t = 2.5$ seconds (when $v = 0$)

   (c) 31.25 m

5 (a) $-\tfrac{1}{4}$ (b) 0   (c) $1\tfrac{3}{4}$

6 Area = $13\tfrac{1}{6}$

7 $a = 1$ and 4

8 $21\tfrac{1}{3}$ metres

9 The graphs $y = 3x^2 - 12$ and $y = 12 - 3x^2$ both intersect the x-axis at $x = \pm 2$.

   By symmetry, the shaded area is twice the area enclosed by the curve $y = 12 - 3x^2$ and the x-axis from $x = -2$ to $x = 2$.

   Shaded area $= 2\displaystyle\int_{-2}^2 (12 - 3x^2)\,dx$

$\qquad\qquad = 2\left[12x - x^3\right]_{-2}^2 = 64$

10   Shaded area $= \int_0^c x^2 \, dx = \left[\tfrac{1}{3}x^3\right]_0^c = \tfrac{1}{3}c^3 = 6$

$\Rightarrow c^3 = 18$

$\Rightarrow c = \sqrt[3]{18} \approx 2.62$

11E $\left[x^3 - x^2\right]_0^a = 0$

$\Rightarrow a^3 - a^2 = 0$

$\Rightarrow a = 0$ (which does not apply here)

or $a = 1$

C   The fundamental theorem of calculus (p. 101)

1D   Integrating a function leads to its integral function.

Differentiating the integral function gives the original function.

2   (a)

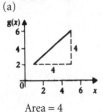

Area = 4

(b)

Area = −6

(c)

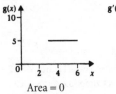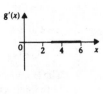

Area = 0

The difference in the y-coordinates of the end points equals the area under the gradient graph.

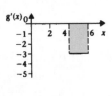

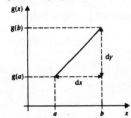

Area of shaded rectangle

$= \dfrac{\text{difference in } y}{\text{difference in } x} \times \text{difference in } x$

$= \text{difference in } y = g(b) - g(a)$

3

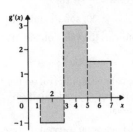

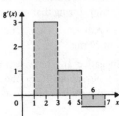

$g(7) = 10$ and $g(1) = 3$, so $g(7) - g(1) = 7$

The result $\displaystyle\int_1^7 g'(x) \, dx = g(7) - g(1)$ is always true.

4 $\displaystyle\int_a^b g'(x) \, dx = g(b) - g(a)$ for any function g whose graph consists of a series of connected line segments.

5E

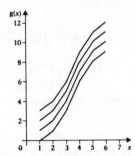

(a)   Any of the graphs shown should give the $(x, g'(x))$ graph shown on p. 104.

(b) Each graph is a simple translation (up or down) of one of the other graphs. There is an infinite number of such graphs, all sharing the same gradient graph.

(c) From the graph on p. 104 you can see that $\int_1^6 g'(x)\,dx = 9$

$\int_1^6 g'(x)\,dx = g(6) - g(1)$ for any correct $(x, g(x))$ graph.

Exercise C (p. 105)

1 (a) (i) 4   (ii) 0
   (b)

The graph has rotational symmetry about $(1, 0)$. The areas shaded are equal.

2 (a) $10x + 3$ (b) $6t^2$

Note that $h(t) = 6t^2$ for *any* integral function of the type $2t^3 + c$ where c is constant.

D The indefinite integral (p. 105)

1D They each differentiate to $2x + 5$.

$\int(2x + 5)\,dx = x^2 + 5x + k$. When evaluating the integral between $x = 1$ and $x = 2$, the constant k will 'cancel out':

$$\int_1^2 (2x + 5)\,dx = \left[x^2 + 5x + k\right]_1^2$$

$$= (14 + k) - (6 + k)$$

$$= 8$$

Hence any of the functions *could* have been used.

Exercise D (p. 107)

1 (a) $\frac{1}{4}x^4 - x + c$

   (b) $\int_1^3 (x + 1)(x - 2)\,dx$

   $= \int_1^3 (x^2 - x - 2)\,dx$

   $= \left[\frac{1}{3}x^3 - \frac{1}{2}x^2 - 2x\right]_1^3 = \frac{2}{3}$

2 (a) $y = \frac{1}{2}x^2 - 4x + c$

   (b) $y = x^3 + \frac{1}{2}x^2 + c$

   (c) $y = \frac{1}{3}x^3 + \frac{1}{2}x^2 + x + c$

   (d) $\dfrac{dy}{dx} = (x + 1)(x - 2) = x^2 - x - 2$

   $\Rightarrow y = \frac{1}{3}x^3 - \frac{1}{2}x^2 - 2x + c$

3 (a) $y = x^3 + 2x^2 + 2$

   (b) $y = \frac{1}{3}x^3 + \frac{1}{2}x^2 + x + 3$

4 (a) $x^3 - x^2 + 5x$

   (b) $(2t + 1)(t - 4) = 2t^2 - 7t - 4$

   $k(t) = \frac{2}{3}t^3 - \frac{7}{2}t^2 - 4t$

10 Summarising data

A Introduction (p. 109)

Exercise A (p. 110)

1 1986, about 22%
   1993, about 33%

   The figure is highest in the North and the North West. It is lowest in East Anglia.

2 (a) (i) 116.5

       (ii) 88.1

   (b) There are clear regional differences in GDP. The highest figures are found in London and the surrounding areas with a fall-off as you move north. Wales and Northern Ireland each have a low GDP in relation to the English regions and to Scotland.

3 (a) (i) About 25%   (ii) about 36%

   (iii) about 25%

(b) No. Note also that the figures are for the clear up of *reported* crime. Much crime is unreported and so cannot be 'cleared up'.

(c) (i) It takes time for a crime to be solved. You could find the percentage clear-up rate by considering at some time the number of crimes reported – say, in a given month – and the number of these crimes solved after, say, six months. Once a suitable method is defined, each region must follow it carefully.

   (ii) Data on *reported* crime could be collected easily from each region and suitably classified. It would be more difficult to obtain information on the hidden pool of unreported crime.

4 (a) Smoking in all regions shown has declined since 1980. There seems to be no obvious regional distinction.

(b) Directing advertising at suitable age groups might be sensible. You would need information on smoking habits, related to age groups and perhaps gender.

B   Types of average (p. 111)

Exercise B (p. 112)

1 (a) Mean $= \frac{1052}{19} = 55.4$ seconds (to 3 s.f.)

   Median $= 52$ seconds

   It would probably be better to quote the mean as this better reflects the individual values, some of which are very low and some high.

(b) Including the value 148 seconds increases the mean to 60 seconds. But the person did not complete the puzzle in 148 seconds (and might have taken much longer than this if he/she had kept trying) so using this figure when finding the mean time to do the puzzle makes it seem 'easier' than it was found to be. On the other hand, disregarding this result and giving the mean for the remaining nineteen people would be understating the difficulty of the puzzle. The median is much less affected by adding in an extreme value (here, in fact, it is still 52 seconds). The median would remain 52 seconds if the person had kept trying and finished the puzzle, however long it took. This does not make the median a better measure if the quickest and slowest performances are thought to be relevant in assessing how difficult the puzzle was found to be.

2 The distribution has two peaks – it is bimodal. Any of the measures of average might be used, but data such as these emphasise that you need to know more about a population than simply a measure of its average value, which can disguise a great deal of hidden detail. There is no particular merit in any of the measures here.

C   Stem and leaf diagrams (p. 113)

1 Bournemouth is slightly sunnier. It has more very bright days but also more very cloudy days. The values for Torquay are more evenly spread out across the distribution.

2 Type B is generally faster, but the speeds of Type A are more consistent.

3 (a) The range of the females' heights is 32 cm. The range of the males' heights is 23 cm. This might suggest that the females' heights are more variable.

(b) (i) **Males**

18	0 2 4
17	1 1 3 3 3 3 4 4 5 5 7 8 9
16	1 4 5 8
15	
14	
13	

17 | 3 means 173 cm

Females

18	
17	0 1
16	1 2 3 4
15	2 4 5 6 6 8 8 8 9 9 9
14	2 3
13	9

14 | 2 means 142 cm

(ii) There is an impression, from the diagrams, that the heights of the females are more variable.

(iii) Males: median = 173.5 cm

Females: median = 158 cm

(iv) The males have the higher median.

(c) **Heights of 40 adults**

```
18 │ 0 2 4
17 │ 0 1 1 1 3 3 3 3 4 4 5 5 7 8 9
16 │ 1 1 2 3 4 4 5 8
15 │ 2 4 5 6 6 8 8 8 9 9 9
14 │ 2 3
13 │ 9
```
16 | 5 means 165 cm

The stem and leaf diagram has two peaks. The distribution is said to be bimodal, as opposed to the unimodal distributions of part (b)(i).

(d) (iv), which corresponds to the stem and leaf plot. Such a distribution often occurs when two distinct populations are mixed.

Exercise C (p. 116)

1
	Class 1		Class 2
		9 │ 1
	7 4 0	8 │ 0 1 3
9 8 8 6 6 5 1	7 │ 1 3 3 5 9
9 6 5 4 2 0	6 │ 2 4 4 8 9
9 8 6 3 1 0	5 │ 1 5 6 8 9
		4 │ 5 8
	1	3 │ 4

| 6 │ 4 means 64 marks
3 │ 5 | means 53 marks

(a) Disregarding the 91 mark in class 2, class 1 seem to have done marginally better, with more marks in the upper 70s and 80s.

(b) Both have approximately symmetrical distributions. The marks for class 1 are slightly more closely bunched than those for class 2.

2
```
3 │ 0 2
2 │ 0 0 0 2 2 2 2 4 4 6 6 8
1 │ 4 5 6 6 7 7 8 8 9
0 │ 9
```

The distribution is slightly skewed, with a 'tail' at the lower end.

D Using cumulative frequency (p. 116)

1 (a) The lower quartile is approximately 12.5 cm. The upper quartile is approximately 18.5 cm.

(b) The interquartile range is approximately 6 cm.

2 Approximately 13.5 cm

3 (a) 16.5 cm   (b) 22 cm

4D

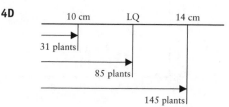

Hence

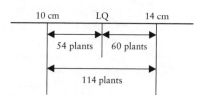

Estimate of lower quartile

$= 10 + \frac{54}{114} \times 4$

$= 11.9$ cm to 1 d.p.

Similarly, estimate of upper quartile = 18.4 cm

Exercise D (p. 119)

1 (a)

Length (mm)	Cumulative frequency
Up to 110	4
Up to 125	14
Up to 140	33
Up to 155	69
Up to 170	112
Up to 185	138
Up to 200	147
Up to 215	150

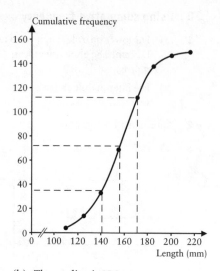

(b) The median is 156 mm.

The interquartile range is 30 mm.

(c) (i)   133 mm   (ii)   152 mm
    (iii) 164 mm   (iv)   183 mm

2 (a) **Males**

Length of stay (days)	Cumulative frequency
up to 5	40
up to 10	98
up to 15	137
up to 20	143
up to 25	147
up to 30	149

Females

Length of stay (days)	Cumulative frequency
up to 5	16
up to 10	32
up to 15	39
up to 20	42
up to 25	45
up to 30	48

(b)

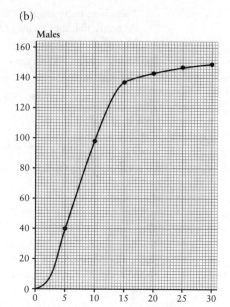

(c) (i)   8 days   (ii)   6.8 days
    (iii) 3.5 days   (iv)   12.5 days

(d) (i)   7.5 days   (ii)   3.8 days
    (iii) 12.9 days (iv)   9.1 days
    (v)   2.6 days   (vi)   16.4 days

E   Box and whisker diagrams (p. 120)

1

	Males	Females
Upper quartile	0.220	0.230
Median	0.185	0.210
Lower quartile	0.165	0.170

2   The range for type A is slightly greater than for type B.

Type A's speeds are generally lower than Type B's.

Type A's speeds are more consistent.

3 (a)

	Males	Females
Upper quartile	177.5	161.5
Median	173.5	158.0
Lower quartile	171.0	154.5

(b)

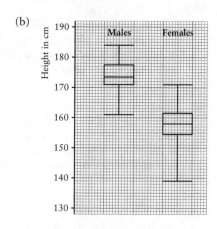

Exercise E (p. 122)

1

	Class 1	Class 2
Upper Quartile	78	74
Median	66	66
Lower Quartile	58	55.5

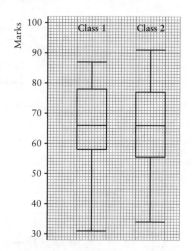

2

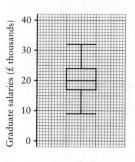

3 (a) The highest recorded temperature was 83 °F, in Copenhagen. London was generally hotter, with a median temperature of 66 °F against Copenhagen's 63 °F. London's lower quartile is only 1 °F less than Copenhagen's upper quartile.

(b) Copenhagen had the greater range of temperatures overall even though the interquartile range for London is much greater than that for Copenhagen. The interquartile range is not particularly useful when planning a trip – you need the full range when deciding what to pack. From that point of view, Copenhagen is the more variable.

London has a more symmetric distribution than Copenhagen.

4 (a) There was very little sunshine in January. There was a much more varied amount in July.

(b)

	January	July
(i) Median	0.4	5.7
(ii) Lower quartile	0	2.6
(iii) Upper quartile	2.1	7.7

(c)

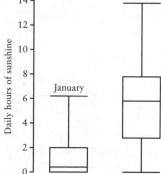

(d) There was a much greater range of sunshine hours in July and the average sunshine was much higher. In January there was no recorded sunshine on at least a quarter of the days.

5 (a) E is the most reliable. 50% of the scripts required at most a $\frac{1}{2}$ mark adjustment.

(b) Drop examiner C, who has greater variability than others in the box section. It is not very easy to make a general adjustment.

(c) Decrease every mark by one.

F Histograms (p. 124)

1D This simple frequency diagram gives a distorted picture of the data. It gives the impression of a large number of screws in the 0–20 mm range. Worse, it suggests that there are 5 screws of length 0–5 mm, another 5 of length 5–10 mm and so on. In fact there are only 5 in the whole 0–20 mm range!

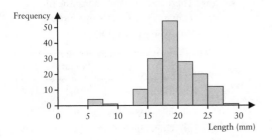

2D

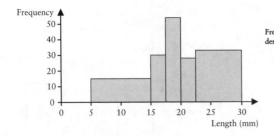

The second bar chart is not a fair representation of the data. The overall shape is very different. For example, it looks as though there are about as many rods in the 22.5–30 mm range as in the 15–22.5 mm range when in fact there are less than a third as many.

3D With the frequency density diagram, there is no distortion as there was in the earlier diagram. This sort of diagram *should* be used when data are grouped into unequal **class intervals**.

4D This seems reasonable as it is likely that some of the eight values in this group are greater than 39; otherwise the data would all fall in the interval 30–39 and this would have been given as the group description.

Exercise F (p. 128)

1 (a) (i) $10 \times 1 = 10$ (ii) $10 \times 2 = 20$

(iii) $20 \times 1 = 20$

(b) Total frequency $= 50$

2 Total frequency $= (25 \times 0.2) + (50 \times 0.4)$
$+ (50 \times 0.2) = 35$

3 (a)

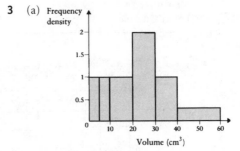

(b)

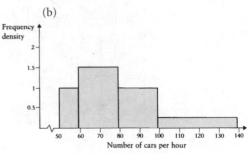

4 (a) See the table in (b). The choice of grouping should reflect the principles established in the previous discussion.

(b)

North			
Rainfall (mm)	Width	Frequency	Frequency density
40–69	30	1	$\frac{1}{30} = 0.033$
70–79	10	4	$\frac{4}{10} = 0.4$
80–89	10	9	$\frac{9}{10} = 0.9$
90–99	10	4	$\frac{4}{10} = 0.4$
100–109	10	11	$\frac{11}{10} = 1.1$
110–119	10	6	$\frac{6}{10} = 0.6$
120–129	10	5	$\frac{5}{10} = 0.5$
130–139	10	1	$\frac{1}{10} = 0.1$
140–149	10	5	$\frac{5}{10} = 0.5$
150–229	80	4	$\frac{4}{80} = 0.05$

South			
Rainfall (mm)	Width	Frequency	Frequency density
40–69	30	10	$\frac{10}{30} = 0.33$
70–79	10	9	$\frac{9}{10} = 0.9$
80–89	10	11	$\frac{11}{10} = 1.1$
90–99	10	8	$\frac{8}{10} = 0.8$
100–109	10	6	$\frac{6}{10} = 0.6$
110–119	10	4	$\frac{4}{10} = 0.4$
120–129	10	1	$\frac{1}{10} = 0.1$
130–139	10	0	0
140–149	10	0	0
150–229	80	1	$\frac{1}{80} = 0.012$

As the readings are to the nearest mm, the true intervals are 39.5–69.5, 69.5–79.5, and so on. The positioning of the bars on the histogram should reflect this.

(c) Rainfall in the north of England

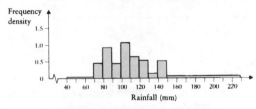

Rainfall in the south of England

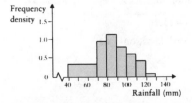

(d) The south of England has more readings in the 40–69 mm range and in general appears to have had a drier month than the north of England. This result needs to be interpreted cautiously as it does not mean that the south has a drier climate than the north. It only indicates what happened in one particular month.

The 100 weather stations chosen were fairly equally divided between the east and the west of England to avoid any east–west differences affecting the result. The line from the Wash to the Bristol Channel was chosen as the north–south boundary for the purposes of this study.

11 Variance and standard deviation

A Averages and spread (p. 131)

1 9.7, 0.13 and 9.3, 0.41

2 (a) 0. The points are all the same and have no spread. This is shown by a standard deviation of zero.

(b) 1.4 (to 2 s.f.)

(c) 1.7 (to 2 s.f.). Set (c) is slightly more spread out than (b) and has a correspondingly higher standard deviation.

(d) 2.8 (to 2 s.f.). Set (d) is twice as spread out as set (b) and has twice the standard deviation.

3 (a) If all the values are increased by the same number, then the mean is also increased by this number but the standard deviation is unchanged.

(b) If all the values are multiplied by the same number, then the mean and the standard deviation are also multiplied by that number.

Exercise A (p. 134)

1 (a) Mean = 54.2,
       standard deviation = 0.473
       (both results to 3 s.f.)

   (b) New mean = 54.2 ÷ 1.10 = 49.3
       (to 3 s.f.)
       New standard deviation = 0.473 ÷ 1.10
       = 0.430 (to 3 s.f.)

2 Mean = 16.0 years
   The standard deviation (0.25 years) is
   unchanged.

3 Fahrenheit mean: $1.8 \times 12 + 32 = 53.6\,°F$
   Fahrenheit standard deviation:
   $1.8 \times 0.5 = 0.9\,°F$

4 Mean $= \dfrac{28 - x}{2}$
   Standard deviation = 2

5 Mean = 130
   Standard deviation = 11

6 Mean = 0
   Standard deviation = 1

7 (a) $a = \dfrac{10}{4.2} = 2.38$

       Applying a multiplier of 2.38
       gives a new mean of 78.5.
       A value of $b = -28.5$ is required
       to make the mean = 50

   (b) Peter's scaled mark is
       $40 \times 2.38 - 28.5 = 66.7$.

B Formulas for variance and standard deviation (p. 135)

1 (a) 2.125
   (b) $68.\dot{2}$

2 The calculation of $(x - \bar{x})^2$ for all values of
   x would prove to be cumbersome for large
   collections of data, making the algorithm
   very labour-intensive! Also, it requires two
   'runs' through the data.

Exercise B (p. 137)

1 Mean = 6.0 years; s.d. = 2.45 years

2 Mean = 51.0 kg; s.d. = 2.2 kg

3 (a) $\sum w = 350$ kg; $\sum w^2 = 25\,000$ kg^2
   (b) Mean = 67.5 kg;

       s.d. $= \sqrt{\dfrac{25\,000 - 80^2}{4} - 67.5^2}$

       = 9.68 kg

4 1116.3 g^2; 2527.5 g^2; 7.1 g

C Variance for frequency distributions (p. 138)

1      $\bar{x} = \dfrac{14.3 \times 1 + 14.4 \times 3 + 14.5 \times 1}{5}$

       = 14.4

   Variance =

   $$\dfrac{(14.3 - 14.4)^2 + 3(14.4 - 14.4)^2 + (14.5 - 14.4)^2}{5}$$

       = 0.004

2D In the general case,

Data values	Frequency of data values	Group total of data values	Group total of squared deviation from $\bar{x}$
x_1	f_1	$x_1 \times f_1$	$(x_1 - \bar{x})^2 \times f_1$
x_2	f_2	$x_2 \times f_2$	$(x_2 - \bar{x})^2 \times f_2$
x_3	f_3	$x_3 \times f_3$	$(x_3 - \bar{x})^2 \times f_3$
$\vdots$	$\vdots$	$\vdots$	$\vdots$
x_n	f_n	$x_n \times f_n$	$(x_n - \bar{x})^2 \times f_n$
Total	$n = \sum f$	$\sum xf$	$\sum (x - \bar{x})^2 f$

   mean, $\bar{x} = \dfrac{\sum xf}{\sum f}$ variance $= \dfrac{\sum (x - \bar{x})^2 f}{\sum f}$

3D The student's notes on using his or her own
    calculator to obtain the mean, variance and
    standard deviation of a frequency
    distribution.

4D Mean = 11.1
    Standard deviation = 9.2

Exercise C (p. 140)

1 (a) The mean is approximately 23.3 and the standard deviation is approximately 12.5.

   (b) The average length of rally has increased; coaching has been of some benefit!

2 (a) The total population is 53 511 000.

   (b) The population mean age is approximately 41 years.

        The population age variance is approximately 580. Therefore, the standard deviation is approximately 24 years.

3 (a) The upper boundary must be taken somewhere! There are so few people aged over 100 that this seems a reasonable upper value.

   (b) The mean is 38.1 years, standard deviation 22.9 years.

   (c) The total population (50 063 000 in 1986) is expected to increase by about $3\frac{1}{2}$ million and the average age is expected to rise from 38 years to 41 years. There is little change in the spread of ages.

4 Taking the upper value as 70 words gives a mean sentence length of 23.4 words and a standard deviation of 11.5 (to 3 s.f.).

   The grouping into intervals mostly of width 10 involves a loss of accuracy. Also, the sample might not be representative.

12 Probability

A Introduction (p. 143)

1

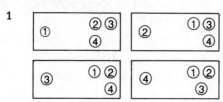

2 There are 6 cases.

3 There are 16 cases.

4 (a) $\frac{4}{16}$ (b) $\frac{2}{16}$ (c) $\frac{6}{16}$

B Compound events (p. 144)

1D The answer $\frac{1}{125}$ can be seen in many ways. For example, imagine that the darts player has a large number of attempts at throwing three darts.

    She would expect to score triple twenty with the first dart on $\frac{1}{5}$ of the occasions.

    On $\frac{1}{5}$ of this reduced number of occasions she would also expect to score triple twenty with the second dart.

    The number of times a triple twenty would be scored on all three throws is $\frac{1}{5} \times \frac{1}{5} \times \frac{1}{5}$ of the total number of attempts.

    In practice, it is likely that scoring triple twenties with the first two darts will affect the chance of scoring triple twenty with the third dart. The chances may be increased if the darts player scores two triple twenties because she is on good form. Alternatively, the chances may be reduced if the first two darts block the triple twenty.

2 $40 \times 40 = 1600$ possible pairs

3 (a) $16 \times 10 = 160$ possible double ones
   (b) (i) $12 \times 10 = 120$ double twos
        (ii) $8 \times 10 = 80$ double threes
        (iii) $4 \times 10 = 40$ double fours
   (c) $160 + 120 + 80 + 40 = 400$

4 (a) P(double one) $= \frac{160}{1600} = \frac{1}{10} = 0.1$
   (b) $\frac{120}{1600} = \frac{3}{40} = 0.075$
   (c) $\frac{400}{1600} = \frac{1}{4} = 0.25$

5 The probability of, say, double two is
   P(Yellow 2 *and* Red 2)
        $= $ P(Y2) $\times$ P(R2)
        $= 0.3 \times 0.25$
        $= 0.075$

   The probability of a double is as follows
   P(double one *or* double two *or* ...)
        $= $ P(double one) $+$ P(double two) $+ \cdots$
        $= $ P(Y1 and R1) $+$ P(Y2 and R2) $+ \cdots$
        $= 0.4 \times 0.25 + 0.3 \times 0.25 + 0.2 \times 0.25$
          $+ 0.1 \times 0.25$
   P(double one *or* double two *or* ...) $= 0.25$

6 Snap occurs when you obtain
(B1 *and* Y1) or (B2 *and* Y2) or (B3 *and* Y3)
So P(Snap) = $(\frac{1}{4} \times \frac{4}{10}) + (\frac{1}{2} \times \frac{3}{10}) + (\frac{1}{4} \times \frac{2}{10})$

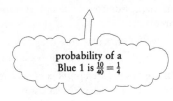

probability of a
Blue 1 is $\frac{10}{40} = \frac{1}{4}$

$= \frac{12}{40} = 0.3$

7 (a) If one happens the other cannot happen. So the events are mutually exclusive. They are not independent as the occurrence of one obviously affects the other.

(b) My cutting an ace and your cutting a king are independent events if the ace is replaced in the pack before you cut. They are *not* mutually exclusive.

(c) If Dan's Delight wins, Andy's Nag cannot – the events are mutually exclusive. They must therefore be dependent as the occurrence of one obviously affects the other.

(d) There is no relationship. The events are independent. They are *not* mutually exclusive.

(e) Since Mrs Smith having toothache is not likely to influence whether Mr Smith has one also, the events are likely to be independent. They are not mutually exclusive.

(f) There is likely to be some connection here and the events are probably not independent, nor are they mutually exclusive.

Exercise B (p. 149)

1 (a) $\frac{1}{36}$ (b) $\frac{11}{36}$ (c) $\frac{5}{18}$

2 (a) $\frac{1}{26}$ (b) $\frac{2}{13}$ (c) $\frac{2}{13}$

3 (a) $\frac{4}{13}$ (b) $\frac{1}{2}$

4 0.005

5 $0.12^2 = 0.0144$

6 $\frac{1}{144}$

7 (a) 0.8464   (b) 0.0064

C Tree diagrams (p. 150)

1 (a) (i) $\frac{1}{64}$ (ii) $\frac{1}{16}$

(b) (i) $\frac{13}{52} \times \frac{12}{51} \times \frac{11}{50} = 0.0129$ (ii) 0.0518

Exercise C (p. 151)

1 (a) 0.382   (b) 0.867   (c) 0.750

(a) $\frac{65}{81}$ (b) $\frac{11}{27}$

Independence has been assumed in arriving at the above answers, but this is probably not justified: if one line is busy, calls may be transferred to a free line.

3 $\frac{90}{156} = \frac{15}{26}$

D Conditional probability (p. 151)

1 (a) 30   (b) 25   (c) 5   (d) 0.01

2 (a) The probability of colour blindness given that the subject is male; 0.05.

(b) The probability of not being colour blind, given that the subject is female; 0.99.

(c) The probability of not being colour blind, given that the subject is male; 0.95.

3 $P(M) \times P(C'|M) = P(M \cap C')$
($0.5 \quad \times \quad 0.95 = 0.475$)

$P(F) \times P(C|F) = P(F \cap C)$
($0.5 \quad \times \quad 0.01 = 0.005$)

$P(F) \times P(C'|F) = P(F \cap C')$
($0.5 \quad \times \quad 0.99 = 0.495$)

Exercise D (p. 155)

1 (a) $\frac{1}{13}$ (b) $\frac{1}{4}$ (c) $\frac{1}{2}$ (d) $\frac{3}{13}$

2 $\frac{2}{3}$ (1, 4 and 6 are not prime; of them, 4 and 6 are multiples of 2.)

3 (a) $\frac{2}{3}$ (b) $\frac{2}{9}$

4 (a) $P(A)P(B|A) = P(A \cap B)$
$0.6 \times 0.5 = P(A \cap B)$
$\implies \quad 0.3 = P(A \cap B)$

(b) $P(B)P(A|B) = P(A \cap B)$

$P(B) \times 0.75 = 0.3$

$P(B) = 0.4$

(c) $P(A \cup B) = P(A) + P(B) - P(A \cap B)$

$= 0.6 + 0.4 - 0.3$

$= 0.7$

5   (a) $P(Y) = 0.25$ (because of independence)

(b) $P(X) = 0.4$

(c) $P(X' \cap Y') = 0.45$

6   (a) $P(A \cap B) = \frac{1}{12}$

(b) $P(A \cup B) = \frac{3}{4}$

(c) $P(A' \cap B') = \frac{1}{4}$

13 Probability distributions

A Random variables (p. 157)

1   (a) Discrete   (b) Discrete

(c) Continuous   (d) Continuous

(e) Discrete   (f) Continuous

Exercise A (p. 160)

1

s	1	2	3	4	5	6
$P(s)$	$\frac{1}{6}$	$\frac{1}{6}$	$\frac{1}{6}$	$\frac{1}{6}$	$\frac{1}{6}$	$\frac{1}{6}$

2

x	0	1	2	3	4 or over
$P(x)$	0.14	0.20	0.51	0.10	0.05

3

s	0	1
$P(s)$	$\frac{1}{2}$	$\frac{1}{2}$

4

y	1	2	3	4	5	6	7	8	9	10
$P(y)$	$\frac{1}{13}$	$\frac{1}{13}$	$\frac{1}{13}$	$\frac{1}{13}$	$\frac{1}{13}$	$\frac{1}{13}$	$\frac{1}{13}$	$\frac{1}{13}$	$\frac{1}{13}$	$\frac{4}{13}$

5

x	0	1	2	3	4	5
$P(x)$	$\frac{6}{36}$	$\frac{10}{36}$	$\frac{8}{36}$	$\frac{6}{36}$	$\frac{4}{36}$	$\frac{2}{36}$

6

h	0	1	2	3
$P(h)$	$\frac{1}{8}$	$\frac{3}{8}$	$\frac{3}{8}$	$\frac{1}{8}$

B The mean and variance of a random variable (p. 160)

1   £800. You should charge at least £2 for each go!

2   Total winnings

$= £(1 \times 400 + 2 \times 300 + 3 \times 200 + 4 \times 100)$

$= £2000$

So mean winnings $= £\frac{2000}{1000}$

$= £2$ per game

3   (a)

b	1	2	3	4
$P(b)$	$\frac{1}{4}$	$\frac{1}{2}$	$\frac{1}{4}$	0

(b) Mean $(\mu) = 2$

Exercise B (p. 165)

1

d	1	2	3	4	5	6
$P(d)$	$\frac{1}{6}$	$\frac{1}{6}$	$\frac{1}{6}$	$\frac{1}{6}$	$\frac{1}{6}$	$\frac{1}{6}$

Mean $(\mu) = 3.5$

Variance $(\sigma^2) = 2.917$

2

x	10	20	50
$P(x)$	0.4	0.4	0.2

Mean $(\mu) = 22$ pence

Variance $(\sigma^2) = 216$

3   $\mu = 2$ (b) $\mu = 1.4$ (c) $\mu = 2$

$\sigma^2 = \frac{2}{3}$ $\sigma^2 = 0.64$ $\sigma^2 = 2\frac{1}{3}$

4

Score x	1	2	3	4	5	6	7	8	9	10
$P(x)$	$\frac{4}{52}$	$\frac{4}{52}$	$\frac{4}{52}$	$\frac{4}{52}$	$\frac{4}{52}$	$\frac{4}{52}$	$\frac{4}{52}$	$\frac{4}{52}$	$\frac{4}{52}$	$\frac{16}{52}$

Mean $= 6.538$, variance $= 9.94$

5   (a) 17p

(b) A 20p coin

Index